Short Bike Rides™
in Eastern Massachusetts

". . . Keeps you organized and informed as you pedal through the back roads."

—*Women's Sports and Fitness* magazine

"Howard leaves no stone unturned in his books. He describes the geography of the region, bicycle safety tips, and the basic accessories you should take with you on bike rides; all add to the pleasure of cycling."

—*Rhode Island Herald*

Also by Howard Stone

Short Bike Rides in Western Massachusetts

Short Bike Rides in Rhode Island

25 Bicycle Tours in Maine

25 Bicycle Tours in the Hudson Valley

SHORT BIKE RIDES SERIES

Short Bike Rides™
in
Eastern Massachusetts

Second Edition

by
Howard Stone

An East Woods Book

The Globe Pequot Press

Old Saybrook, Connecticut

Cover design by Saralyn D'Amato-Twomey

Photographs on pages 268 and 354 courtesy of the Massachusetts Department of Commerce and Development, Division of Tourism. All other photographs courtesy of the author.

Library of Congress Cataloging-in-Publication Data

Stone, Howard.
    Short bike rides in eastern Massachusetts / by Howard Stone. — 2nd ed.
        p.   cm.
    "An East Woods book."
    Includes bibliographical references
    ISBN 0-7627-0077-7
    1. Bicycle touring—Massachusetts—Guidebooks. 2. Massachusetts—Guidebooks. I. Title.
    GV1045.5.M4S766 1997
    796.6'4'09744—dc21   96-50083
                                                                                         CIP

Manufactured in the United States of America
Second Edition/Second Printing

♻ This text and cover are printed on recycled paper.

Contents

The numbers on this map refer to rides in this book.

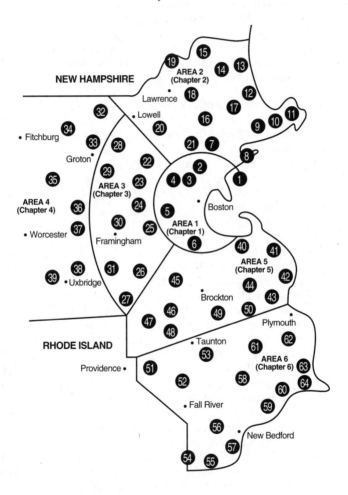

Acknowledgments

This book could never have come to fruition without a lot of help. My wife, Bernice, provided continual encouragement, support, and late-night snacks. Many members of the Narragansett Bay Wheelmen kept me company while I was researching the rides by providing good cheer, taking notes, and patiently putting up with endless hours of backtracking and rechecking intersections. Dominique Coulombe, my supervisor, allowed me to work flexible hours so that I could take advantage of the daylight to research the rides. Jeanne LaFazia helped me interpret the intricacies of the laws of Massachusetts. Carla Petersen helped me type the manuscript. Dozens of local residents told me about hidden back roads and interesting places to see. I would also like to thank Kevin and Anita Clifford for putting me up overnight at various times.

Some of the photographs were supplied by the Massachusetts Department of Commerce and Development, Division of Tourism. Mr. Leon White gave me full access to the photo collection and helped me choose scenes that would best capture the various landscapes of the state.

A few of the rides were originally mapped out as a whole or in part by the following members of the Narragansett Bay Wheelmen, to whom I extend my thanks:

Bill McIlmail, Ride 59
Ed Ames, Ride 54
Chick Mead, Ride 60

Phil Maker, Ride 52
Steve McGowen, Ride 56
Wes Ewell, Ride 57

Preface to the Second Edition

The second edition of *Short Bike Rides in Eastern Massachusetts* covers the same basic area as the first edition, with a new chapter added for the outer western suburbs of Boston. To keep the book to approximately the same size, I have deleted the most urban and least scenic rides from the first edition. The region west of Worcester and Fitchburg is covered in the companion volume *Short Bike Rides in Western Massachusetts*. The material in this book is arranged in the same basic format as the earlier edition, with an introductory description, a map, and point-to-point directions for each ride. The directions are somewhat more detailed to make them as easy to follow as possible.

Many of the rides have been modified slightly to improve scenery and safety or to avoid badly deteriorated roads. Some of the starting points for rides in earlier editions now have parking for "customers only" or for short time periods. In these cases I have changed the starting point to a location where parking is no problem.

Introduction

This book is a guide to bicycling in the portion of Massachusetts within reasonable commuting distance of Boston, covering the area between the Cape Cod Canal and a north–south line just east of Worcester and Fitchburg. The region, along with the sections of Rhode Island and New Hampshire just over the state lines, offers ideal cycling. Massachusetts is blessed with an impressive network of thousands of back roads, most of them paved but not heavily traveled. Beyond the built-up metropolitan areas, which compose a very small percentage of the state, the landscape is rural enough to give the cyclist a sense of remoteness and serenity, and yet the nearest town, village, or grocery store is never more than a few miles away. The terrain is refreshingly varied for a relatively small state.

East of Boston lies the seacoast, one of the state's most scenic features. Most of the Massachusetts coast is beautiful and relatively unspoiled, with smooth, sandy beaches, windswept dunes, and extensive salt marshes. Outside Boston is a broad belt of affluent suburbs with gracious homes and estates surrounded by acres of gently rolling, open land. Southeast of Boston, toward Cape Cod, is a landscape of cranberry bogs and scrub pine. Beyond the metropolitan area, as the land becomes genuinely rural about 25 or 30 miles outside the city, lie lake-dotted forests, rolling apple orchards, and old mill villages.

Bicycling is an ideal way to appreciate the New England landscape's unique intimacy. The back roads turn constantly as they hug the minute contours of the land, forcing your orientation down to a small scale. Every turn and dip in the road may yield a surprise—a weathered barn, a pond, a stream, a little dam or falls, a hulking old mill right out of the Industrial Revolution, a ragged stone wall, or a pasture with grazing cattle or horses. Most of the smaller town centers are architectural gems, with the traditional stately white church and village green flanked by the town hall, a handsome brick or stone library, and graceful old wooden homes.

Geography of the Region

Not counting Cape Cod, Massachusetts is basically a rectangle that extends upward and downward at its eastern edge. The eastern side of the rectangle is notched inward by the U-shaped cup of Massachusetts Bay, with Boston lying at the innermost point. The area covered by this book measures about 90 miles from north to south and 60 miles from east to west.

In general the region is fairly flat with an occasional hill. Most of the rides traverse at least one or two hills, sometimes steep or long enough that you'll want to walk them. Yet no hills are long enough to be really discouraging, and for every uphill climb there's a corresponding downhill run. The large majority of the hills you'll encounter are less than half a mile long, the steepest portion limited to a couple of hundred yards or less.

Culturally Massachusetts has a long and proud history, beginning with the Pilgrim settlement in Plymouth in 1620. The first armed encounters of the Revolutionary War occurred a century and a half later in Concord and Lexington. The deep and sheltered waters of the harbors bordering Newburyport, Gloucester, Salem, Boston, and New Bedford spawned thriving seaports, fisheries, and maritime commerce in Colonial times and into the nineteenth century. Today, these same harbors, along with the many smaller coves and inlets piercing the coast, are filled with motor yachts and sailboats. The Industrial Revolution got a head start in Massachusetts when Lowell and Holyoke, two of the first planned industrial cities in the country, evolved before the Civil War. In later years, between the end of the Civil War and the turn of the century, hundreds of mills were built along the swift-flowing Merrimack, Blackstone, Quaboag, and numerous other rivers, employing thousands of immigrants from Europe and French Canada.

Today, hundreds of smaller towns and villages in Massachusetts make up some of the state's most appealing and architecturally fascinating hallmarks. As you bike through a town, try to notice each building along the green. First you'll see the graceful white church, usually built before 1850, often on a little rise, standing proudly above the rest of the town. Next look for the town hall, probably a handsome, white-pillared, Colonial-style building or an ornate wooden or stone Victorian one. Near the town hall you'll frequently find the library, a gracious brick or stone building dating from the turn of the century or the two decades before it. The small-town library is almost always recognizable, generally built to appear dignified yet inviting, with wide steps, a portico framing the front door, and often a dome or rounded roof.

Another building worth noticing is the schoolhouse. In the smaller towns, the schools are typically handsome old wooden or brick buildings, sometimes with graceful bell towers or cupolas. In some towns, such as Fairhaven, the high school is an architectural showpiece.

Mill towns at first may look depressing, but there is always some architectural beauty to be found. The mills themselves are often fascinating old Victorian structures, forbidding but ornamented with cornices and clock towers. Next to the mill is usually a small millpond with a little dam or falls. Many mill towns have orderly rows of identical two- or three-story wooden houses, originally built for the workers during the late 1800s. Unfortunately fire, neglect, and vandalism claim several mills each year, but a growing consciousness has arisen about preserving and maintaining these unique and impressive buildings. Many old mills have been recycled into apartments, condominiums, or offices.

Geographically, eastern Massachusetts is divided into six fairly distinct areas, and this book covers all of them except for Cape Cod. Boston and its close suburbs, lying within the Route 128 semicircle and extending along the coast as far as Lynn to the northeast and Quincy to the southeast, is the most densely populated part of the state. Immediately north of Boston is a cluster of cities that are as densely populated as Boston itself—Cambridge, Somerville, Everett, Chelsea, Medford, Malden, Revere, and Winthrop. Beyond this urban cluster, Boston itself, Lynn, and Quincy, the area consists primarily of affluent communities with gracious older homes and estates and a surprising amount of protected, lake-dotted woodland—including the Lynn Woods, Middlesex Fells, and Blue Hills reservations.

I've defined the North Shore as the land between the coast slanting northeastward from Lynn and the west bank of the Merrimack River where it enters New Hampshire. The North Shore has the most extensive concentration of old wealth in the state, expressed in its mansions, estates surrounded by acres of gently rolling meadows, and hundreds of tidy horse farms with simple white fences bordering large fields. The coastline is the nicest in the state, with mansions and estates lining most of the stretch between Lynn and Ipswich. North of Cape Ann are extensive salt marshes and Crane Beach, one of the finest in the state. Salem, Marblehead, Gloucester, and Newburyport are historic communities where you'll find narrow streets lined with old wooden homes and broad avenues boasting the impressive Federal-style mansions of early merchants and sea captains. The wide Merrimack River, which at the turn of

Town Hall, Swansea

the century was the textile center of the country, enters the state from Nashua, New Hampshire, and flows through the three early mill cities of Lowell, Lawrence, and Haverhill, evenly spaced about 10 miles apart. East of Haverhill the river flows through an idyllic, undeveloped landscape of gentle green hills.

I've defined the South Shore as the shoulder of coast extending southeastward from Weymouth to Kingston Bay just north of Plymouth, inland to the northeast corner of Rhode Island, and bordered on the south by Route 44 between Providence and Plymouth. The South Shore is more built up and suburban than the North Shore. The coast is a varied mixture of estates and fine homes in Duxbury and Cohasset; summer beach colonies with rows of cottages and more modest homes in Marshfield, Scituate, and Hull; and vast salt marshes along the mouth of the North River between Marshfield and Scituate. Inland from Kingston Bay is a large cluster of lakes and ponds, and here you start to see the cranberry bogs that are a distinguishing feature of the southeastern part of the state. At the western edge of the region is the jewelry capital of the United States, along the axis from Attleboro to Pawtucket and Providence, Rhode Island.

Southeastern Massachusetts includes everything south of the South Shore, excluding Cape Cod. This region has unique characteristics—sandy soil, scrub pine, cranberry bogs, generally flat and often swampy terrain, and cedar-shingled houses with peaked roofs. In general this area provides the easiest bicycling in the state. The historical center of the region is of course Plymouth, with its collection of landmarks and sites related to the Pilgrim settlement. The southern coast is delightful, with unspoiled beaches and a string of elegant small towns that at one time were shipbuilding communities and are now yachting and sailing centers. In the middle of the southern coast is New Bedford, the nation's prime whaling port during the mid-1800s and today the home of the East Coast's largest fishing fleet.

The western suburbs compose the broad belt of Massachusetts between the North Shore and the South Shore east of Worcester and Fitchburg. I've divided them into halves separated roughly by Interstate 485. East of this highway, the predominant landscape is graciously suburban and punctuated by a large number of towns, most of them enjoyable. Many of the western suburbs are affluent, with prosperous farms and spacious homes on large wooded lots. Bicycling in this area is a pleasure, with gently rolling terrain that does not become hilly until you get west of Framingham. The best-known historic sites in this region are the green in Lexington, the Old North Bridge in Concord, and the Wayside Inn in Sudbury. Not far from Route 128 are the two truly rural and unspoiled towns closest to Boston, Carlisle and Dover. West of Concord is the prime apple-growing region of the state, with dozens of orchards stretching along the hillsides in Stow, Bolton, Harvard, and Boxboro.

West of Interstate 495 the landscape becomes genuinely more rural and hillier. Biking in the farther western suburbs is more challenging, but the lovely countryside makes the cycling worthwhile. Most of the small towns are elegant, unspoiled jewels. The Wachusett Reservoir, with its massive dam at the northern end in Clinton, is the second largest lake in the state. The southern half of the region is drained by the Blackstone River, running southeastward from Worcester to Woonsocket, Rhode Island. A series of fascinating old mill towns right out of the Industrial Revolution lies along the banks of the river and its tributaries. In this area is Purgatory Chasm, a deep cleft in the earth formed by some glacial cataclysm. The Blackstone Valley is currently being developed by the state into a linear historical park.

Massachusetts is fortunate to benefit from an active heritage of preserving the land and historic sites that began in the nineteenth century, before preservation was even considered in many other parts of the country. The state park system, run by the Department of Environmental Management, is admirable. A unique feature of the state park system is the renovation of old mills and factories, along with their adjacent waterways, into interpretive museums and visitor centers called Heritage State Parks. The names of two organizations, the Trustees of Reservations (TOR) and the Society for the Preservation of New England Antiquities (SPNEA), appear frequently in our descriptions of the rides. The first body is dedicated to acquiring and maintaining scenic areas, and it does the job admirably. TOR reservations are never shabby or shopworn, as so many public areas are; instead, they are impeccably clean and well landscaped. Some of the finest natural areas in the state, such as Crane Beach in Ipswich and World's End in Hingham, are TOR properties. The second body aims to acquire, preserve, and open to the public historic homes and mansions. Like TOR, it does a superb job. SPNEA properties are, however, open during limited hours, usually afternoons in the summer. Largely a volunteer and member-supported organization, it simply

6

does not have the funds to keep longer hours. In addition to these two bodies, dozens of other local historical societies and conservationist groups, including the Massachusetts Audubon Society, maintain historic houses and areas of greenspace.

One final geographic feature you'll encounter across the state is the drumlin, a small, sharp hill left behind by the glaciers. Most drumlins are elliptical, like a football sliced lengthwise along the middle. They are usually less than a mile long and less than 200 feet high and lie along a northwest-southeast or north-south axis, the direction of glacial flow. The biggest concentration of drumlins lies within 10 miles of Boston. Most of those near the ocean, such as Orient Heights in East Boston or World's End in Hingham, offer outstanding views. Other clusters of drumlins are scattered across the state. In rural areas such as West Newbury, Groton, and Lunenburg, they transform the land into a rippling sea of rolling hills with broad pastures and orchards sweeping up and over them, providing some of the most inspiring and scenic bicycling in the state.

About the Rides

Ideally, a bicycle ride should be a safe, scenic, relaxing, and enjoyable experience that brings you into intimate contact with the landscape. In striving to make this goal possible, I've routed the rides along paved secondary and rural roads, avoiding main highways, cities, and dirt roads as much as I could. I've also tried to make the routes as safe as possible. Routes containing hazards, such as very bumpy roads or dead stops at the bottom of steep hills, have been avoided whenever reasonable alternate routes were available. Any dangerous spots remaining on a recommended route have been clearly indicated in the directions by a **CAUTION** warning. I've included scenic spots such as dams, falls, ponds, mill villages, ocean views, and open vistas on the rides whenever possible.

Nearly all the rides have two options—a shorter one averaging about 15 miles and a longer one that is usually between 25 and 30 miles long. All the longer rides are extensions of the shorter ones, with both options starting off at the same place. A few rides have no shorter option, and several have three alternatives. All the rides make a loop or figure-eight rather than backtracking along the same route. For each ride, I include both a map and directions.

If you've never ridden any distance, the thought of riding 15 or, heaven forbid, 30 miles may sound intimidating or even impossible. I want to emphasize, however, that *anyone* in normal health can ride 30 miles and enjoy it if he or she gets mildly into shape first. You can accomplish this painlessly by riding at a leisurely pace for an hour several times a week for two or three weeks. At a moderate pace, you'll ride about 10 miles per hour. If you think of the rides by the hour rather than the mile, the numbers are much less frightening.

To emphasize how easy bicycle riding is, most bike clubs have a 100-mile ride, called a Century, each fall. Dozens of ordinary people try their first Century without ever having done much biking and finish it, and enjoy it! Sure, they're tired at the end, but they've accomplished the feat and loved it. (If you'd like to try one, the biggest and flattest Century in the Northeast is held in southeastern Massachusetts on the Sunday after Labor Day—ask at any good bike shop for details.)

Not counting long stops, a 15-mile ride should take about two hours at a leisurely speed, a 20- to 25-mile ride about three hours, and a 30-mile ride about four hours. If you ride at a brisk pace, subtract an hour from these estimates.

A few of the rides in this book have short (half a mile or less) sections of dirt road, or go a block or two along streets that are one-way in the wrong direction. This was occasionally necessary when there was no simple alternate route or to avoid making the directions needlessly complicated. If you come to a dirt road, get the feel of it first. If it's hard-packed, you can ride it without difficulty, but if it's soft, you should walk instead because it's easy to skid and fall unless you're on a mountain bike. If you encounter a one-way street in the opposite direction, *always* get off your bike and walk, using the sidewalk if there is one. It's illegal and also very dangerous to ride against traffic because motorists simply aren't expecting you, especially if they are pulling out of a driveway or side street.

For every ride I've recommended a starting point, but you can start anywhere else along the route if it's more convenient. This is sometimes the best choice, especially if you live in Boston but don't have a car and would like to try the rides within biking distance of the city.

I have intentionally not listed the hours and fees of historic sites because they are subject to so much change, often from one year to the next. If it's a place you've heard of, it's probably open from 10 A.M. to 5

8

P.M., seven days a week. Unfortunately many of the less frequently visited spots have limited hours—often only weekday afternoons during the summer, perhaps one day during the weekend. A few places of historic or architectural interest, such as the Rocky Hill Meetinghouse in Amesbury, are open only by appointment. The reason is a matter of funding and staffing. Most historic sites are maintained by voluntary contributions and effort, and it's simply impossible to keep them staffed more than a few hours a day or a few months a year. If you really want to visit a site, call beforehand and find out the hours.

You may wonder why no larger cities are on the rides. The reason is twofold. First, most cities just aren't very pleasant to bike through. Do you really want to ride along congested streets lined with businesses and tenements, just to see a few points of interest? Second, once you get to the points of interest, there is usually no safe place to keep your bike. The best way to explore a city is on foot, so that you can look at the architecture of each building and visit places without having to worry about traffic or having your bike stolen. If you really want to explore a city—and Lowell, Lawrence, Fall River, New Bedford, and, of course, Boston are worth exploring—visit it by car or public transportation and leave your bike at home.

About the Maps

The maps are reasonably accurate, but they are not necessarily strictly to scale. Congested areas may be enlarged in relation to the rest of the map for the sake of legibility. All the maps contain these conventions:

1. Route numbers are circled.
2. Small arrows alongside the route indicate direction of travel.
3. The longer ride is marked by a heavy line. The shorter ride is marked by a dotted line where the route differs from that of the longer ride.
4. I've tried to show the angle of forks and intersections as accurately as possible.

Enjoying the Rides

You'll enjoy biking more if you add a few basic accessories to your bike and bring a few items with you.

1. **Handlebar bag with transparent map pocket on top.** It's always helpful to have some carrying capacity on your bike. Most handlebar bags are large enough to hold tools, a lunch, or even a light jacket. If you have a map or directions in your map pocket, it's much easier to follow the route. You simply glance down to your handlebar bag instead of fishing the map or directions out of your pocket and stopping to read them safely. You may also wish to get a small saddlebag that fits under your seat, or a metal rack that fits above the rear wheel, to carry whatever doesn't fit in the handlebar bag.

Always carry things on your bike, not on your back. A knapsack raises your center of gravity and makes you more unstable; it also digs painfully into your shoulders if you have more than a couple of pounds in it. It may do for a quick trip to the grocery store or campus but never for an enjoyable ride where you'll be on the bike for more than a few minutes.

2. **Water bottle.** It's vital to carry water with you, especially in hot weather. On any ride of more than 15 miles, and any time the temperature is above 80 degrees, you will get thirsty, and if you don't drink enough water, you will dehydrate. On longer rides through remote areas, or on a hot day, bring two or three water bottles. Put only water in your water bottles—it quenches thirst better than any other liquid.

3. **Basic tools.** Always carry a few basic tools with you when you go out for a ride, just in case you get a flat or a loose derailleur cable. Tire irons, a 6-inch adjustable wrench, a small pair of pliers, a small standard screwdriver, and a small Phillips-head screwdriver are all you need to take care of virtually all roadside emergencies. A rag and a tube of hand cleaner are useful if you have to touch your chain. If your bike has any Allen nuts (nuts with a small hexagonal socket on top), carry metric Allen wrenches to fit them. Cannondale makes a handy one-piece kit with four Allen wrenches, along with standard and Phillips-head screwdrivers.

4. **Pump and spare tube.** If you get a flat, you're immobilized unless you can pump up a new tube or patch the old one. Installing a brand new tube is less painful than trying to patch the old one on the road. Do the patching at home. Pump up the tire until it's hard, and you're on your way. Carry a spare tube in your handlebar bag, or wind it around the seat post, but make sure it doesn't rub against the rear tire.

If you bike a lot and don't use a mountain bike, you'll get flats—it's a fact of life. Most flats are on the rear wheel because that's where most of your weight is. You should, therefore, practice taking the rear wheel off and putting it back on the bike, and taking the tire off and putting it on the rim, until you can do it confidently. It's much easier to practice at home than to fumble at it by the roadside.

5. **Dog repellent.** When you ride in rural areas you're going to encounter dogs, no two ways about it. Even if you don't have to use it, you'll have peace of mind knowing you have something like ammonia or commercial dog spray to repel an attacking dog if you have to. More on this later.

6. **Bicycle computer.** A bicycle computer provides a much more reliable way of following a route than depending on street signs or landmarks. Street signs are often nonexistent in rural areas or are rotated 90 degrees by mischievous kids. Landmarks like "turn right at green house" or "turn left at Ted's Market" lose effectiveness when the green house is repainted red or Ted's Market goes out of business. Most computers indicate not only distance but also speed, elapsed time, and cadence (pedal strokes per minute). The solar-powered models last a long time before the batteries need replacement.

7. **Bike lock.** This is a necessity if you're going to leave your bike unattended. The best locks are the rigid, boltcutter-proof ones such as Kryptonite and Citadel. The next best choice is a strong chain or cable that can't be quickly severed by a normal-sized boltcutter or hacksaw. A cheap, flimsy chain can be cut in a few seconds and is not much better than no lock at all.

In urban or heavily touristed areas, always lock both wheels as well as the frame to a solid object and take your accessories with you when you leave the bicycle. Many a cyclist ignoring this simple precaution has returned to the vehicle only to find one or both wheels gone, along with the pump, water bottle, and carrying bags.

8. **Rear-view mirror.** Available at any bike shop, this marvelous safety device enables you to check the situation behind you without turning your head. Once you start using a mirror, you'll feel defenseless without it. Most mirrors are designed to fit on either a bike helmet or the handlebars. Some fit directly onto the temple piece of eyeglasses.

9. **Bike helmet.** Accidents happen, and a helmet will protect your head if you fall or crash. Bike helmets are light and comfortable, and more and more cyclists are using them.

10. **Food.** Always bring some food with you when you go for a ride.

It's surprising how quickly you get hungry when you're biking. Some of the rides in this book go through remote areas with no food along the way, and that country store you were counting on may be closed on weekends or out of business. Fruit is nourishing and includes a lot of water. A couple of candy bars will provide a burst of energy for the last 10 miles if you're getting tired. (Don't eat candy or sweets before then—the energy burst lasts only about an hour, and then your blood-sugar level drops to below where it was before and you'll be really weak.)

11. **Bicycling gloves.** Gloves designed for biking, with padded palms and no fingers, will cushion your hands and protect them if you fall. For maximum comfort, use handlebar padding also.

12. **Kickstand.** Using a kickstand is the most convenient way to stand your bike upright without leaning it against a wall or other object. Keep in mind that a strong wind may knock your bike over and that in hot weather a kickstand may sink far enough into asphalt to topple your bike.

13. **Bike rack.** It is easier to use a bike rack than to wrestle your bike into and out of your car or trunk. Racks that attach to the back of the car are most convenient—do you really want to hoist your bike over your head onto the roof? If you use a rack that fits onto the back of the car, make sure that the bike is at least a foot off the ground and that the bicycle tire is well above the tailpipe. Hot exhaust blows out tires!

14. **Light.** Bring a bicycle light and reflective legbands with you in case you are caught in the dark. Ankle lights are lightweight and bob up and down as you pedal, giving additional visibility.

15. **Toilet paper.**

16. **Roll of electrical tape.** You never know when you'll need it.

If you are not concerned with riding fast, the most practical bicycle for recreational riding is either a mountain bike or a hybrid between a mountain bike and a sport bike. Most people find them more comfortable than sport bikes because the riding position is more upright. The gearing is almost always lower than it is on sport bikes, which makes climbing hills much easier. (If you buy a mountain bike, be sure to get one with 18 or 21 speeds.) Mountain bikes usually have thumb-operated shift levers, so you don't have to move your hands when shifting gears. The fatter, thicker tires are very resistant to punctures. Mountain bikes are very stable—you're less likely to skid or fall if you should go off the road into soft dirt or if you hit an obstacle like a sand patch, pothole, sewer grate, or bad bump. Mountain bikes are rugged and resistant to damage; for example, a pothole will often dent the rim of a sport bike but will not usually hurt a mountain bike. The only disadvantage of mountain bikes is that they are a little slower than other bicycles because of the wider tires and less streamlined riding position.

If most of your riding is on pavement, you don't need standard mountain bike tires, which are about 2 inches wide with a deep, knobby tread. Use narrower tires (often called city tires or cross-training tires), which are $1\frac{3}{8}$ or $1\frac{1}{2}$ inches wide with a fairly smooth tread.

Take advantage of your gearing when you ride. It's surprising how many people with 21-speed bikes use only two or three of their gears. It takes less effort to spin your legs quickly in the low or middle gears than to grind along in your higher ones. For leisurely biking, a rate of about 80 revolutions per minute, or slightly more than one per second, is comfortable. If you find yourself grinding along at fewer than 70 RPMs, shift into a lower gear. Time your RPMs periodically on a watch with a second hand or your bicycle computer—keeping your cadence up is the best habit you can acquire for efficient cycling. You'll be less tired at the end of a ride, and will avoid strain on your knees, if you use the right gears.

If you have a 10- or 12-speed bike, you'll find it much easier to climb hills if you get a freewheel (the rear cluster of gears) that goes up to 34 teeth instead of the standard 28 teeth. You may also have to buy a new rear derailleur to accommodate the larger shifts, but the expense will be more than worthwhile in terms of ease of pedaling. For the ultimate in hill-climbing ease, you need an 18- or a 21-speed bicycle. The smaller the inner front chainwheel, the lower the low gear. I recommend a small chainwheel with 24 or 26 teeth.

When approaching a hill, always shift into low gear *before* the hill, not after you start climbing it. If it's a steep or long hill, get into your lowest gear right away and go slowly to reduce the effort. Don't be afraid to walk up a really tough hill; it's not a contest, and you're out to enjoy yourself.

Here are a few more hints to add to your cycling enjoyment: Adjust your seat to the proper height and make sure that it is level. Test for proper seat height by pedaling with your heels. Your leg should barely straighten out (with no bend) at the bottom of the downstroke. If your leg is bent, the seat is too low. If you rock from side to side as you pedal, the seat is too high.

Pedal with the balls of your feet, not your arches or heels, over the spindles. Toe clips are ideal for keeping your feet in the proper position on the pedals; they also give you added leverage when going uphill. The straps should be *loose* so that you can take your feet off the pedals effortlessly. In proper pedaling position, your leg should be slightly bent at the bottom of the downstroke.

Eat before you get hungry, drink before you get thirsty, and rest before you get tired. A good rule of thumb is to drink one bottle of water per hour. To keep your pants out of your chain, tuck them inside your socks. Wear pants that are as seamless as possible. Jeans or cut-offs are the worst offenders; their thick seams are uncomfortable. For maximum comfort, wear padded cycling shorts or pants, with no underwear. Use a firm, good-quality seat. A soft, mushy seat may feel inviting, but as soon as you sit on it, the padding compresses under your weight so that you're really sitting on a harsh metal shell.

If you have to use the bathroom, the simplest solution is to get out of sight off the road. A footpath or one-lane dirt road that curves out of sight into the woods is ideal. Most fast-food restaurants have easily accessible restrooms. If a restaurant is of the "Please wait to be seated" variety or has facilities "for customers only," either walk in briskly or order a snack. Most gas stations have restrooms; most convenience stores and country stores do not, but they will sometimes accommodate you if you ask urgently.

Using the Maps and Directions

Unfortunately a book format does not lend itself to quick and easy consultation while you're on your bike. The rides will go more smoothly if you don't have to dismount at each intersection to consult the map or directions provided in this book. You can solve this problem by making a photocopy of the directions and carrying it in your map pocket and dismounting occasionally to turn the sheet over or to switch sheets. Most people find it easier to follow the directions than the map.

In the directions, I have indicated the name of a road if there was a street sign at the time I researched the route; I designated the road as "unmarked" if the street sign was absent. Street signs have a short life span—a couple of years on the average—and are often nonexistent in rural areas. Very frequently, the name of a road changes without warning at a town line, crossroads, or other intersection.

Using a bicycle computer is virtually essential to enjoying the rides. The directions indicate the distance to the next turn or major intersection. Because so many of the roads are unmarked, you'll have to keep track accurately of the distance from one turn to the next. It is helpful to keep in mind that a tenth of a mile is 176 yards, or nearly twice the length of a football field.

In the written directions, it is obviously not practical to mention every single intersection. Always stay on the main road unless directed otherwise.

In addition to distances and a description of the next intersection, the directions also mention points of interest and situations that require caution. Any hazardous spot—for example, an unusually busy intersection or a bumpy section of road—has been clearly indicated by a **CAUTION** warning. It's a good idea to read over the entire tour before taking it in order to familiarize yourself with the terrain, points of interest, and places requiring caution.

In the directions certain words occur frequently, so let me define them to avoid any confusion.

To "bear" means to turn diagonally, somewhere between a 45-degree angle and going straight ahead. In these illustrations, you bear from road A onto road B.

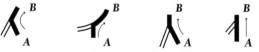

To "merge" means to come into a road diagonally, or even head-on, if a side road comes into a main road. In the examples, road A merges into road B.

A "sharp" turn is any turn sharper than 90 degrees; in other words, a hairpin turn or something approaching it. In the examples, it is a sharp turn from road A onto road B.

Safety

It is an unfortunate fact that thousands of bicycle accidents occur each year, with many fatalities. Almost all cycling accidents, however, are needless and preventable. Most accidents involve children under sixteen and are caused by foolhardy riding and failure to exercise common sense. The chances of having an accident can be reduced virtually to zero by having your bike in good mechanical condition, using two pieces of safety equipment (a rear-view mirror and a helmet), being aware of the most common biking hazards, and not riding at night unless prepared for it.

Before going out for a ride, be sure your bike is mechanically sound. Its condition is especially worthy of attention if you bought the bike at a discount store, where it was probably assembled by a high school kid with no training. Above all, be sure that the wheels are secure and the brakes work.

Be certain that your shoelaces are firmly tied, or use footwear with Velcro closures. A loose shoelace can wrap around the pedal axle or get caught in the chain, trapping you on the bicycle.

Invest in a rear-view mirror and a bicycle helmet, both available at any bike shop. Most mirrors attach to either your helmet or your handlebars and work as well as a car mirror when properly adjusted. Having a mirror means that when you come to an obstacle such as a pothole or a patch of broken glass, you can tell at a glance whether or not it's safe to swing out into the road to avoid it. On narrow or winding roads you can always be aware of the traffic behind you and plan accordingly. Best of all, a mirror eliminates the need to peek back over your shoulder—an action that is not only awkward but also potentially dangerous because riders sometimes unconsciously veer toward the middle of the road while peeking.

A bicycle helmet is the cyclist's cheapest form of life insurance. A helmet not only protects your head if you land on it after a fall but also protects against the sun and the rain. More and more cyclists are wearing them, so you shouldn't feel afraid of looking odd if you use one. Helmets are light and comfortable; once you get used to one, you'll never even know you have it on.

While on the road, use the same old common sense that you use while driving a car. Stop signs and traffic lights are there for a reason—

obey them. At intersections, give cars the benefit of the doubt rather than trying to dash out in front of them or beat them through the light. Remember, they're bigger, heavier, and faster than you are. And you're out to enjoy yourself and get some exercise, not to be king of the road.

Several situations are inconsequential to the motorist but potentially hazardous for the bicyclist. When biking, try to keep aware of these:

1. **Road surface.** Not all roads in Massachusetts are silk-smooth. Often the bicyclist must contend with bumps, ruts, cracks, potholes, and fish-scale sections of road that have been patched and repatched numerous times. When the road becomes rough, the only prudent course of action is to slow down and keep alert, especially going downhill. Riding into a deep pothole or wheel-swallowing crack can cause a nasty spill. On bumps, you can relieve some of the shock by getting up off the seat.

2. **Sand patches.** Patches of sand often build up at intersections, sharp curves, the bottoms of hills, and sudden dips in the road. Sand is very unstable if you're turning, so slow way down, stop pedaling, and keep in a straight line until you're beyond the sandy spot.

3. **Storm-sewer grates.** Federal regulations have outlawed thousands of hazardous substances and products but unfortunately have not yet outlawed the storm sewer with grates parallel to the roadway. This is a very serious hazard because a cyclist catching the wheel in a slot will instantly fall, probably in a somersault over the handlebars. Storm sewers are relatively rare in rural areas but always a very real hazard.

4. **Dogs.** Unfortunately man's best friend is the cyclist's worst enemy. When riding in the country you will encounter dogs, pure and simple. Even though many communities have leash laws, they are usually not enforced unless a dog really mangles someone or annoys its owner's neighbors enough that they complain—a rare situation because the neighbors probably all have dogs too.

The best defense against a vicious dog is to carry a commercial dog spray called Halt, which comes in an aerosol can and is available at most bike shops. Repellent is effective only if you can grab it instantly when you need it—*don't* put it in your handlebar pack, a deep pocket, or any place else where you'll have to fish around for it. For Halt to work you have to squirt it directly into the dog's eyes, but if the dog is close enough to really threaten you, it's easily done.

The main danger from dogs is not being bitten but rather bumping into them or instinctively veering toward the center of the road into on-coming traffic when the dog comes after you. Fortunately almost all dogs have a sense of territory and will not chase you more than a tenth of a mile. If you're going along at a brisk pace and you're in front of the dog when it starts to chase you, you can probably outrun it and stay ahead until you reach the animal's territorial limit. If you're going at a leisurely pace, however, or heading uphill, or the dog is in the road in front of you, the only safe thing to do is dismount and walk slowly forward, keeping the bike between you and the dog, until you leave its territory. If the dog is truly menacing, or there's more than one, repellent can be comforting to have.

If you decide to stay on the bike when a dog chases you, always get into a low gear and spin your legs as quickly as possible. It's hard for a dog to bite a fast-rotating target. Many cyclists swing their pump at the animal, but this increases the danger of losing control of your bike. Often, yelling "Stay!" or "No!" in an authoritative voice will make a dog back off.

A word of caution about using commercial dog spray: It can be legally argued that dog spray comes under the Massachusetts firearms law, which carries a mandatory one-year jail sentence for carrying an un-licensed firearm. Such a case would probably not hold up in court, but because of the potential hazard, a zealous police officer might give you a hassle if he or she noticed it on your bike. The law states in Section 10 of Chapter 269, "Whoever . . . carries . . . a firearm . . . as defined in Section 121 of Chapter 140 . . . shall be punished by imprisonment. . . ." When you go to the definition in Section 121 of Chapter 140, it says, "Firearm shall mean a pistol, revolver or other weapon of any description loaded or unloaded, from which a shot or bullet can be discharged." A court would have to decide whether or not dog spray fits this definition.

5. **Undivided, shoulderless four-lane highways.** This is the most dangerous type of road for biking. If traffic is very light there is no prob-lem, but in moderate or heavy traffic the road becomes a death trap un-less you ride assertively. The only safe way to travel on such a road is to stay in or near the center of the right lane, rather than at the edge, forc-ing traffic coming up behind you to pass you in the left lane. If you hug the right-hand edge, some motorists will not get out of the right lane, brushing past you by inches or even forcing you off the road. Some drivers mentally register a bicycle as being only as wide as its tire, an un-settling image when the lane is not much wider than a car.

ʋeral rides in this book contain short stretches along highways. If is heavy enough to occupy both lanes most of the time, the only afe thing to do is walk your bike along the side of the road.

Railroad tracks. Tracks that cross the road at an oblique angle are a severe hazard because you can easily catch your wheel in the slot between the rails and fall. NEVER ride diagonally across tracks—either walk your bike across or, if no traffic is in sight, cross the tracks at right angles by swerving into the road. When riding across tracks, slow down and get up off the seat to minimize the shock of the bump.

7. **Oiled and sanded roads.** Many communities occasionally spread a film of oil or tar over the roads to seal cracks and then spread sand over the road to absorb the oil. The combination is treacherous for biking. Be very careful, especially going downhill. If the tar or oil is still wet, you should walk or you'll never get your bike clean.

8. **Car doors opening into your path.** This is a severe hazard in urban areas and in the center of towns. To be safe, any time you ride past a line of parked cars, stay 4 or 5 feet away from them. If oncoming traffic won't permit this, proceed very slowly and notice whether the driver's seat of each car is occupied. A car pulling to the side of the road in front of you is an obvious candidate for trouble.

9. **Low sun.** If you're riding directly into a low sun, traffic behind you may not see you, especially through a smeared or dirty windshield. Here your rear-view mirror becomes a lifesaver because the only safe way to proceed is to glance constantly in the mirror and remain aware of conditions behind you. If you're riding directly away from a low sun, traffic coming toward you may not see you and could make a left turn into your path. If the sun is on your right or left, drivers on your side may not see you, and a car could pull out from a side road into your path. To be safe, give any traffic that may be blinded by the sun the benefit of the doubt, and dismount if necessary. Because most of the roads you'll be on are winding and wooded, you won't run into blinding sun frequently, but you should be aware of the problem.

10. **Kids on bikes.** Little kids riding their bikes in circles in the middle of the road and shooting in and out of driveways are a hazard: The risk of collision is always there because they aren't watching where they're going. Any time you see kids playing in the street, especially if they're on bikes, be prepared for anything and call out "Beep-beep" or "Watch out" as you approach. If you have a loud bell or horn, use it.

19

11. **Wet leaves.** In the fall, wet leaves are very slippery. Avoid turning on them.

12. **Metal-grate bridges.** When wet, the metal grating becomes very slippery, and you may be in danger of falling and injuring yourself on the sharp edges. If the road is wet, or early in the morning when there may be condensation on the bridge, please walk across.

A few additional safety reminders: If bicycling in a group, ride single file and at least 20 feet apart. Use hand signals when turning—to signal a right turn, stick out your right arm. If you stop to rest or examine your bike, get both your bicycle and yourself *completely* off the road. Sleek black bicycle clothing is stylish, but bright colors are safer and more visible.

Finally use common courtesy toward motorists and pedestrians. Hostility toward bicyclists has received national media attention; it is caused by the 2 percent of discourteous cyclists (mainly messengers and groups hogging the road) who give the other 98 percent—responsible riders—a bad image. Please do not be part of the 2 percent!

Bicycles and Public Transportation

Thanks to the efforts of the Bicycle Coalition of Massachusetts, bicycles are currently allowed on some of the routes of the Massachusetts Bay Transit Authority (the T) on weekends and off-peak hours. You must obtain a bicycle permit first from the MBTA Senior and Access Pass Office at 10 Boylston Place in downtown Boston (adjacent to the Transportation Building) between 8:30 A.M. and 4:00 P.M. on weekdays. Permits are also available at selcted retail outlets; for more information call the MBTA (617–222–3200) or visit its Website (www.mbta.com/bikepass/html). The permit costs $5.00 and is good for four years. Bikes are allowed only on the three in-town lines using subway cars—the Red, Blue, and Orange Lines—and on commuter rail trains (the Purple Line). Bikes are not allowed on trolleys (the Green Line) or MBTA buses.

It must be emphasized that this program was implemented with some reluctance by MBTA officials, and that it may be either expanded or curtailed at any time. The Bicycle Coalition of Massachusetts urges cyclists to use the program, so that the MBTA will see that there is continued interest in it. The more cyclists take advantage of the program, the more likely it will be continued or expanded in the future.

The only other public transportation practical for bicycles are the ferries that run from Boston Harbor to East Boston, Hingham, Hull, Provincetown, and Gloucester. Bikes are allowed on Amtrak trains and most inter-city buses only if boxed.

Cyclists who depend on public transportation may wish to consider a folding bicycle that fits into a small bag. Several brands, which are sturdy yet easily assembled and disassembled, are available at better bike shops. Folding bikes are suitable for most of the rides in this book. It may take a little while to get used to the steering and handling because of the small wheels.

Bikeways

Bikeways, or bicycle paths, are few and far between in eastern Massachusetts, although many are being planned. The Minuteman Bikeway between Cambridge and Bedford, completed in 1993, is a welcome addition; it is incorporated into ride number 4. (Two other rides in this book, numbers 63 and 64, utilize the bikeway along the Cape Cod Canal.) In the Boston area, bikeways run along both sides of the Charles River in the Back Bay and in Cambridge. In good weather they are jammed with pedestrians and joggers. The Southwest Corridor Bikeway runs 4 miles from the Forest Hills T station in Jamaica Plain to Back Bay Station, paralleling the T Red Line tracks and the Amtrak line. It runs through marginal neighborhoods and crosses some busy streets. Another bikeway originates from the Alewife T station in Cambridge and follows an abandoned railroad line to Davis Square in Somerville.

Bikeways are a mixed blessing. If well designed and well maintained, like the Cape Cod Rail Trail or the East Bay Bicycle Path in Rhode Island, they are a pleasure. If poorly designed or maintained, they are much more dangerous than the roads that they're supposed to avoid. Many bikeways are too narrow or have curves that are too sharp, and many have unsafe road crossings. Unless maintenance is vigilant, a bikeway will rapidly fill up with leaves, glass, and debris; and the surface will deteriorate. In good weather, all bikeways in populated areas will be used by pedestrians, joggers, rollerskaters, skateboarders, children, dogs, and other noncyclists.

The Bicycle Coalition of Massachusetts is actively striving to improve and increase bikeways. If you'd like to join in their efforts, contact them at 214A Broadway, Cambridge, MA 02139 (phone 617–491–RIDE).

Feedback

I'd be very grateful for any comments, criticisms, or suggestions about the rides in this book. Road conditions change, and a new snack bar or point of interest may open up along one of the routes. An intersection may be changed by road construction or improvement, or a traffic light may be installed. I'd like to keep the book updated by incorporating changes as they occur or modifying a route if necessary in the interest of scenery or safety. Many of the changes in this edition are in response to riders' suggestions. Please feel free to contact me through the Globe Pequot Press, 6 Business Park Road, Old Saybrook, CT 06475-0833 with any revision you think helpful.

Chapter 1:
The Immediate Suburbs of Boston

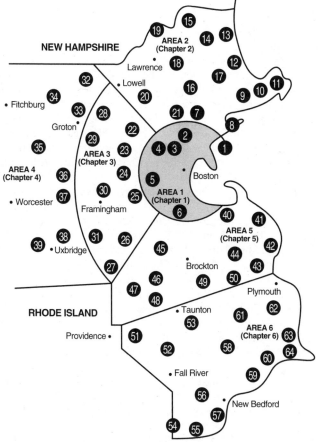

The numbers on this map refer to rides in this book.

Nahant

Number of miles: 7

Terrain: Rolling, with several short, steep hills.

Food: Grocery and snack bar near center of town.

Start: Nahant Beach parking lot, on the east side of the causeway from Lynn to Nahant. On beach days get here early; the huge lot fills up by 10 o'clock. Do not park in Nahant itself; you'll get a ticket. If you wish, you can park in Lynn just north of the rotary at the beginning of the causeway and bike along the beach on the bike path. This adds 3 miles to the ride. On beach days the bike path will be clogged with pedestrians.

How to get there: From the south, head north on Route 1A into Lynn. When Route 1A turns left, continue straight on main road for ½ mile to rotary. Bear right at rotary onto the causeway to Nahant. The parking lot is to the left of the causeway.

If you're coming from the west on Route 128, exit onto Route 129 East (exit 44B). Follow Route 129 East about 5 miles to the ocean (Lynn Shore Drive on right). Turn right and go 1 mile to rotary. Go ⅔ around it onto the causeway to Nahant. The parking lot is to the left of the causeway.

If you're coming from the north on Interstate 95, exit onto Route 1 South (exit 44). Follow Route 1 South about a mile to Route 129 East. Follow Route 129 East about 5 miles to the ocean (Lynn Shore Drive on right). Turn right and go 1 mile to rotary. Go ⅔ around it onto the causeway to Nahant. The parking lot is to the left of the causeway.

This is a short ride that makes up in coastal scenery for what it lacks in distance. It's easy to spend half a day biking those 7 miles if you take time to poke around the rocky ledges and remains of old forts along the shore, especially at the eastern tip of the island.

Nahant is an island 2 miles off the coast of Lynn and Revere, about 2 miles long and ½ mile wide, connected to Lynn by a causeway. It contains some of the most pleasant and scenic bicycling close to Boston. Nahant is a wealthy community with fine homes and a number of mansions lining its rocky, convoluted coastline. For most of the ride you will be within sight of the ocean, and as you head along the southern shore you'll see the Boston skyline, 10 miles away, rising up across the water. Traffic on Nahant is refreshingly light because it is an island with a small population (only 4,000) and no public parking.

For a longer trip, the Nahant ride can easily be added to ride number 8, Lynn– Swampscott–Marblehead, for a total of 29 miles.

Directions for the ride

1. From the Nahant end of the parking lot, head along the main road, following the ocean on your right. Go $\frac{1}{2}$ mile to fork immediately after the Coast Guard station on your left (Castle Road bears right).

2. Bear right on Castle Road and go $\frac{7}{10}$ mile to small crossroads shortly after school on left (Colby Way is straight ahead). You will now do a small counterclockwise loop and return to this point after $\frac{6}{10}$ mile.

3. Turn sharply right at crossroads up a little hill. Go $\frac{6}{10}$ mile to this same intersection (Colby Way on left), making four 90-degree left turns. At the third turn is Fort Buckman, a park on a rocky outcropping with fine ocean views. It used to be a military installation originally built during the Spanish-American War. When you leave the park, you'll go up a short, steep hill. As you complete the loop, notice the square stone tower built into a house at the top of the hill on your left.

4. When you complete the loop, turn right at crossroads and go $\frac{1}{4}$ mile to Flash Road on right, just past the school.

5. Turn right on Flash Road and go $\frac{3}{10}$ mile to fork (Spring Road bears both left and right).

6. Bear right at fork and go $\frac{2}{10}$ mile to Emerald Road, which bears right.

7. Bear right on Emerald Road and go $\frac{2}{10}$ mile to end (merge left onto Willow Road, unmarked, at ocean).

8. Bear left on Willow Road, following the ocean on your right. After $\frac{4}{10}$ mile you'll cross Wharf Street, which goes to the town wharf. Continue $\frac{3}{10}$ mile to Vernon Street (unmarked) on right, at small round traffic island.

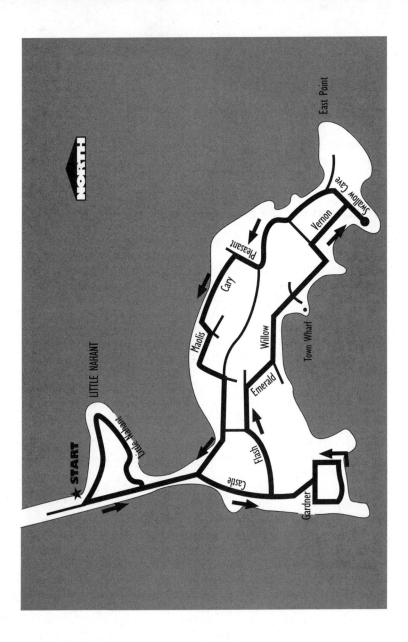

9. Turn right on Vernon Street and go $^2/_{10}$ mile to end (Swallow Cave Road, unmarked).

10. Turn right on Swallow Cave Road and go $^1/_{10}$ mile to end, in front of a mansion. You'll pass two old lookout towers on your left. A path on the left side of the gate leads 100 yards to a small cave hollowed out by the sea. At high tide the ocean spills into the cave.

11. Head back on Swallow Cave Road. After $^2/_{10}$ mile you'll pass the Northeastern University Marine Science Center on your right. This area encompasses East Point, the magnificent rockbound far tip of Nahant. Fascinating old bunkers are built into the rocky ledges. A road leads to the top of the bunkers, providing superb views.

12. From the Marine Science Center, continue $^1/_2$ mile to Pleasant Street on right. It passes between the library and town hall.

13. Turn right on Pleasant Street and go $^1/_{10}$ mile to Cary Street, your second left (dead end if you go straight).

14. Turn left on Cary Street and go $^4/_{10}$ mile to small crossroads (Maolis Road, unmarked), just after you turn 90 degrees inland. The road on the right is very narrow.

15. Turn right at crossroads onto Maolis. After $^1/_{10}$ mile the road turns 90 degrees left (dead end if you go straight). Turn left and go $^2/_{10}$ mile to crossroads and stop sign.

16. Turn right at crossroads and go $1^1/_{10}$ miles to Little Nahant Road on right (it goes up a steep hill). It's the first right after the Coast Guard station. You will now go around Little Nahant, a small island connected to the causeway just north of Nahant itself.

17. Turn right on Little Nahant Road and go $^2/_{10}$ mile to end, at top of steep hill (Simmons Road on left).

18. Turn right at end (still Little Nahant Road) and immediately curve sharply to the left, staying on the main road. Go $^7/_{10}$ mile to end, at yield sign. The entrance to the beach parking lot is on your right when you come to the end.

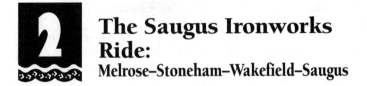

The Saugus Ironworks Ride:
Melrose–Stoneham–Wakefield–Saugus

Number of miles: 18 (11 with shortcut omitting Stoneham and Wake-field)

Terrain: Gently rolling with several short, sharp hills.

Food: Groceries and restaurants in the towns.

Start: Square One Mall, at the junction of Route 1 and Essex Street in Saugus, on the west side of Route 1. Take the Essex Street exit toward Melrose. The exit is just north of Route 99 and about 4 miles south of Route 128 (I–95). Park at the Essex Street entrance to the mall.

On this ride you explore four pleasant middle-class communities about 10 miles directly north of Boston. The region is far enough from the city to be suburban rather than urban, with stretches of greenery, gracious residential neighborhoods, and roads that are not clogged with traffic (except for parts of Saugus near Route 1). All four towns have attractive, well-defined centers with handsome churches, city halls, and other public buildings. The historical highlight of the ride is the Saugus Ironworks, one of the earliest industrial enterprises in America; it dates from around 1650.

The ride starts from the outskirts of Saugus, which is best known for its 4-mile-long commercial strip on Route 1, the busiest in Massachusetts. After less than a mile, you'll enter the pleasant residential community of Melrose, where a cluster of fine old buildings—the town hall, two handsome churches with a school between them, and the graceful stone Soldiers and Sailors Memorial Hall, used as an auditorium—grace the main street. Adjoining the downtown area is delightful Ell Pond, with a park spreading along its northern shore. From here, the route leads a short way across the Stoneham town line, where you'll go through a portion of the Middlesex Fells Reservation, a large expanse of wooded hills and ponds. You'll go along Spot Pond, which is completely surrounded by forest except for the Stone Zoo. From here you head into the center of town, with a compact business block and two distinctive white churches.

From Stoneham, the route climbs past gracious old houses and descends briskly into Wakefield, the most affluent of the four communities and one of the most visually pleasing suburbs inside the Route 128 semicircle. The center of town, a New England classic, could almost be from a rural town 20 miles farther from Boston. The large triangular green, at the southern end of Lake Quannapowitt, is framed by stately Colonial-style homes, a classic white church, and a handsome stone one. Across from the green lies a beautifully landscaped park stretching along the lakeshore, complete with a graceful old bandstand in the middle.

From Wakefield you'll head into Saugus, where the marvelous Victorian town hall will greet you as you pull into the center of town. Just outside of town is the Saugus Ironworks, a splendid example of historical reconstruction that is part of the National Park system. With meticulous attention to detail, the furnace, forge, massive waterwheels, and the dam across the Saugus River have been restored to working order. And to top all this off, it's free. From the Ironworks it's about 2 miles to the end of the ride.

Directions for the ride: 18 miles

1. Turn right onto Essex Street and go $1^{8}/_{10}$ miles to traffic light (Lebanon Street).
2. Go straight at light for $^{2}/_{10}$ mile to another traffic light (Main Street). This is the center of Melrose. Notice the fine stone church on your right at the intersection.
3. Turn right on Main Street and go $^{4}/_{10}$ mile to fork where Green Street (unmarked) bears right, immediately after Ell Pond on left. Here the short ride goes straight and the long ride bears right.
4. Bear right on Green Street and go less than $^{2}/_{10}$ mile to traffic light (Lynn Fells Parkway, unmarked).
5. Turn left at traffic light. Just ahead is another light (Main Street again). Continue straight for $1^{3}/_{10}$ miles to the third traffic light (Pond Street on right), not counting the blinking lights at the beginning. A sign may point right to MDC Zoo and Route 28.
6. Turn right at light and go $^{3}/_{10}$ mile to end, at stop sign at top of hill.

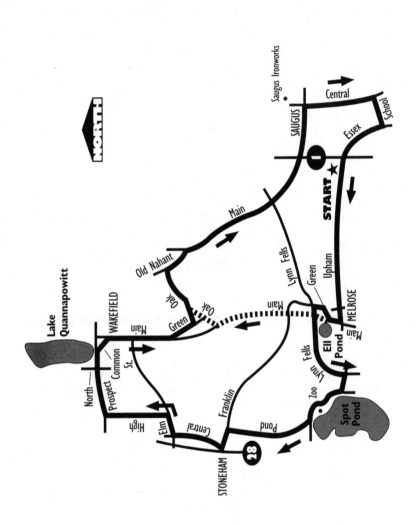

7. Bear right at end and go $^6/_{10}$ mile to Pond Street, which bears right. You'll follow Spot Pond on your left and pass the Stone Zoo.

8. Bear right on Pond Street and go 1 mile to end.

9. Turn left at end and go $^3/_{10}$ mile to end, in the center of Stoneham.

10. Turn sharply right at end on Central Street (unmarked), passing fire station on right. (Don't turn 90 degrees right on Route 28, a wide, busy road.) Go $^1/_2$ mile to third traffic light (Elm Street, unmarked).

11. Turn right on Elm Street and go $^2/_{10}$ mile to High Street on left.

12. Turn left on High Street and go 1 mile to crossroads and stop sign (Prospect Street). You'll climb and then descend steeply.

13. Turn right on Prospect Street and go $^9/_{10}$ mile to traffic light at bottom of hill (North Avenue). As you're coming down the hill, a little red schoolhouse is on the left, built in 1847.

14. Continue straight for $^3/_{10}$ mile to Common Street, which bears right at the Wakefield town green. You'll see Lake Quannapowitt on your left.

15. Bear right on Common Street and go $1^1/_{10}$ miles on Main Street to Green Street, which bears left uphill. At the beginning you'll pass the magnificent First Baptist Church on the right and go through downtown Wakefield. Just before Green Street on the left is J. J. Rounds Park, a rocky outcropping providing a fine view of Crystal Lake. A lookout tower on the top has been torn down, another victim of vandalism and neglect.

16. Bear left on Green Street and go $^1/_2$ mile to Oak Avenue on left. If you come to a fork, you've gone 1 block too far.

17. Turn left on Oak Avenue and go $^9/_{10}$ mile to end, at yield sign (Old Nahant Road). **CAUTION:** The end is at bottom of steep hill.

18. Turn right on Old Nahant Road and go $^1/_4$ mile to end.

19. Turn right at end onto Main Street. After $2^1/_{10}$ miles you'll cross Route 1 on an overpass. **CAUTION:** Watch for traffic entering and exiting Route 1. Continue $^8/_{10}$ mile to a rotary with a monument in the center of Saugus. The Victorian town hall is on the far side of the intersection.

20. Turn left at rotary and go $^2/_{10}$ mile to the Saugus Ironworks on right.

21. Leaving the Ironworks, backtrack to the rotary in the center of town. Continue straight on Central Street for $^8/_{10}$ mile to School Street on right, midway up short hill.

22. Turn right on School Street and go $^4/_{10}$ mile to end (Essex Street, unmarked).

23. Turn right on Essex Street and go $^1/_2$ mile to fork where one road goes straight and the other bears left.

Saugus Ironworks

24. Bear left at fork. **CAUTION** here—much of the traffic coming up behind you will be going straight, to get onto Route 1 North. Go almost $^4/_{10}$ mile to mall entrance on right. **CAUTION:** Just past the overpass above Route 1, watch for traffic entering and leaving the highway.

Directions for the ride: II miles 〰〰〰〰

1. Follow directions for the long ride through number 3.
2. Continue straight on Main Street for $1\frac{1}{2}$ miles to Oak Street on right, at traffic light. It's shortly after an attractive brick school on the right.
3. Turn right on Oak Street and just ahead, curve left on the main road. Go $^1/_{10}$ mile to fork just after stop sign (Green Street bears left, Oak Street bears right).
4. Bear right on Oak Street and go $^9/_{10}$ mile to end, at yield sign (Old Nahant Road). **CAUTION:** The end is at bottom of steep hill.
5. Follow directions for the long ride from number 18 to the end.

Woburn–Winchester–Arlington–Belmont

Number of miles: 19 (13 without Arlington–Belmont extension)
Terrain: The short ride is gently rolling. The long ride is rolling with several steep hills, one a real monster almost $^4/_{10}$ mile long.
Food: Grocery stores and restaurants in the towns.
Start: Parking lot at the corner of Winn Street and Wyman Street in Burlington, at the Woburn town line, across from church (don't park at the church itself). The start is $^1/_2$ mile south of Route 128 (take exit 34, Winn Street). If you live in or near Boston and don't have a car, you can start from the center of Arlington or Belmont.

Just northwest of Cambridge, the older, well-to-do suburbs stretching out to Route 128 provide surprisingly pleasant biking. The area is suburban in the gracious sense of the word, with well-spaced older homes on well-landscaped lots and tree-lined streets. A series of rolling hills across Winchester, Arlington, and Belmont add effort to biking but also heighten the attractiveness of the area. Adding variety to the landscape are Horn Pond in Woburn and the long, slender Mystic Lakes 2 miles south. The Minuteman Bikeway, the longest bicycle trail in the state outside of Cape Cod, passes through the region but is not on the route. The bikeway is on ride 4.

The ride starts from the town line of the pleasant, fairly affluent community of Woburn. After a mile, you'll go through the compact downtown area and then pass the pride of the town, the magnificent Gothic-style stone library designed by H. H. Richardson and built in 1878. It's one of the finest in the state, and it's worth going inside to see its high vaulted ceilings and wooden alcoves. Just outside the town you'll bike along Horn Pond. The former Middlesex Canal passed next to it, and during the canal's heyday in the early 1800s, boatloads of Bostonians would visit the pond for a day's outing. From here it's a short ride to Winchester, another pleasant community, this one with two delightful duck ponds adjoining the center of town. Just outside of Winchester is a relaxing ride along the shore of the Mystic Lakes, two ponds connected like sausages by a narrow neck of land. The Mystic River flows as a small stream from the southern end of the lakes, dramatically increasing in size until it enters Boston Harbor.

The ride now turns north, paralleling the opposite shore of the Mystic Lakes in Arlington and then Winchester again. Here you'll pass through gracious older residential neighborhoods and then back into Woburn, where you'll bike along the other side of Horn Pond through a large lakefront park. The last 2 miles run through a surprisingly undeveloped area, where you'll pass several nurseries and greenhouses.

The long ride heads farther south into Belmont, wealthiest of the communities on the ride. It has a fair amount of greenspace and open fields in the western edge of the town, including the Rock Meadow Reservation, the Habitat Institute for the Environment (a wildlife sanctuary with nature trails), and an Audubon sanctuary. Any one of these spots is a good place to relax after the steep climb out of town. You'll then cross back into Arlington, where you'll climb more gradually to the highest point in the area, a 375-foot hill crowned by a stately concrete water tower. Two blocks off the route there's a superb view of Boston from a playground sloping along the hillside.

After a fast downhill plunge, you can detour $^2/_{10}$ mile off the route to see the Old Schwamb Mill, a wooden building that was a mill during the 1800s and is now an arts and crafts center. From here you'll climb into the wealthy, wooded western edge of Winchester and rejoin the short ride about a mile before you come to Horn Pond.

Directions for the ride: 19 miles ◆◆◆◆◆◆◆◆◆◆◆◆◆

1. Turn right (south) on Winn Street and go $1^2/_{10}$ miles to stop sign in the center of Woburn (Pleasant Street on right). It's one-way in the wrong direction if you go straight.
2. Turn right on Pleasant Street and go $^2/_{10}$ mile to Arlington Road, which bears left at traffic light. You'll pass the library on your right.
3. Bear left on Arlington Road (don't turn sharply left on Warren Avenue) and go $^9/_{10}$ mile to crossroads and stop sign at the end of Horn Pond.
4. Go straight at crossroads for $^1/_{10}$ mile to a dead end, and then go

straight ahead onto a narrow bicycle path. **CAUTION:** Watch for glass and bumps. Follow the path 100 yards to end, then continue straight on another paved road.

5. Follow the paved road $3/10$ mile to Horn Pond Brook Road, which bears left.

6. Bear left on Horn Pond Brook Road for 100 yards to a dead end, and then go straight onto another bike path.

7. Follow the path $3/10$ mile to the end. You'll ride along Horn Pond Brook on your left. Wedge Pond, a delightful little duck pond, will be in front of you when you reach the end.

8. Jog left at end and immediately right at traffic light (Main Street). Go $1/4$ mile to end (Church Street). At the end, notice the graceful white church 100 yards to your right.

9. Turn left at end under railroad bridge and immediately bear right (still Main Street). **CAUTION** here—cross traffic does not have to stop. This is downtown Winchester. Go $1/10$ mile to traffic light (Mystic Valley Parkway, unmarked). Immediately before the light on your left is another tiny duck pond with the water cascading over curving stone steps. It's worth crossing the street to see this delightful spot.

10. Turn right at light on Mystic Valley Parkway and go $6/10$ mile to end.

11. Turn right at end and go $1/10$ mile to your first left.

12. Turn left on this road (still Mystic Valley Parkway) and go $1 8/10$ miles to a small rotary (Route 60, High Street). You'll ride along the Mystic Lakes.

13. Turn right at rotary and go 100 yards to another rotary. Continue straight on Route 60 for $1/2$ mile to end, at traffic light (Mystic Street). Here the short ride turns right and the long ride turns left.

14. Turn left at end (still Route 60). **CAUTION:** Busy intersection. Go $1/10$ mile to traffic light (Massachusetts Avenue). This is downtown Arlington. You'll see the Minuteman Bikeway on your right immediately before the light.

15. Cross Massachusetts Avenue onto Pleasant Street. After $9/10$ mile you'll cross the Route 2 overpass. Continue 1 mile to your third traffic light (Concord Avenue), not counting the lights at the overpass. This is the center of Belmont. Notice the old brick town hall on your left at the intersection.

16. Turn right on Concord Avenue up a very steep hill and go $1 2/10$ miles to Winter Street, which bears right.

17. Bear right on Winter Street and go $^2/_{10}$ mile to crossroads and blinking light (Marsh Street).

18. Turn right on Marsh Street and go $^9/_{10}$ mile to rotary.

19. Bear left at rotary onto Park Avenue and go $1^2/_{10}$ miles to traffic light at bottom of steep hill (Massachusetts Avenue). **CAUTION:** This intersection comes up suddenly while you're going downhill. At the top of the hill is the big water tower. If you go to the back of the tower and head a couple of blocks downhill on Eastern Avenue, which runs perpendicular to the route, you'll come to a playground with a splendid view of Boston.

20. Cross Massachusetts Avenue and go $^1/_{10}$ mile to a six-way intersection. Here the ride goes straight uphill, but if you turn right for $^2/_{10}$ mile and then take your first left on Mill Lane, you'll see the old red wooden Schwamb Mill.

21. At the six-way intersection, continue straight uphill (don't bear right on Bow Street). Go $^3/_{10}$ mile to traffic light (Summer Street).

22. Cross Summer Street and go $^1/_{10}$ mile to stop sign (merge left).

23. Bear left at stop sign and then immediately bear right uphill on Forest Street. Go $^4/_{10}$ mile to fork at top of hill where the main road (Ridge Street) bears left.

24. Bear left on Ridge Street. After $^1/_4$ mile Lockeland Road bears right, but continue straight for $^1/_2$ mile to crossroads and stop sign (Johnson Road).

25. Turn right on Johnson Road and go 1 mile to traffic light (Route 3, Cambridge Street).

26. Continue straight for $^4/_{10}$ mile to where the main road curves 90 degrees right and Woodside Road turns left.

27. Turn left on Woodside Road (**CAUTION** here) and go $^2/_{10}$ mile to Chesterford Road, which bears left. You'll pass Winter Pond.

28. Bear left on Chesterford Road and go $^2/_{10}$ mile to end, at stop sign.

29. At end, go straight ahead onto a blocked-off lane that runs along the west shore of Horn Pond (you'll see the pond on your right after a short distance). After $^7/_{10}$ mile you'll come to a parking lot. At the far end of the lot curve right, following the pond, and go $^4/_{10}$ mile to the end of the blocked-off section (Water Street on left). **CAUTION:** Watch for glass, joggers, and pedestrians.

30. At end of blocked-off section, continue straight for $^2/_{10}$ mile to end (Pleasant Street, unmarked).

31. Turn left at end and go less than $^2/_{10}$ mile to fork (Burlington Street bears right).

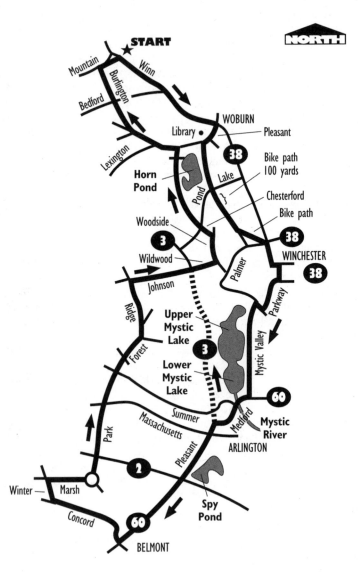

32. Bear right on Burlington Street and go $^4/_{10}$ mile to three-way fork. A greenhouse is on the left at the intersection.

33. Bear right at fork (still Burlington Street) and go $^3/_{10}$ mile to cross-roads and stop sign (Bedford Road, unmarked).

34. Go straight at crossroads for $^4/_{10}$ mile to end (Mountain Road).

35. Turn right on Mountain Road and go $^1/_{10}$ mile to Wyman Street (un-marked) on right. It's immediately after Manor Avenue on right.

36. Turn right on Wyman Street and go less than $^2/_{10}$ mile to parking lot on left.

Directions for the ride: 13 miles

1. Follow directions for the 19-mile ride through number 13.

2. Turn right at the end onto Mystic Street (Route 3). Go $2^6/_{10}$ miles to Wildwood Street, which crosses Route 3 at traffic light.

3. Turn right on Wildwood Street and go $^4/_{10}$ mile to where the main road curves 90 degrees right and Woodside Road turns left.

4. Follow directions for the long ride from number 27 to the end.

The Minuteman Bikeway:
Arlington–Lexington–Bedford–Burlington–Woburn–Winchester

Number of miles: 23
Terrain: Gently rolling.
Food: Grocery stores and restaurants just off the route in Lexington and Bedford. Neighborhood grocery in Woburn.
Start: Center of Arlington, at the corner of Massachusetts Avenue and Mystic Street (Route 60), a mile east of Route 2. The municipal parking lots next to the starting point are free on weekends.

CAUTION:

The Minuteman Bikeway is very heavily used on weekends in good weather by both cyclists and noncyclists. Keep alert for walkers, joggers, rollerskaters, children, and dogs. When passing, call out "Passing on your left" or "Coming through" in a clear voice. The trail also crosses some busy roads. Keep your pace moderate. I suggest getting an early start so that you can enjoy the bikeway before it becomes busy.

This ride explores the same general area as ride 3, but immediately west of it. The route follows the Minuteman Bikeway, the longest bicycle trail in the state outside of Cap Cod, for most of its length—an 8⁶/₁₀-mile stretch between Arlington Center and Bedford. The trail, which was completed in 1993, follows a former Boston and Maine railroad line. Because of this fact, the scenery along the bikeway is what one would expect to see from a train. The trail is isolated from the communities through which it passes as it slips behind homes, factories, and warehouses. The bikeway passes in back of the handsome storefronts and public buildings in the centers of Arlington and Lexington; to see them you have to get off the trail onto Massachusetts Avenue. The bikeway is well designed and wide enough to be safe, but it is heavily used, and caution is necessary (see **CAUTION** notice at beginning of ride directions).

The ride begins by following the trail from Arlington to Bedford. After 1½ miles you'll come within 100 yards of the Old Schwamb Mill, a wooden building that has been producing high-quality picture frames since 1864. Workshops in crafting Shaker furniture are held across the street. About 3 miles ahead you'll skirt downtown Lexington and pass near Battle Green, where the first skirmish of the American Revolution took place in 1775. Facing the green is the Buckman Tavern, where the Minutemen assembled for battle. In Bedford, the northwestern terminus of the trail, you'll head ½ mile into the center of town. Bedford is a pleasant residential community with an unusually large and elegant white church.

From Bedford you'll follow quiet secondary roads to Burlington and then Woburn, both attractive residential towns. In Woburn you'll ride along Horn Pond through a large lakeside park on a road blocked off to cars. Just beyond Horn Pond the route enters the affluent town of Winchester, where you'll enjoy a relaxing ride along the shore of the Mystic Lakes, two ponds connected by a narrow neck of land. From the southern end of the Mystic Lakes it's less than a mile to the starting point.

Directions for the ride:

1. From the corner of Massachusetts Avenue and Mystic Street (Route 60) in the center of Arlington, head northwest on the Minuteman Bikeway, paralleling Massachusetts Avenue on your left. Go 8.6 miles to end, in Bedford. (Before beginning this route, read the **CAUTION** notice in the Start section of the ride description.)

After 1½ miles, the trail passes within 100 yards of the Old Schwamb Mill and Shaker workshop center. If you'd like to visit them, watch for a street paralleling the bikeway on the left (Frazer Road). It's just after an athletic field on the right. Get on Fraser Road (it's safest to walk off the bikeway). Turn right as you leave the bikeway and immediately curve left away from it. The mill and workshop center are just ahead.

Continuing along the trail, after 6/10 mile you'll see a ballfield on the right. A footpath leads from the far side of the field 50 yards to the Arlington Reservoir, a small secluded pond straddling the Arlington-Lexington town line. The trail skirts downtown Lexington 2 6/10 miles farther

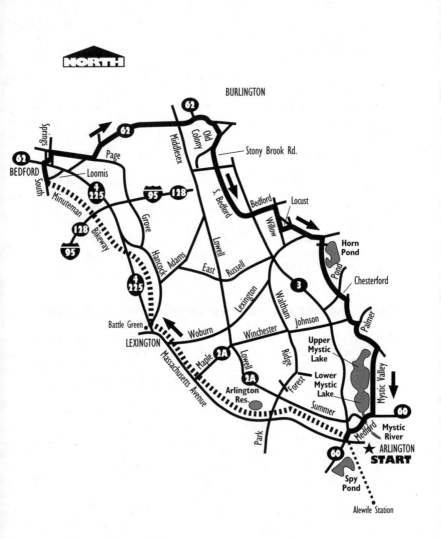

on, on your left. Battle Green, where the first shots of the Revolutionary War were fired, is at the western end of the downtown area. You'll cross above Route 128 about 2 miles past downtown Lexington; from here it's another 2 miles to the end of the bikeway.

2. At the end of the bike trail, turn 90 degrees right uphill on South Road, which is unmarked. (Don't turn sharply right on Loomis Street.) Go $^4/_{10}$ mile to traffic light (Route 62), in the center of Bedford. Notice the impressive white church on your left at the intersection.

3. Cross Route 62 and go $^1/_{10}$ mile to fork (Springs Road bears right).

4. Bear right at fork and go less than $^2/_{10}$ mile to end (merge left at stop sign).

5. Bear left at stop sign and go $^1/_4$ mile to crossroads and stop sign (Pine Hill Road on left, Page Road on right).

6. Turn right on Page Road and go $^7/_{10}$ mile to stop sign (merge head-on onto Route 62).

7. Go straight on Route 62 for $^2/_{10}$ mile to where Route 62 curves sharply left and Page Road goes straight.

8. Curve left on Route 62 and go $^3/_{10}$ mile to fork where Route 62 bears right.

9. Bear right on Route 62 and go $1^8/_{10}$ miles to traffic light after large athletic field on left (Middlesex Turnpike).

10. Cross Middlesex Turnpike. After $^6/_{10}$ mile Route 62 turns left, but continue straight, passing a distinctive modern church on right. Go $^7/_{10}$ mile to where the main road curves sharply left and Terrace Hall Avenue turns right.

11. Curve left on main road and go $^2/_{10}$ mile to Old Colony Road, which turns right up a short, steep hill.

12. Turn right on Old Colony Road and go $^3/_{10}$ mile to end (Lexington Street, unmarked).

13. Turn right at end and go almost $^6/_{10}$ mile to Stony Brook Road on left. The main road curves sharply right at the intersection.

14. Turn left on Stony Brook Road and go almost $^4/_{10}$ mile to traffic light.

15. Continue straight for $1^1/_{10}$ miles to Route 3 (Cambridge Street), at traffic light.

16. Go straight for almost $^6/_{10}$ mile to another traffic light (Willow Street). You'll pass an old-fashioned little grocery store on the left.

17. Turn right on Willow Street and go $^3/_{10}$ mile to Locust Street on left, just after school on right.

18. Turn left onto Locust Street and go $^2/_{10}$ mile to end (merge right; no stop sign). There's a greenhouse on the right at the intersection.

19. Bear right at end and go $^4/_{10}$ mile to end.

20. Turn left at end and go less than $^2/_{10}$ mile to Woburn Parkway on right.

21. Turn right on Woburn Parkway and go $^2/_{10}$ mile to end (Water Street on right).

22. At end, go straight ahead onto a blocked-off lane that follows the shore of Horn Pond. Go $^4/_{10}$ mile to parking lot on left.

23. Turn left into lot. At the far end continue straight, following the pond on your left. Go $^3/_{10}$ mile to fork at far end of pond. **CAUTION:** Watch for pedestrians.

24. Bear right uphill at fork, passing electric power station on left. Go $^3/_{10}$ mile to end of blocked-off road.

25. At end of blocked-off road, continue straight onto Chesterford Road. Go $^2/_{10}$ mile to end (merge right at stop sign).

26. Bear right at end and go $^1/_2$ mile to crossroads, at second stop sign (Palmer Street on left, Fletcher Street on right). You'll pass Winter Pond at the beginning.

27. Turn right on Fletcher Street and go $^2/_{10}$ mile to traffic light (Church Street).

28. Continue straight for $^4/_{10}$ mile to crossroads (Ginn Street on left, Mystic Valley Parkway on right). It's just before you go under a railroad bridge.

29. Turn right on Mystic Valley Parkway and go $1^8/_{10}$ miles to a small rotary (Route 60, High Street). You'll ride along the Mystic Lakes on your right.

30. Turn right at rotary and go 100 yards to another rotary.

31. Continue straight for $^1/_2$ mile to end, at traffic light (Mystic Street). Route 60 turns left there.

32. Turn left at end (**CAUTION:** busy intersection). Go $^1/_{10}$ mile to traffic light (Massachusetts Avenue), in the center of Arlington. If you wish, you can follow the southeastern section of the Minuteman Bikeway $1^3/_{10}$ miles to the Alewife T station and backtrack to Arlington Center. You'll pass Spy Pond, which is surrounded by houses and apartments. To get on this section of the bikeway, cross Massachusetts Avenue diagonally (it's safest to walk), follow it 100 yards to the first right (Swan Place), turn right, and turn immediately left onto the bikeway.)

Newton–Brookline

Number of miles: 22 (15 without Brookline–Arnold Arboretum–Jamaica Pond extension)

Terrain: Gently rolling, with several hills, including two steep ones.

Food: Numerous groceries and restaurants.

Start: Commuter rail parking lot at the corner of Auburn Street and Woodland Avenue, alongside the Massachusetts Turnpike, in the Auburndale section of Newton.

An alternate starting point, closer to Boston, is one of the side streets just off the Jamaicaway opposite Jamaica Pond. If you start the ride here, begin by heading along the bike path next to the Jamaicaway. Go to direction 30 for the long ride.

How to get there: From Route 128, get off at Route 30 (exit 24). Turn right (east) at end of ramp and go ²/10 mile to Auburn Street, which bears right at traffic light. Bear right and go ³/10 mile to parking lot on right, just after Woodland Road on right. If you're heading west on Commonwealth Avenue, turn left on Lexington Street (the first traffic light after the bridge over the Massachusetts Turnpike). Go 100 yards to your first right, Auburn Street. Turn right and go ¼ mile to parking lot on left.

On weekdays the lot fills with commuters. If the lot is full, start from the corner of Concord Street and Route 16 (follow directions 1 through 3). Park on Concord Street facing away from Route 16.

This ride takes you exploring in two affluent suburbs immediately west of Boston filled with large, gracious homes from the nineteenth and early twentieth centuries. The long ride heads across the Boston line to the Arnold Arboretum, a large, beautifully landscaped park with rolling, grassy hillsides and 6,000 varieties of trees, shrubs, and flowers from all over the world.

The ride starts from Newton, a classic "streetcar suburb" that evolved with public rail transportation during the second half of the nineteenth century. This sparked the construction of residential areas, generally

45

aimed at a well-to-do market, beyond the confines of Boston itself yet easily accessible to the city for daily commuting. Newton is pleasant to bicycle through, with tree-lined, curving streets and spacious older wooden or brick homes surrounded by attractively landscaped yards. You'll bike past Boston College, with its dignified stone Gothic-style buildings, and return along broad, gracefully curving Commonwealth Avenue, with a grassy island in the middle for its entire length.

The long ride heads farther east across Brookline, which geographically should be part of Boston because it is surrounded by the city along three-quarters of its perimeter. The southern half of Brookline is even more elegant than Newton, with a broad belt of mansions and estates just south of Route 9. You'll pass through this idyllic area and then head to the Arnold Arboretum. The most spectacular time to visit it is around Mother's Day, when thousands of lilacs and other flowers bathe the hillsides in a pink and purple haze. Just up the road from the Arboretum is Jamaica Pond, with the built-up Boston neighborhood of Jamaica Plain on one side and estates just across the Brookline border on the other.

From Jamaica Pond you'll angle back across Brookline through more estates and gracious residential areas where it's hard to believe that you're only 5 miles from downtown Boston. You'll pass the Frederick Law Olmsted National Historic Site, a rambling old building that was for many years the home and office of the country's foremost landscape architect of the nineteenth century. Olmsted is most famous for designing Central Park in New York City. He also designed an elaborate, linear park system for Boston, including Franklin Park, Jamaica Pond, the Muddy River between Brookline and Jamaica Plain, and the Back Bay Fens. Some of his original plans are on display at the site, which is currently open from Friday through Sunday.

Just ahead, a couple of blocks off the route, you can visit the Longyear Museum, an elegant stone mansion with exhibits relating to the life of Mary Baker Eddy, founder of Christian Science. The beautifully landscaped grounds, with gardens, gazebos, fountains, and statuary, provide a lovely rest stop at the top of a hill. Newbury College, a private two-year institution, is next to the museum. You'll descend to Beacon Street and enjoy a relaxing run along the Chestnut Hill Reservoir, which is framed by two ornate Victorian stone pumping stations. Just beyond the reservoir you'll join the route of the short ride past Boston College and along Commonwealth Avenue to the end.

Directions for the ride: 22 miles

1. Turn left out of parking lot and immediately turn left on Woodland Road, crossing the bridge over the Massachusetts Turnpike. Go ¼ mile to crossroads and blinking light (Grove Street).

2. Turn right on Grove Street. After ²/10 mile the main road curves sharply left. Continue 1¹/10 mile to end (Concord Street, unmarked). **CAUTION** at the entrance and exit ramps for Route 128. You will pass the Riverside MBTA Station, a convenient spot for taking public transportation into Boston.

3. Turn left on Concord Street and go ²/10 mile to end (Route 16).

4. Turn left on Route 16 and go ³/10 mile to the entrance road to Interstate 95 South, at traffic light. On this stretch you'll parallel the Charles River on your right. This area is called Newton Lower Falls.

5. Turn 90 degrees right at traffic light, passing the Pillar House on your left. (Don't turn sharply right onto Wales Street–Walnut Street.) Just ahead, go underneath the highway onto Quinobequin Road. This is a great winding road with the Charles River on your right. After 1½ miles you'll go underneath Route 9. Just beyond Route 9 is another bridge, a graceful, slender concrete span called Echo Bridge. To verify the accuracy of the name, walk to the bank of the Charles directly beneath the bridge and holler. A walkway runs along the top of the bridge, providing a fine overview of the river, which flows between two hills and a dam just upstream.

6. From Echo Bridge, continue up a short, steep hill to stop sign at the top (merge right). This area is called Newton Upper Falls.

7. Bear right at stop sign and go ½ mile to second traffic light (Oak Street, unmarked).

8. Turn right on Oak Street and go ³/10 mile to end, at traffic light (Needham Street).

9. Jog left and immediately right (almost straight) onto Christina Street. Go ½ mile to end (Wallace Street, unmarked). **CAUTION:** Bumps and potholes at the railroad crossing.

10. Turn left at end and go ²/10 mile to end (Winchester Street, unmarked).

11. Turn right on Winchester Street and go ⁶/10 mile to end (Nahanton Street).

12. Turn left on Nahanton Street and go ⁷/10 mile to end (merge right on Dedham Street).

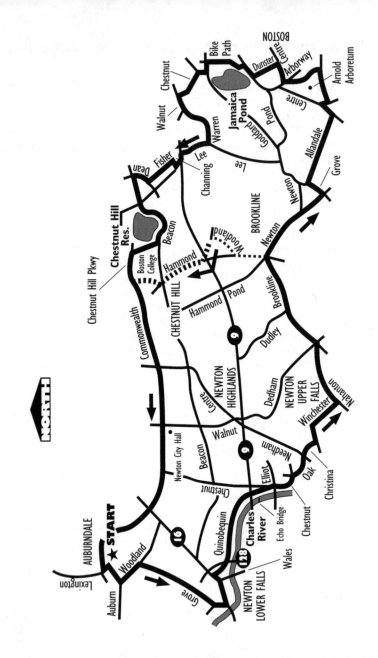

13. Bear right on Dedham Street and go ¹⁄₁₀ mile to traffic light (Carlson Avenue on right, Brookline Street on left).

14. Turn left on Brookline Street and go 1½ miles to rotary. Here the short ride goes two-thirds around onto Hammond Street, and the long ride bears right.

15. Bear right at rotary onto Newton Street, a divided parkway. It's the second road off the rotary. Go ⁴⁄₁₀ mile to fork where West Roxbury Parkway bears right and uphill.

16. Bear right uphill and go ³⁄₁₀ mile to rotary at bottom of hill.

17. Go three-quarters around the rotary onto Grove Street. Go ²⁄₁₀ mile to Allandale Road on right.

18. Turn right on Allandale Road and go 1¹⁄₁₀ miles to end (Centre Street). The second half of this road is in Boston, but the area is so undeveloped you'd never know it.

19. Turn left at end and go ²⁄₁₀ mile to the entrance to Arnold Arboretum on right. It comes up suddenly as you're going downhill—don't whizz past it.

20. Turn sharply right into the Arboretum. Just beyond the gate there's a road on your left. Turn left and go ⁴⁄₁₀ mile to fork at bottom of hill. **CAUTION:** Watch for pedestrians and joggers.

21. Bear left at fork and go ½ mile to end (Arborway, unmarked). The visitors center is on your left just before the end.

22. Turn left on Arborway, using service road on the far side. (To cross the Arborway, use the crosswalk just to the right of the exit gate.) Go ¹⁄₁₀ mile to crossroads (Centre Street).

23. Turn right on Centre Street and go 200 yards to Dunster Road, your third left.

24. Turn left on Dunster Road and go ³⁄₁₀ mile to end (Pond Street, unmarked). This is the Jamaica Plain section of Boston.

25. Turn right on Pond Street and immediately merge head-on into the Jamaicaway. **CAUTION:** Be sure to use the sidewalk. Go ²⁄₁₀ mile to traffic light. This is one of the busiest roads in the state, and if you don't use the sidewalk, you'll get killed.

26. Cross the Jamaicaway at traffic light and turn right onto the bike path that goes alongside the Jamaicaway on your right. (Don't bike on the path right next to the pond, which is for pedestrians only.) Go ⁴⁄₁₀ mile to traffic light (Perkins Street).

27. Turn left on Perkins Street and go less than $^2/_{10}$ mile to Chestnut Street (unmarked) on right, at traffic light.

28. Turn right on Chestnut Street and go 100 yards to rotary.

29. Bear left at rotary and go $^1/_{10}$ mile to fork where High Street bears right and the main road bears slightly left.

30. Stay on main road for $^2/_{10}$ mile to fork where Kendall Street bears right and Chestnut Street (unmarked) bears left.

31. Bear left on Chestnut Street and go $^2/_{10}$ mile to crossroads and stop sign (Walnut Street).

32. Turn left on Walnut Street and go $^2/_{10}$ mile to fork at top of hill. Notice the handsome stone church on your left at the fork.

33. Bear left at fork and immediately bear left again on Warren Street. Go $^7/_{10}$ mile to end, at rotary (Lee Street, an unmarked divided road). Just beyond the fork you'll pass the Frederick Law Olmsted National Historic Site on your right.

34. Bear right on Lee Street and go less than $^4/_{10}$ mile to end (Route 9). You'll pass the Brookline Reservoir on the right.

35. Turn left on Route 9 and go 100 yards to traffic light (Chestnut Hill Avenue, unmarked, on right).

36. Turn right on Chestnut Hill Avenue, and immediately turn right again on Channing Road. Go $^1/_{10}$ mile to end (Fisher Avenue).

37. Turn left on Fisher Avenue and go $^1/_2$ mile to stop sign and blinking light (Dean Road). **CAUTION:** You'll reach this intersection while you're going downhill. At the top of the hill you'll pass the Fisher Hill Reservoir, hidden behind an embankment, on the left. Newbury College is immediately after the reservoir. The Longyear Museum is 2 blocks to your right just past the top of the hill; to get to it turn right on Holland Road, bear right uphill on Seaver Street and turn sharply right to the museum.

38. Turn right on Dean Road and go $^4/_{10}$ mile to Beacon Street, at traffic light. It's all downhill! When you get to Beacon Street, notice the handsome stone church on the left.

39. Turn left on Beacon Street and go $1^3/_{10}$ miles to Chestnut Hill Parkway (unmarked) on right, at end of reservoir. **CAUTION:** After $^4/_{10}$ mile you'll go through Cleveland Circle, a busy commercial area with diagonal trolley tracks at the main intersection. Then you'll follow the Chestnut Hill Reservoir on your right and pass two imposing Victorian waterworks buildings on your left.

40. Turn right on Chestnut Hill Parkway, still following the pond on your right, and go ½ mile to traffic light (Commonwealth Avenue). You curve sharply right just before the light. Boston College is on your left.

41. Turn left on Commonwealth Avenue. **CAUTION:** There are more dangerous trolley tracks at the intersection; walk your bike. Follow Commonwealth Avenue 4^8/$_{10}$ miles to Lexington Street, the first traffic light after the bridge over the Massachusetts Turnpike (sign may point left to Auburndale Center). Whenever possible, use the service road to the right of the center island. There is a tough hill at the beginning, followed by a long downhill, which is the infamous "Heartbreak Hill" on the Boston Marathon route. The marathoners, of course, are going in the opposite direction. Farther on you'll pass the ornate red-brick city hall on your left.

42. Turn left on Lexington Street and go 100 yards to your first right, Auburn Street. This is the center of Auburndale.

43. Turn right and go ¼ mile to parking lot on left.

Directions for the ride: 15 miles 🐛🐛🐛🐛🐛🐛

1. Follow directions for the long ride through number 14.

2. Go two-thirds around the rotary onto Hammond Street, the third road off the rotary. (If you come to Hammond Pond Parkway, unmarked, you've gone too far around.) Go ^{4}/$_{10}$ mile to Woodland Road, which bears right.

3. Bear right on Woodland Road and go ½ mile to end, at yield sign.

4. Turn left at end of Woodland Road and go ^{3}/$_{10}$ mile back to Hammond Street (unmarked), at crossroads and stop sign.

5. Turn right on Hammond Street and immediately cross Route 9 at traffic light. **CAUTION:** Busy intersection. Go ^{3}/$_{10}$ mile to Beacon Street (unmarked), at traffic light. You'll go through Chestnut Hill, the area where Brookline, Newton, and the Brighton section of Boston meet.

6. Cross Beacon Street, bearing right on the far side of the intersection onto College Road (it's one-way in the wrong direction if you go directly across). Go ^{3}/$_{10}$ mile to traffic island (Commonwealth Avenue, unmarked), passing Boston College on your right.

7. Turn left on Commonwealth Avenue at far side of traffic island. Go 4^4/$_{10}$ miles to Lexington Street, the first traffic light after the bridge over the Massachusetts Turnpike (sign may point left to Auburndale Center). Whenever possible, use the service road to the right of the center island.

You'll go down "Heartbreak Hill" of Boston Marathon fame and then pass the ornate city hall on your left.

8. Turn left on Lexington Street and go 100 yards to your first right, Auburn Street. This is the center of Auburndale, a section of Newton.

9. Turn right and go ¼ mile to parking lot on left.

The Blue Hills Ride:
Milton–West Quincy

Number of miles: 18 (11 with shortcut)
Terrain: Rolling, with one long, tough hill and several short ones.
Food: Howard Johnson's near end.
Start: Trailside Museum, Route 138, Milton, 1 mile north of Route 128.
It's just after the ski area.

Directly south of Boston is an area that's a pleasant surprise. Instead of
dreary suburbs or industrial barrens, there are old mansions and gracious estates, a long, stately parkway with a broad, grassy island down
the middle, and the elegant town center of Milton. Surrounding all this is
the wonderful Blue Hills Reservation, the largest protected expanse of
greenspace in the metropolitan area, yet very close to Boston. Five miles
long, the reservation contains one of the most prominent natural features
in the Boston area, the range of rugged wooded hills rising to a height of
630 feet at its western end on top of Great Blue Hill. Foot trails hop from
hill to hill, providing some superb views; horseback riders and cross-
country skiers can enjoy 65 miles of bridle paths. Also on the grounds
are a natural history museum, an Audubon Society education center, and
two ponds.

The ride starts at the Trailside Museum, a natural history museum
run by the Massachusetts Audubon Society, at the foot of Great Blue Hill.
It contains both live and stuffed animals and birds native to Massachusetts. Large animals are exhibited outdoors. From behind the museum a trail leads ½ mile to the summit, where an observation tower
affords one of the best views to be found of Boston and vicinity. You'll
head past estates and rolling hillsides to the center of Milton, a New England jewel with a large green framed by the town hall and two classic
white churches.

From here you'll parallel the Neponset River estuary along a hillside
with magnificent views. Sloping down the hill to the water's edge is
Hutchinson Field, a lush, grassy meadow with a vista of the river and the

Boston skyline. The field is one of the properties of the Trustees of Reservations, whose main office is next door. Across the street is the imposing Captain Robert Bennett Forbes House, which contains exhibits of the China trade (Forbes made his fortune that way). Just ahead you'll enter the Blue Hills Reservation and traverse its entire length on smooth roads winding through the woods, passing Houghtons Pond, which has a beach. At the end you'll go by more estates along a tiny lane just over the Canton town line.

Directions for the ride: 18 miles

1. Turn right (north) out of parking lot and go ²/₁₀ mile to Canton Avenue (unmarked), which bears right (sign may say TO HYDE PARK).

2. Bear right on Canton Avenue and stay on main road 1³/₁₀ miles to Atherton Street on left. It's ½ mile past Dollar Lane on left. There's a graceful stone gatehouse on the right just past Dollar lane.

3. Turn left on Atherton Street and go less than ²/₁₀ mile to traffic light (Route 138).

4. Cross Route 138 and go ⁴/₁₀ mile to crossroads and stop sign (Brush Hill Road).

5. Turn right at crossroads onto Brush Hill Road and go 1²/₁₀ miles to end (merge right at stop sign).

6. Bear right at end onto divided highway and go ²/₁₀ mile to Brook Road (unmarked), which bears right.

7. Bear right on Brook Road and go ¹/₁₀ mile to traffic light (Route 138).

8. Cross Route 138 and go ¹/₁₀ mile to stop sign and a divided parkway (Blue Hills Parkway, unmarked).

9. Turn right on parkway and go 1²/₁₀ miles to stop sign where the divided road ends (Canton Avenue, unmarked). Here the short ride goes straight and the long ride turns left.

10. Turn left on Canton Avenue and go 1 mile to traffic light at five-way intersection. The Milton town green is on your left just before the light.

11. Bear left at light, staying on Canton Avenue (don't turn 90 degrees left on Reedsdale Road). **CAUTION** bearing left. Go ⁴/₁₀ mile to diagonal crossroads and stop sign (Brook Road).

12. Cross Brook Road and go ⁷/₁₀ mile to end (Adams Street). Get in lowest gear at end.

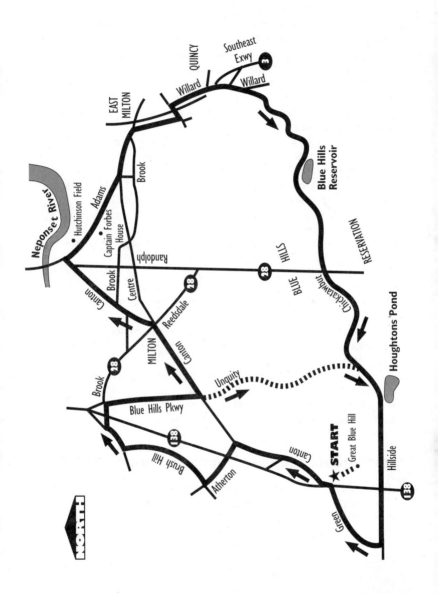

13. Turn 90 degrees right on Adams Street and go 1½ miles to traffic light immediately before the bridge over Interstate 93 (sign says TO INTERSTATE 93 SOUTH). You'll pass Hutchinson Field on your left and the Robert Bennett Forbes House on your right after ²/10 mile.

14. Bear right at light, paralleling Interstate 93 on left, and go ⁶/10 mile to crossroads (Robertson Street; a sign may say TO EAST MILTON, WEST QUINCY).

15. Turn left at crossroads and go ¹/10 mile to traffic light (Willard Street).

16. Turn right on Willard Street and go ½ mile to fork where the main road bears right underneath Interstate 93.

17. Bear right on main road and go ³/10 mile to fork where Willard Street bears right and the ramp onto Interstate 93 bears left.

18. Bear right at fork. Just ahead is another fork. Bear right again, following sign that may say TO MILTON, CANTON, BLUE HILLS. Go 1³/10 miles to end (merge right at stop sign). Most of this stretch is uphill.

19. Bear right at stop sign and go 1⁶/10 miles to traffic light (Route 28). You'll pass the Blue Hills Reservoir on your left. Half a mile ahead is a small parking area on the right with a fine view of Boston. From here it's all downhill to Route 28.

20. Cross Route 28 and go 1³/10 miles to fork where the main road bears slightly left.

21. Bear slightly left at fork and go ²/10 mile to end (merge left at stop sign).

22. Bear slightly left at end and go 1½ miles to traffic light (Route 138). You'll pass Houghtons Pond on your left at the far end of a large parking lot after ½ mile.

23. Go straight at light for ⁷/10 mile to Green Street, a small crossroads just beyond the Blue Hills Office Park on left.

24. Turn right at crossroads and go 1²/10 miles to end (Route 138).

25. Turn right on Route 138. The museum is just ahead on your left.

Directions for the ride: 11 miles

1. Follow directions for the long ride through number 9.

2. Go straight at crossroads onto Unquity Road (unmarked). Go 3⁸/10 miles to traffic light (Route 138). You'll pass Houghtons Pond on your left at the far end of a large parking lot after about 2½ miles.

3. Follow the directions for the long ride from number 23 to the end.

Chapter 2:
The North Shore

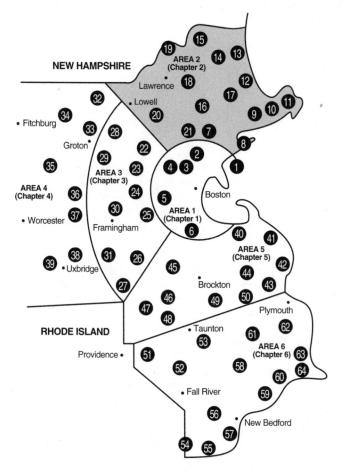

The numbers on this map refer to rides in this book.

7 Lynnfield–North Reading–Saugus

Number of miles: 23 (16 without North Reading loop)
Terrain: Gently rolling.
Food: Several grocery stores and restaurants. 99 Restaurant near end.
Start: Hunter Place, a small office center at the junction of Route 129 and Walnut Street in Saugus. It's ⁴/₁₀ mile west of Route 1.
How to get there: From Route 1, exit west onto Route 129. Go ⁴/₁₀ mile to Hunter Place on right.

This is a tour of affluent residential areas north of Boston. After going along two ponds, the ride passes through the elegant town center of Lynnfield and the traditional New England town of North Reading. The landscape is midway between rural and suburban and very pleasant for biking. If you're looking for a fairly easy and relaxing ride, this is a good choice.

The ride starts from Saugus, which is best known for its potently visual commercial strip along Route 1. (The Saugus Ironworks is not on the route, but you can see it on ride 2.) Within ½ mile you'll cross the town line into Lynnfield and ride along Hawkes Pond. Soon you'll pass Pillings Pond and arrive at the classic town center of Lynnfield, the wealthiest of the three communities on the ride. The large, triangular green is graced by a stately white church, and on the green itself stands a meetinghouse built in 1714.

From Lynnfield you'll proceed on lightly traveled side roads to the charming town center of North Reading. The large green, complete with bandstand, slopes uphill to a white church with a clock tower built in 1829. Just past the green is the town hall, a striking Victorian building. The return trip to Saugus follows pleasant secondary roads through a different section of Lynnfield. You'll ride along the opposite shore of Pillings Pond on a road not much wider than a bicycle path.

The short ride omits the western loop and does not go through North Reading.

Directions for the ride: 23 miles

1. Turn right out of parking lot onto Walnut Street (don't get on Route 129 West, Water Street). Go 1⁴/10 miles to traffic light (Salem Street), just before you go under Route 128. You'll go along Hawkes Pond on the right.

2. Go straight at light for ⁷/10 mile to Thomas Road on right. It goes up a short hill.

3. Turn right on Thomas Road and go ⁴/10 mile to end.

4. Turn left at end and go 1½ miles to end, in the center of Lynnfield. You'll pass Pillings Pond on your right. Just before the end go straight (don't bear left), passing the green on your left.

5. Turn left at end onto Main and go ⁴/10 mile to Chestnut Street on right.

6. Turn right on Chestnut Street and go 1⁷/10 miles to end (Lowell Street). After ⁴/10 mile, notice the old house on the left with a steep-pitched roof and small, diamond-paned windows. At the end, the short ride turns right and the long ride turns left.

7. Turn left at end onto Lowell Street and stay on main road for 1⁴/10 miles to crossroads and stop sign, at blinking light (Haverhill Street).

8. Turn left at crossroads and go 1¹/10 miles to Franklin Street on right.

9. Turn right on Franklin Street and go ¼ mile to small crossroads (Pearl Street). It's just after Partridge Road on right.

10. Turn right on Pearl Street and go ⁴/10 mile to Route 28, at stop sign.

11. Cross Route 28 onto Mill Street, bearing right as you go through the intersection. **CAUTION:** Route 28 is very busy. Follow main road for ½ mile to end. **CAUTION:** Watch for potholes at the beginning.

12. Turn right at end and go ²/10 mile to traffic light (Route 28 again).

13. Continue straight for ⁶/10 mile to crossroads and stop sign (Route 62).

14. Turn right on Route 62 and go 1⁴/10 miles to fork where Route 62 (unmarked here) bears left and Park Street bears right, at gas station. You'll go through the center of North Reading shortly before the fork, passing the green and former town hall (now a library), built in 1875, on your left.

15. Bear right on Park Street and go 1 mile to end.

16. Turn left at end onto Lowell Street, up a short hill. Go ⁴/10 mile to traffic island where Chestnut Street turns right and the main road curves left.

17. Curve left on Lowell Street and go 1 mile to crossroads and stop sign (Main Street).

18. Turn right on Main Street and go ⁸/10 mile to Essex Street on left. It's just after a grocery store with gasoline pumps on the left.

19. Turn left on Essex Street and go $\frac{9}{10}$ mile to Pillings Pond Road on right, after high school.

20. Turn right on Pillings Pond Road and go $\frac{6}{10}$ mile to fork where Oak Ridge Terrace, a narrow lane, bears left.

21. Bear left at fork, following the shore of Pillings Pond on your right. Go $\frac{3}{10}$ mile to small unmarked crossroads where Walsh Road turns left and Edgemere Road turns right. Both roads are so narrow that they look like driveways. If you come to Birch Road on the left, you've gone 100 feet too far.

22. Turn right at crossroads, following pond on right. Go $\frac{1}{2}$ mile to end (Wildewood Drive on left).

23. Turn right at end and go $\frac{4}{10}$ mile to end.

24. Turn right at end and go $\frac{1}{10}$ mile to crossroads and stop sign (Sumner Street, unmarked).

25. Turn left at crossroads onto Sumner Street and go $\frac{1}{2}$ mile to end (Salem Street), just after you go underneath Route 128.

26. Turn right on Salem Street and go $\frac{8}{10}$ mile to traffic light (Walnut Street, unmarked). The 99 Restaurant, on the left shortly before the light, is an excellent lunch stop.

27. Continue straight for $\frac{8}{10}$ mile to Montrose Avenue on left, just after the entrance road to Interstate 95 South on right. A good snack bar is on the left just before the intersection.

28. Turn left on Montrose Avenue and go $\frac{9}{10}$ mile to end (Route 129). **CAUTION:** Watch for potholes.

29. Turn left at end and go $1\frac{6}{10}$ miles to stop sign where Route 129 East bears right. The starting point is on the left at the intersection. **CAUTION:** Watch for bumps and potholes. The road is currently under construction.

Directions for the ride: 16 miles ～～～～～～

1. Follow directions for the long ride through number 6.

2. Turn right at end onto Lowell Street and go 1 mile to crossroads and stop sign (Main Street).

3. Follow directions for the long ride from number 18 to the end.

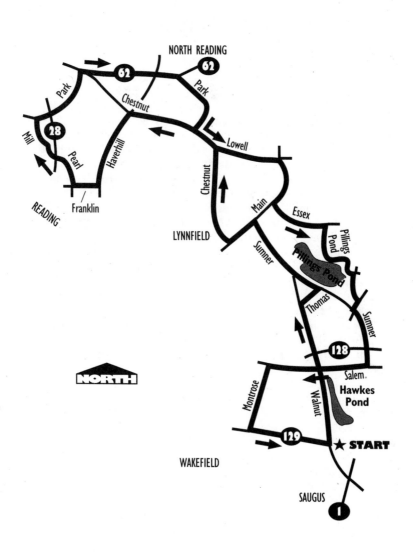

8 Lynn–Swampscott–Marblehead

Number of miles: 20
Terrain: Gently rolling.
Food: Numerous stores and restaurants on the route.
Start: Lynn Shore Drive in Lynn, just north of the causeway to Nahant.
How to get there: From the south, head north on Route 1A into Lynn. When Route 1A turns left, continue straight on main road for ½ mile to rotary. Go three quarters of the way around the rotary. Park as soon as it's legal or on the service road on the left (inland) side of road.

If you're coming from the west on Route 128, exit onto Route 129 East (exit 44B). Follow Route 129 East about 3 miles to Route 107 (Western Avenue). Cross Route 107 onto Chestnut Street and follow it for 1²/₁₀ miles to traffic light (Lewis Street on left, Broad Street on right). Turn right on Broad Street and go ²/₁₀ mile to Nahant Street on left, at second traffic light. Turn left on Nahant Street (you have to go a little past it and make a U-turn), and go ⁴/₁₀ mile to end, at ocean. Turn right immediately before end on Beach Road and park where legal.

If you're coming from the north on Interstate 95, exit onto Route 1 South (exit 44). Follow Route 1 South about a mile to Route 129 East. Pick up the directions for coming from the west, at "Follow Route 129 East about 3 miles . . ."

This is a tour of the nicest coastline close to Boston if you don't count Nahant. (You can do the Nahant ride too—from the starting point go along the bike path on the east side of the causeway to Nahant. Added distance is 9 miles.) The area is similar to Cape Ann but only half the distance from Boston, with beautiful stretches of shoreline graced by elegant mansions and estates, some rocky headlands, and the maze of narrow streets lined with restored antique homes in the center of Marblehead. The town lies along a peninsula jutting northeastward into the Atlantic. Just east of it is Marblehead Neck, a bowling-pin-shaped island 1 mile long and ½ mile wide, rimmed with elegant homes and connected to the mainland by a causeway. Between the two are the deep, sheltered waters of Marblehead Harbor, one of the yachting and sailing capitals of New England. The view of Marblehead across the harbor from the Neck, sloping up a low hillside crowned by Abbott Hall, the proud Victorian town hall that dominates the town, is inspiring.

You start the ride by heading up the Lynn shoreline, the best face of this otherwise drab industrial city, with a well-landscaped strip of parkland along the ocean on your right and gracious older homes and apartment buildings on your left. You then continue up the coast through Swampscott, an affluent community with attractive older homes, many quite elegant, lining the shore and the hillsides rising from it.

From Swampscott it's a short ride into Marblehead. First you'll go around the Neck. At its northern tip is Chandler Hovey Park, a beauty spot with a nearly 360-degree view of the sea and a tall old lighthouse. Then you'll go around Marblehead itself, where you're much better off on a bike than in a car as you weave along its narrow streets without worrying about finding a parking place. You'll pass Abbott Hall, the ornate town hall built in 1876, which contains an impressive painting, *The Spirit of '76*, commissioned for the American Centennial. Just ahead are two delightful waterfront parks, Chandler Park and Fort Sewell. The latter commands a small peninsula and contains the remains of a Revolutionary fort. Just north of town is Old Burial Hill, one of the state's outstanding historic cemeteries, with many slate headstones, dating back to the 1700s and even earlier, stretching up the terraced hillside.

Directions for the ride

1. Head north on Lynn Shore Drive, following the ocean on your right. Go $1^6/10$ miles to Puritan Road, which bears right at traffic light along the ocean. After $1^1/10$ miles you'll pass the Swampscott town green on your left, with the town hall a block inland.
2. Bear right on Puritan Road and stay on main road for $1^2/10$ miles to end (Atlantic Avenue, Route 129). Several dead-end lanes on the right lead to the rocky coastline past elegant homes and estates.
3. Turn right on Route 129, and immediately go straight ahead (don't bear left on Humphrey Street). Go $1^2/10$ miles to traffic light (Clifton Avenue).

4. Continue straight for $8/10$ mile to Gallison Avenue on right. It's the next street after Vassar Road.

5. Turn right on Gallison Avenue and go $1/10$ mile to Orchard Street, your first left.

6. Turn left on Orchard Street and go $3/10$ mile to your second crossroads and stop sign. It's a one-way street going right.

7. Turn right at crossroads and go $1/10$ mile to end, at yield sign (merge right).

8. Bear right at end and go $7/10$ mile across the causeway to Marblehead Neck. There's a fork at the end of the causeway (Harbor Avenue bears left, Ocean Avenue bears right).

9. Bear right at fork and go $14/10$ miles to a little traffic circle. Shortly before the circle, a paved footpath on the right leads $1/10$ mile to Castle Rock, which provides a stunning view of the rugged, Mainelike coastline.

10. Bear right at traffic circle and go $3/10$ mile to Chandler Hovey Park, at the northern tip of the neck.

11. Leaving the park, turn right on Kimball Street and go $2/10$ mile to end.

12. Turn right at end and go $1/10$ mile to the little traffic circle (Harbor Avenue bears right).

13. Bear right at traffic circle and go $1/4$ mile to crossroads just beyond the crest of a little hill (Ballast Lane).

14. Turn right at crossroads, going along the shore of Marblehead Harbor on your right. Go $1/2$ mile to end (merge to your right at stop sign). The brick building with the tall clock tower on the far side of the harbor is Abbott Hall, the town hall.

15. Bear right at end and go $8/10$ mile to traffic light (Atlantic Avenue). You'll cross the causeway in the opposite direction.

16. Turn right at traffic light and go $1/4$ mile to Chestnut Street on right, just after church on left.

17. Turn right on Chestnut Street. After $2/10$ mile the street turns 90 degrees left along the water, then left again. Continue 100 yards to Gregory Street on right.

18. Turn right on Gregory Street and go $2/10$ mile to Waldron Street on left, at top of little hill.

19. Turn left on Waldron Street and go $1/10$ mile to fork (Waldron Court, a dead end, bears left).

20. Bear right at fork. Just ahead, turn right at end and go 100 yards to

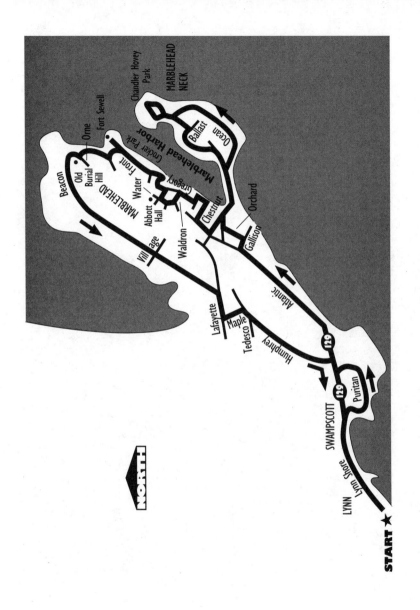

Marblehead Harbor

your first right, Lee Street. At this intersection, the ornate brick building on the far-left corner is the town hall, Abbott Hall.

21. Turn right on Lee Street and go 100 yards to end (merge left at stop sign).

22. Bear left at end (still Lee Street) and go 100 yards to stop sign.

23. Turn right downhill at stop sign and immediately turn right again on Water Street. Go 100 feet to bottom of hill, where the main road turns 90 degrees left onto Front Street.

24. Turn left at bottom of hill. On your right is Crocker Park, a rocky outcropping with a magnificent view of the harbor. Continue straight, following the water on your right, for 6/10 mile to Fort Sewell at end.

25. Leaving Fort Sewell, backtrack 1/10 mile to a forced right turn (it's one-way in the wrong direction if you go straight).

26. Turn right and go 1/10 mile to where the main road turns left and a smaller road, Orne Street (unmarked), bears right. A sign may point left TO LYNN, BOSTON.

27. Bear right on Orne Street and follow main road 4/10 mile to end (Norman Street on left, Beacon Street on right). After 1/4 mile the Old Burial Hill is on your left. It was founded in 1638 and is a great place to compare old gravestones. Across the road is still another waterfront park, Fountain Park.

28. Turn right at end and go 1⁸/10 miles to traffic light (Village Street). You'll pass Dolliber Cove on your right at the beginning.

29. Go straight at light for 8/10 mile to end (merge to your right onto Lafayette Street, unmarked, at another traffic light).

30. Bear right on Lafayette Street and go 1/4 mile to Maple Street, which turns sharply left at traffic island.

31. Turn sharply left on Maple Street and go 2/10 mile to traffic light.

32. Bear right at light on Humphrey Street. (Don't turn 90 degrees right on Tedesco Street.) Go 1½ miles to end, at yield sign (merge right on Route 129).

33. Bear right on Route 129 and go 2½ miles back to start, following the ocean on your left.

Estates and Estuaries:
Beverly–Manchester–Wenham–Essex–Hamilton

Number of miles: 26 (16 without Manchester–Essex–Hamilton extension)
Terrain: Gently rolling, with one short, sharp hill.
Food: Grocery in Beverly. Groceries and restaurants in Manchester. Grocery and restaurant in Essex. The local specialty here is clams.
Start: Hamilton-Wenham commuter rail parking lot, corner of Route 1A and Walnut Road, Hamilton, at the Wenham town line. It's 3 miles north of Route 128, next to the Hamilton Shopping Center. The entrance is on Walnut Road.

The region northeast of Beverly is the North Shore at some of its finest: a magnificent landscape of rocky coastline with mansions perched above it; the broad, gently rolling fields of gentleman farms and old-moneyed estates; and gracious horse farms partitioned by white wooden fences. The town centers are classic New England gems. A fine network of smooth, little-traveled secondary roads weaving across the landscape provides bicycling at its best.

The ride starts off by heading a few miles along winding lanes to the ocean in Beverly. Like others across the state, Beverly is a two-sided community. The negative side, which you won't come anywhere near, is a congested, unattractive commercial area surrounded by factories and closely stacked houses. The positive side is the eastern half of the city and the northernmost section along the Wenham line, consisting primarily of woods, some gracious residential neighborhoods, and the magnificent Atlantic shore. The two easternmost communities of Pride's Crossing and Beverly Farms have been havens for Boston's landed gentry since the railroad was built in the 1800s. In the wedge of land between Route 127 and the ocean, dozens of mansions rise in isolated splendor at the end of 1/4-mile-long driveways.

Your first encounter with the shore comes at Lynch Park, commanding a promontory jutting into the ocean. As city parks go it is a pleasure—clean, well landscaped, and well maintained. Just east of the park on the next point stands a handsome lighthouse built in 1871. A mile up the coast is Endicott College, a women's school and one of the most spectacularly located in the state. Several of its buildings are elegant mansions perched directly on the rocky shoreline.

From here it's a short ride through Pride's Crossing, with its touristy country store at the railroad crossing, then Beverly Farms and on into Manchester, where you'll loop along the water on a little lane before coming into town.

Manchester is a gracious seaside town with more oceanfront estates belonging to Boston's bluebloods; fine old homes on the streets adjacent to the center of town; and beautiful Singing Beach, one of the North Shore's nicest. In the town center is the handsome town hall and a graceful white church dated 1809.

From Manchester you'll have a smooth run into Essex, another delightful town with a cluster of antique shops along the main street. If you like clams you're in the right place—all the restaurants serve clams that were on the ocean floor only hours before. The best-known spot is Woodman's, on the left as you're heading down Route 133. The remainder of the town consists of vast salt marshes extending along the estuaries of the Essex and Castle Neck rivers, wooded hills, and some broad farms.

After you leave Essex, the remainder of the ride goes through a little bit of Ipswich and then across Hamilton, passing through magnificent horse-farm and estate country. Hamilton is another gracious, well-to-do community where many of the residents are likely to feed the family horse in the morning. You'll pass Asbury Grove, a Methodist campground containing small, Gothic-style cottages and a central tabernacle. It is similar to Oak Bluffs in Martha's Vineyard but not as extensive or ornamented. Asbury Grove was founded in 1858.

Hamilton's best-known landmark is the Myopia Hunt Club, an extensive estate founded in 1875 that is the major center for polo in the state. Polo matches are held on Sunday afternoons at 3 o'clock and are fascinating to watch. If you'd like to go to them after the ride, the Club is on Route 1A ½ mile north of the starting point.

The short ride bypasses Manchester, Essex, and Hamilton by taking a direct route from Beverly Farms back to the start. You'll pass through a long slice of Wenham, going by Gordon College, beautifully situated on an unspoiled lake, and then past horse farms and country estates.

Directions for the ride: 26 miles

1. Turn right out of parking lot onto Walnut Road and go $1^1/_{10}$ miles to crossroads and stop sign (Larch Row).

2. Go straight at crossroads. You'll immediately pass an unusual Gothic-style church on your right. Go $^7/_{10}$ mile to Grover Street on left.

3. Turn left on Grover Street and go $1^1/_{10}$ miles to end (Essex Street, Route 22).

4. Turn right at end and go $^2/_{10}$ mile to Groce Street (unmarked), which turns sharply left just before a gas station on left.

5. Turn sharply left on Groce Street and immediately right on Standley Street. Go $^7/_{10}$ mile to fork where Common Lane turns left and Foster Street bears right.

6. Bear right on Foster Street and go $^3/_{10}$ mile to another fork, where Cole Street turns right and Boyles Street bears left across railroad tracks.

7. Bear left across tracks and go $^7/_{10}$ mile to traffic island where Lakeshore Avenue turns right. **CAUTION:** Bumpy spots.

8. Bear left at traffic island, and immediately bear left again on Cross Street (unmarked). Go $^3/_{10}$ mile to end (Route 127).

9. Turn right on Route 127 and go $^1/_{10}$ mile to Woodbury Street, which bears left. It's your second left.

10. Bear left on Woodbury Street and go $^2/_{10}$ mile to crossroads and stop sign.

11. Turn left at crossroads. Just ahead is the entrance to Lynch Park. The view from the point is impressive.

12. Just past the park exit, bear slightly left at fork on Neptune Street (don't turn 90 degrees left on Evergreen Drive). Go $^3/_{10}$ mile to end (Neptune Street on left, Pickman Road on right). If you want to look at the lighthouse, turn right at first crossroads on Bayview Avenue and go $^2/_{10}$ mile.

13. Turn right at end and go $^3/_{10}$ mile to end (Route 127).

14. Turn right on Route 127. After $^2/_{10}$ mile Route 127 curves sharply right. Continue along Route 127 for 3 miles to Hale Street, which turns left immediately after the third railroad crossing. **CAUTION:** These are dangerous diagonal railroad crossings with frequent train traffic. Walk your bike over them. The short ride turns left on Hale Street, and the long ride goes straight.

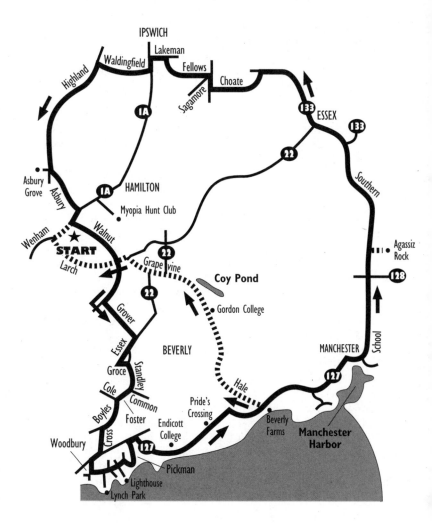

15. Continue along Route 127 for $1\frac{1}{10}$ miles to Harbor Street on right, at a traffic island. The Old Corner Inn is on the far side of the intersection.

16. Turn right on Harbor Street and go $\frac{2}{10}$ mile to end, immediately after a little railroad bridge.

17. Turn right at end and go $\frac{2}{10}$ mile to where the road becomes private, just beyond the beautiful rockbound inlet called Black Cove. Make a U-turn here and backtrack to Route 127. If you wish, you can bear right when you come to the road that crosses the railroad bridge and go $\frac{1}{4}$ mile to the end at Tucks Point, a small peninsula at the mouth of Manchester Harbor. Here you'll find a yacht club and a small waterfront park with a gazebo.

18. Turn right on Route 127 and go $\frac{8}{10}$ mile to School Street (unmarked), which bears left in the center of Manchester opposite the town hall/police station and the classical white church. A sign at the intersections points left to Essex.

19. Bear left on School Street and go $4\frac{1}{10}$ miles to end (Route 133). After $1\frac{7}{10}$ miles you'll see a dirt turnoff on the right. From here a path leads $\frac{1}{4}$ mile to Agassiz Rock, a large boulder on a hilltop.

20. Turn left on Route 133 and go $\frac{1}{2}$ mile to fork where Route 133 bears right and Route 22 bears left. You'll go through the center of Essex. At the fork the ride bears right, but if you bear left for $\frac{2}{10}$ mile you'll come to the town hall, a portly wooden Victorian monstrosity with the fattest clock tower in Massachusetts.

21. Bear right on Route 133 and go $1\frac{9}{10}$ miles to Choate Street on left, just before top of hill.

22. Turn left on Choate Street and go $1\frac{3}{10}$ miles to end. **CAUTION:** Bumps and potholes.

23. Turn right at end and go $\frac{1}{10}$ mile to your second left, Fellows Road. (The first left bears left.)

24. Turn 90 degrees left on Fellows Road (don't turn sharply left on Sagamore Road). Go $1\frac{2}{10}$ miles to end.

25. Turn left at end and go $\frac{3}{10}$ mile to end (Route 1A).

26. Turn left on Route 1A and go $\frac{2}{10}$ mile to Waldingfield Road on right.

27. Turn right on Waldingfield Road and go 1 mile to end (Highland Street, unmarked). **CAUTION:** Bumps and potholes.

28. Turn left on Highland Street and go $2\frac{8}{10}$ miles to crossroads and blinking light (Asbury Street on left). Here the ride turns left, but if you turn right you'll enter Asbury Grove. The center of the campground is set back ¼ mile from the road.

29. Turn left on Asbury Street and go 1 mile to end (Route 1A).

30. Turn right on Route 1A and go ²/10 mile to shopping center on left. **CAUTION:** Dangerous diagonal railroad tracks as you turn left. Either turn immediately before them or walk across.

Directions for the ride: 16 miles ~~~~~~~~~

1. Follow directions for the long ride through number 14.

2. Turn left immediately after railroad tracks on Hale Street and go 4⁴/10 miles to end (Larch Row). Hale Street becomes Hart Street, which in turn becomes Grapevine Road. The lane along the lake behind Gordon College is delightful.

3. Turn left on Larch Row and go ¹/10 mile to crossroads.

4. Continue straight for 1⁶/10 miles to end (Route 1A, Main Street). Here the ride turns right, but if you turn left, after ³/10 mile you'll come to the lovely town center of Wenham. On the left is the Claflin-Richards House, built in 1664, and an adjoining museum of nineteenth-century dolls, toys, and games.

5. Turn right on Route 1A and go ⁷/10 mile to shopping center on right, at the intersection with Walnut Road. **CAUTION:** Dangerous diagonal railroad tracks at the intersection; please walk across.

Manchester Harbor

Gateway to Cape Ann:
West Gloucester–Essex–Manchester–Magnolia

Number of miles: 23

Terrain: Gently rolling, with two short hills.

Food: Grocery stores and restaurants in the towns. The regional favorite dish is clams, especially in Essex.

Start: Junction of Routes 127 and 133 in Gloucester, just west of the bridge over the Blynman Canal. Park on Route 127 on the ocean side of the road.

How to get there: From Route 128, exit east onto Route 133 (take exit 14). Go 3 miles to end (Route 127). Bear left on Route 127 and park.

The area just west of Cape Ann has the glorious seascape scenery of the cape itself without the tourists and the traffic. Like Cape Ann, the region is characterized by gracious old towns; the rocky coastline with mansions and estates perched above it in baronial splendor; little sandy beaches tucked between craggy headlands; and lonely, unspoiled salt marshes along the northern shore.

The ride starts from West Gloucester, the less urban portion of the city on the western side of the canal that separates Cape Ann from the mainland. You will head westward along the rural, unspoiled northern shore past woods, small farms, and salt marshes to Essex, another picturesque community. In the center of town, just off the route, are several antiques shops, snack bars serving clams dredged up from the ocean floor only hours before, and the mouth of the Essex River, filled with small fishing boats. From Essex it's a smooth run to Manchester. At the town line you'll pass Agassiz Rock, a large glacial boulder on top of a hill. The area is maintained by the Trustees of Reservations.

Manchester is a stately seaside community with a graceful white church, built in 1809, dominating the center of town. Also in town are the Trask House, an elegant Federal-period mansion, and an old cemetery filled with weathered slate gravestones dating back to 1800 and before. Just south of town is Smith Point, a rockbound, steep-spined

75

peninsula rimmed with mansions of Boston Brahmins and landed gentry. The northern shore of the neck offers fine views of boat-filled Manchester Harbor. As you leave Smith Point you visit Singing Beach, one of the North Shore's finest, a wide, graceful curve of smooth but squeaky (singing) sand with rocky headlands at each end and a succession of mansions gracing the water's edge.

From Manchester you'll follow the coast across the Gloucester town line into Magnolia, a gracious nineteenth-century resort community with a row of smart shops and a delightful lane hugging the shore of the small peninsula on which the village is located. Just up the road a short trail leads to the shore, where you'll get a view of Rafe's Chasm, a spectacular narrow defile in the cliffs rising from the sea about 75 feet deep. A little farther on is one of the North Shore's most distinctive landmarks, the Hammond Museum, often called the Hammond Castle. It is a medieval-style castle, complete with moat and drawbridge, spectacularly located on the oceanfront cliffs. It was built in 1928 by John Hays Hammond, inventor of systems to control the movement of vehicles from a distance by radio and an avid collector of medieval artifacts. Until legislation prohibited the practice, it was fashionable for the wealthy to plunder the European landscape for bits and pieces of old castles and palaces, which is exactly what Hammond did to construct his own. Inside is a fascinating collection of medieval furniture, tapestries, armor, and other relics. The centerpiece of the castle is a magnificent organ with more than 8,000 pipes, on which concerts are given during the summer. From behind the building you can see Normans Woe, the offshore rocks made famous by Longfellow's "The Wreck of the Hesperus."

From the Castle it's about 2 miles to the canal separating Cape Ann from the mainland. Just before the canal is Stage Fort Park, a dramatic oceanfront expanse that's worth exploring.

Directions for the ride

1. Head west on Route 133. Go 2⁴/10 miles to Concord Street on right (sign may say TO WINGAERSHEEK MOTEL AND BEACH).
2. Turn right on Concord Street. After ½ mile you'll go underneath Route 128. Continue ⁷/10 mile to Atlantic Street on right. Here the ride goes straight, but if you turn right and go 2 miles, you'll come to

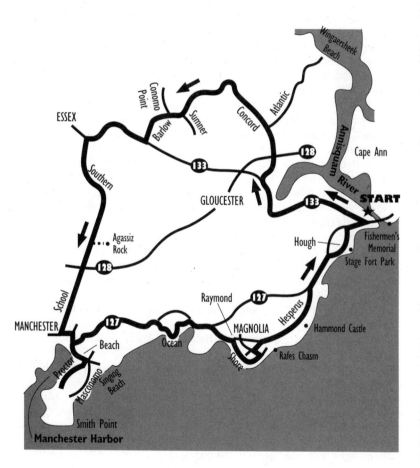

Wingaersheek Beach. Atlantic Street is a pleasant, narrow road winding along salt marshes.

3. Continue straight on Concord Street for $2^1/10$ miles to fork where the right-hand road goes over a little bridge and Summer Street bears left. **CAUTION:** Bumps and potholes.

4. Bear right at fork. After $4/10$ mile Conomo Point Road (unmarked) bears right, but curve left on main road and go $6/10$ mile to end (Route 133).

5. Turn right on Route 133 and go $1^3/10$ miles to Southern Avenue on left. It's shortly after Grove Street, also on left. You'll pass Farnham's on your right; this is a well-known restaurant specializing in clams. When you get to Southern Avenue, the ride turns left, but if you go straight for $1/2$ mile, you'll come to the center of Essex, where you can browse through several antiques shops.

6. Turn left on Southern Avenue and go $4^1/10$ miles to end (Route 127), in the center of Manchester. After $2^4/10$ miles, you'll see a small dirt turnoff on the left. From here a path leads $3/10$ mile to Agassiz Rock, a large boulder on a hilltop.

7. Turn left on Route 127. Just ahead it jogs right and immediately left.

8. Where Route 127 turns left, go straight ahead across the railroad tracks onto Beach Street. Go $4/10$ mile to crossroads at top of hill (Masconomo Street). Just past the tracks on your right is a little park overlooking Manchester Harbor.

9. Turn right on Masconomo Street. Just ahead is a fork. Bike along each branch until the road becomes private, then backtrack to Beach Street. The right-hand branch leads $1/2$ mile to a fine view of Manchester Harbor, and the left-hand branch winds $6/10$ mile to Lobster Cove, a small inlet bound by rocky headlands.

10. Turn right on Beach Street and go $2/10$ mile to end. This is Singing Beach.

11. Make a U-turn and go $7/10$ mile back to Route 127 (Summer Street on right).

12. Turn right on Route 127 and go $1^6/10$ miles to Ocean Street, which bears right.

13. Bear right on Ocean Street and go $9/10$ mile to end (Route 127 again). You'll go along two little coves—the first one is called White Beach, the second one Black Beach.

14. Turn right on Route 127 and go $4/10$ mile to Raymond Street, which bears right (sign may say TO MAGNOLIA).

15. Bear right on Raymond Street and go ½ mile to crossroads with tall streetlight in the middle (Magnolia Avenue on left). This is Magnolia, which is part of Gloucester.

16. Turn 90 degrees right at crossroads onto Shore Road, following the ocean on your right. Go ⁷⁄₁₀ mile to end (merge to the right onto a wider road). You will turn sharply left here.

17. Turn sharply left at end and go ¹⁄₁₀ mile to crossroads at top of hill (Lexington Avenue).

18. Turn right on Lexington Avenue and go ²⁄₁₀ mile to end (Hesperus Avenue, unmarked). You'll go through the Magnolia business district.

19. Turn right at end. After ½ mile you'll see a small dirt parking lot and metal fence on your right. From here a path leads ¼ mile to the ocean for the view of Rafe's Chasm.

20. Continue on Hesperus Avenue 1²⁄₁₀ miles to end (Route 127). The Hammond Castle will be on your right after ½ mile.

21. Turn right on Route 127 and go ⁷⁄₁₀ mile to Hough Avenue on right. A sign may say VISITOR INFORMATION CENTER.

22. Turn right on Hough Avenue and go ½ mile to end, at stop sign (merge right on Route 127). You'll go through Stage Fort Park, a large oceanfront park.

23. Bear right on Route 127 and go ²⁄₁₀ mile to starting point. (If you continue straight on Route 127, the bridge over the Blynman Canal to Cape Ann is immediately ahead. Just beyond the bridge is the famous statue of the weathered fisherman at the helm of his boat.)

Cape Ann:
Gloucester–Rockport

Number of miles: 27 (11 with East Gloucester area only, 20 with short-cut from Rockport)

Terrain: Gently rolling, with a few short hills.

Food: Numerous groceries and snack bars along the way.

Start: Junction of Routes 127 and 133 in Gloucester, just west of the bridge over the Blynman Canal. Park on Route 127 on the ocean side of the road.

How to get there: Same as ride 10.

CAUTION:

On good weekend days Cape Ann is crowded with people and traffic. It's not much of a hazard because it won't be moving much faster than you. The main hazards are car doors opening into your path, drivers pulling out in front of you without looking, and having your bike stolen. Don't leave your bike unlocked, and if you leave it, take your accessories with you (pump, handlebar bag, tools, and the rest).

You've probably been to Cape Ann. If you haven't, everything you've heard about it is true. It's one of the most popular places to visit in the state, and with good reason. Nowhere else on the coast do four distinct elements—a working fishing port; historic communities filled with graceful, well-maintained old buildings; a glorious coastline with dozens of picturesque coves and rocky headlands and curving beaches; and a major artists' colony and crafts center—blend into such a thoroughly appealing and satisfying composite. And the only way to fully experience it—to smell the sweet, freshly caught fish; to feel the power of surf crashing against rocks; to let the impression of each mansion and each little cove and beach imprint itself on your mind—is to tour it on a bicycle.

Much of Cape Ann's unique charm stems from its refreshingly unspoiled condition despite the annual onslaught of millions of visitors. Except for a couple of ugly motels on the East Gloucester shore and the cutesy-fake strip of shops on Bearskin Neck in Rockport, you will see none of the unsightly commercial development and ripoff tourist traps that mar so many other naturally beautiful areas across the country. No sleazy fast-food joints or shabby rows of beach cottages despoil the shore; instead you'll find gracious older homes, delightful old villages gracing the inlets and hillsides along the Cape's northern shore, and sometimes nothing manmade at all.

To fully enjoy the trip, pick a comfortable day, ideally not on a weekend, and take the whole day to find out what Cape Ann has to offer. Explore the historic old center of Gloucester, visit the forty-room Beauport mansion, poke around the art galleries on Rocky Neck, walk out to tips of land like the breakwater at the end of Eastern Point or rockbound Halibut Point at the northern extremity of the cape. When you get back to Gloucester, step onto the old wharves and watch the day's catch being unloaded. Don't try to rush—Cape Ann is too special for that.

You'll circle the cape in a counterclockwise direction, heading first by the famous Fishermen's Memorial, a statue of the hardy fisherman gripping the helm of his boat. It was erected in 1923 during Gloucester's tricentennial. You'll go along the wharves and by fish-processing plants lining the inner harbor. A couple of blocks inland from the harbor is the old center of town, which is worth a look. The graceful Victorian town hall, built in 1871, and the handsome library are New England classics. Also gracing downtown are several fine churches and elegant old homes.

You'll now head down to Eastern Point, the estate-lined peninsula forming the southern tip of Cape Ann. First you'll visit Rocky Neck, center of the artists' colony. A mile farther down is Beauport, one of the state's most impressive mansions. Its forty rooms overflow with antiques and decorative artwork from every period of American history. It was the home of Henry Davis Sleeper, a prominent interior designer and antique collector early in the century. Maintained by the Society for the Preservation of New England Antiquities, it is unfortunately not open on weekends except in September and October, and then only in the afternoon. It's open on weekdays all day from May through October.

At the southern end of Eastern Point is an Audubon sanctuary, a Coast Guard Station, a graceful old lighthouse, and a ½-mile-long breakwater extending nearly halfway across the entrance to Gloucester Har-

Rockport Harbor with the peak-roofed building that is referred to as Motif Number One

bor. You'll now head up the eastern shore of the Cape, hugging the ocean on one of the finest coastal roads in the state. As you proceed to Rockport you'll go inland just a bit, then hug the shore again on little lanes.

Rockport is visually a delight, with the tiny boat-clogged harbor, complete with Motif Number One, the red fishing shack that has long been a favorite subject for painters and photographers. Even the cutesy gift shops look properly old and weathered from the back. The gently curving beach, with the graceful churches and old white houses of the town stretching behind it, is delightful. A mile north of Rockport you can climb 200-foot-high Pigeon Hill for a magnificent view of the town. Just ahead is Halibut Point, the northern tip of Cape Ann, an impressive spot where the surf washes onto broad, flat rocks. It's maintained by our old friends, the Trustees of Reservations.

Beyond Halibut Point you'll cross the town line back into Gloucester and go through a string of unspoiled little villages—Lanesville, Bay View, Annisquam, and Riverdale. From here it's a short distance back to the starting point with the best downhill run on the ride.

Directions for the rides: 27 and 20 miles 〰️〰️〰️

1. Head east on Route 127 over the bridge. Just ahead on the right is the Fishermen's Memorial statue.
2. Continue on Route 127. After $2/10$ mile, Route 127 jogs right and immediately left. Continue $1/4$ mile to Harbor Loop on right.
3. Turn right on Harbor Loop and go $3/10$ mile to end (Route 127 again). This is a small loop closer to the harbor.
4. Turn right on Route 127 and go $1/2$ mile to fork where Route 127 bears left.
5. Bear right at fork and go $1/10$ mile to another fork, at traffic light.
6. Bear right uphill at traffic light (sign may say TO EAST GLOUCESTER). Go $1 1/10$ miles along the water to Rocky Neck Avenue on right (sign may say TO ROCKY NECK ART COLONY).
7. Turn right on Rocky Neck Avenue. Go $4/10$ mile to end, then backtrack to main road. The small Rocky Neck peninsula is the center of the Gloucester art colony.
8. Leaving Rocky Neck, turn right and go $1/2$ mile to a smaller road that bears right along the water through a pair of stone pillars. Here the ride

bears left, but if you bear right and go $^6/_{10}$ mile, the Beauport mansion is on your right. Just past the mansion, a private road continues $^6/_{10}$ mile to the Eastern Point Audubon Sanctuary and the Coast Guard station just beyond it at the tip of the peninsula. People are allowed to use the road to get to the Audubon Sanctuary. **CAUTION:** Watch for speed bumps.

On summer weekends, a guard may be stationed at the beginning of the road leading to the Beauport mansion. If you are stopped, say that you are going to the Audubon Sanctuary and the guard will wave you through.

9. Bear left on main road and go $2^7/_{10}$ miles to crossroads and stop sign at bottom of hill (Bass Avenue). You'll pass a graceful stone church on your right at the beginning; then you'll enjoy a spectacular ride along the ocean. At Bass Avenue the 11-mile ride turns left and the longer rides go straight.

10. Go straight at crossroads for 1 mile to fork where Rockport Road bears right and the main road bears left.

11. Bear left on main road and go $1^8/_{10}$ miles to South Street, which turns sharply right at traffic island. It's at the top of a long, gradual hill.

12. Turn sharply right on South Street and go $^4/_{10}$ mile to Penzance Road on left, just before ocean.

13. Turn left on Penzance Road. After $^6/_{10}$ mile the main road bears left, and a dead-end road (Old Penzance Road) goes straight. Stay on main road for $^1/_4$ mile to Eden Road on right.

14. Turn right on Eden Road, following the ocean on your right, and go $^8/_{10}$ mile to end (Route 127A). **CAUTION:** The first half of Eden Road is very bumpy; slow down and enjoy the scenery.

15. Turn right on Route 127A and go $^3/_{10}$ mile to Marmion Way on right.

16. Turn right on Marmion Way, and just ahead bear right at fork on main road. Go $^8/_{10}$ mile to small crossroads midway up a hill (Richards Avenue on left, Old Garden Road on right). You'll pass an old metal radio tower on your right.

17. Turn right on Old Garden Road and go $^4/_{10}$ mile to crossroads and stop sign (Highland Avenue).

18. Turn right on Highland Avenue and go $^3/_{10}$ mile to end. On your right is tiny Rockport Harbor. The small red wooden building on the opposite shore with the peaked roof is Motif Number One, one of the most frequently painted places in the country.

19. Turn right at end of Highland Avenue. After $^2/_{10}$ mile the road widens

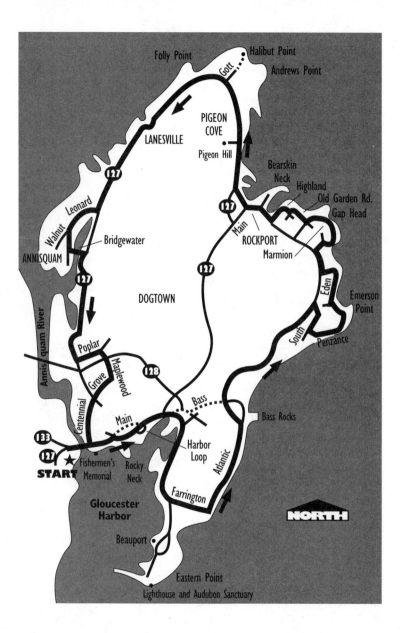

into Dock Square and a narrow lane turns right onto Bearskin Neck. This is the heart of Rockport. On a nice day you'll have to walk your bike through the throngs of tourists swarming amid the clutter of craft shops, boutiques, and ice cream stands.

20. From Bearskin Neck, continue on the main road for $^2/_{10}$ mile to fork where Main Street bears left and Beach Street bears right. Here the ride bears right, but you can cut it short to 20 miles by bearing left for $^3/_{10}$ mile to stop sign and then going straight on Route 127 for about $3^1/_2$ miles back to Gloucester.

21. Bear right at fork, following the ocean on your right. Go $^4/_{10}$ mile to end, at stop sign (merge to your right onto Route 127).

22. Bear right at end and go $1^8/_{10}$ miles to Gott Avenue (unmarked) on right. Route 127 curves left at the intersection, and a sign may point right TO STATE PARK.

After $^6/_{10}$ mile you'll see Landmark Lane on your left. This road climbs a steep hill with a broad, grassy park at the top and a magnificent view of Rockport and the surrounding coastline. If you turn right on Gott Avenue, just ahead a path leads $^4/_{10}$ mile to Halibut Point.

23. Leaving Halibut Point, continue along Route 127 for $2^9/_{10}$ miles to Leonard Street on right (sign may say TO ANNISQUAM VILLAGE). There's a church on the far corner.

24. Turn right on Leonard Street and go $^4/_{10}$ mile to fork (Walnut Street bears right uphill). You are now entering Annisquam.

25. Bear left downhill at fork and go $^2/_{10}$ mile to Bridgewater Street (unmarked) on left, immediately after Rogers Lane on right.

26. Turn left on Bridgewater Street. You'll immediately come to a footbridge that crosses Lobster Cove. The ride crosses the bridge, but if you wish, you can make a small clockwise loop by turning right at the bridge, following the cove on your left. Go $^3/_{10}$ mile to end (Leonard Street), turn right, and continue less than $^2/_{10}$ mile to Bridgewater Street on right.

27. Cross the footbridge. At the far end of the bridge, continue 100 feet to end (merge right on Route 127).

28. Bear right on Route 127 and go $2^4/_{10}$ miles to Poplar Street on left, immediately before rotary.

29. Turn left on Poplar Street and go $^4/_{10}$ mile to Maplewood Avenue on right. The main road bears left at the intersection. If you're adventurous, you can visit Dogtown, the wooded, uninhabited interior of Cape Ann, which is dotted with cellar holes of eighteenth-century dwellings. To get

Lobsterman's cottage in Rockport

there, turn left on Cherry Street just before Maplewood Avenue. Go $^7/_{10}$ mile to a lane bearing right up a steep hill, and follow the lane until it becomes dirt. A mazework of paths weaves through the scrubby, rolling landscape. It's very easy to get lost.

30. Turn right on Maplewood Avenue and go $^2/_{10}$ mile to the second crossroads (Grove Street), just before an old factory on left.

31. Turn right on Grove Street. Just ahead you'll see a large cemetery on your left. Parallel the cemetery for $^3/_{10}$ mile to end.

32. At end of Grove Street jog left and immediately right on Centennial Avenue. Go $^6/_{10}$ mile to end (Route 127). **CAUTION:** Bumpy railroad bridge at the beginning. You'll enjoy a fast descent.

33. Turn right on Route 127 and cross the bridge back to starting point.

Directions for the ride: 11 miles

1. Follow directions for the long ride through number 9.

2. Turn left on Bass Avenue and go $^1/_2$ mile to traffic light where Route 128 turns right.

3. Go straight at light for $^3/_{10}$ mile to fork at top of hill.

4. Bear right at fork on Main Street into the business district. Go $^6/_{10}$ mile through downtown Gloucester until you rejoin Route 127. **CAUTION:** Watch for traffic and pedestrians. If you wish, you can turn right on Pleasant Street and then take your next left on Middle Street, which goes past the Victorian city hall and other old buildings.

5. Go straight on Route 127 for $^4/_{10}$ mile across the bridge back to starting point.

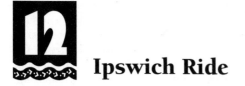

Ipswich Ride

Number of miles: 21 (11 with Crane Beach section only, 11 with Great Neck section only)

Terrain: Flat, with a tough climb to the Crane estate on Castle Hill and a couple of short, steep hills on Great Neck.

Food: Numerous stores and restaurants in the center of Ipswich. The local specialty is clams. Goodale Orchards, noted for wonderful cider doughnuts, other homemade pastries, and fresh cider in the fall.

Start: Free municipal parking lot behind the business block at the corner of Route 1A and Topsfield Road in downtown Ipswich. Entrance to the lot is on Hammatt Street, which is off Route 1A, 1 block north of Topsfield Road.

Ipswich ranks as one of the most beautiful towns in the state, both architecturally and geographically. If you're a historic-house enthusiast, you'll exult: The town has more pre-Revolutionary homes—some going back to the 1600s—than any other locale north of Williamsburg, Virginia. Beyond the center of town is an unspoiled mixture of wooded hills; broad, gently rolling horse farms and gracious country estates; vast salt marshes stretching to the horizon; the Great Neck peninsula rising steeply from the bay; and magnificent 4-mile-long Crane Beach, New England's finest beach north of Cape Cod.

The ride starts from the center of Ipswich, lying between a north green and a south green and surrounded by a marvelous variety of buildings, all painstakingly restored and maintained, spanning every architectural style from early Colonial days to the turn of the century. You'll head first to Crane Beach through an idyllic landscape of salt marshes, horse paddocks, and estates. A quarter mile from the beach, the majestic Crane mansion, resembling a palace from the Italian Renaissance, crowns Castle Hill. The wide beach is unique in that it is almost completely unspoiled—no hot dog stands, no cottages, no anything except sand, dunes, and lots of people on a hot day. The beach, along with the Castle Hill estate, is owned by our friends the Trustees of Reservations.

89

From Crane Beach you'll return to the center of town and then head through an endless expanse of salt marshes to the Great Neck peninsula, just north of Crane Beach. Rising steeply from the bay as a succession of four round drumlins, the peninsula is bordered by salt marshes on the west, the broad Plum Island Sound on the north, the southern tip of Plum Island on the east, and Crane Beach on the south. The roads rimming the peninsula offer spectacular views of this varied and beautiful seascape. From Great Neck you return through the salt marshes to Ipswich.

Directions for the ride: 2I miles

1. Turn right out of lot onto Hammatt Street and go to end (Route 1A).
2. Turn right on Route 1A and go $^4/_{10}$ mile to where the main road curves 90 degrees right. After $^1/_{10}$ mile you will cross the Ipswich River over the Choate Bridge, built in 1764. This graceful stone arch is one of the oldest original bridges in the country. At the sharp curve the John Whipple House is on your right. It is a fine example of Colonial architecture. Built in 1640, it has numerous period furnishings and an herb garden. Across the road is the Thomas Franklin Waters Memorial, a Federal-era mansion with articles from the China trade and a carriage collection. Both buildings are open to visitors.
3. Curve 90 degrees right on main road and go 100 yards to Argilla Road on left.
4. Turn left on Argilla Road and go $^1/_2$ mile to Heartbreak Road on right.
5. Turn right on Heartbreak Road and go $^7/_{10}$ mile to end (Route 133).
6. Turn left on Route 133 and go $1^1/_{10}$ miles to Northgate Road on left (sign says TO CASTLE HILL, CRANE BEACH).
7. Turn left on Northgate Road and go $^7/_{10}$ mile to end.
8. Turn right at end (you're back on Argilla Road) and go $2^4/_{10}$ miles to the entrance to Crane Beach. You'll pass Goodale Orchards on the right after $^3/_{10}$ mile. During the summer, there is unfortunately a beach fee for bicycles that is more than nominal. If you plan to spend some time here, the fee is worth it, considering the beauty of the area and the fact that your money is supporting the Trustees of Reservations, without whom the place would probably be another Hampton Beach. During the off-season the fee is nominal and the attendant may wave you through.
9. Leaving Crane Beach, backtrack on Argilla Road $^1/_4$ mile to the entrance to Castle Hill on right. If the estate is open, the climb to the top is

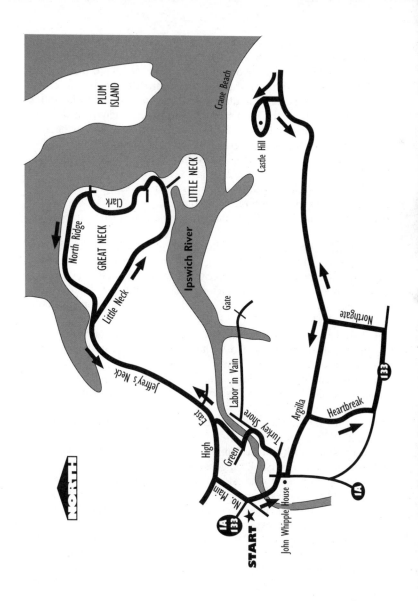

unquestionably worth the effort. You'll be rewarded by the view of the mansion along the smooth lawn, which undulates between two groves of trees in a rippling green ribbon for nearly ½ mile between the mansion and the cliff overlooking the ocean. From the edge of the cliff a panorama of sea, marsh, and dune spreads before you. At the far end of the lawn, a path on the right leads down to (accurately named) Steep Beach. Unfortunately Castle Hill is open very limited hours, because most of the time the estate is rented for private functions.

10. From Castle Hill, continue on Argilla Road and stay on the main road for 4 miles to end (Routes 1A and 133).

11. Turn right at end and go 100 yards to crossroads where the main road turns left and Poplar Street turns right.

12. Turn right on Poplar Street and go ¹/₁₀ mile to first left, Turkey Shore Road.

13. Turn left on Turkey Shore Road and go ¼ mile to the first left (Green Street, unmarked), which crosses the Ipswich River. Here the ride turns left; but if you wish, you can continue straight for ⁹/₁₀ mile to a rustic wooden bridge over an inlet—it's a delightful spot. (Shortly after Green Street, the main road turns 90 degrees right at stop sign onto Labor in Vain Road.)

14. Turn left on Green Street and go 50 yards, then right on Water Street at the far side of the bridge. Go ⁴/₁₀ mile along the river to the far end of the parking lot for the town wharf.

15. At the end of the lot, jog left and then immediately right onto the main road. Go ¹/₁₀ mile to fork where the main road (Jeffrey's Neck Road) bears left.

16. Bear left on the main road and go 1⁷/₁₀ miles to another fork (North Ridge Road bears left).

17. Bear right at fork and go ½ mile to another fork where the main road bears right and Plover Hill Road goes straight up a steep hill.

18. Bear right on main road and go ⁹/₁₀ mile to another fork where the right-hand branch goes over a causeway. On the far side of the causeway is Little Neck, a small ellipse about ¼ mile across and filled with attractive older summer homes. This area is private.

19. Bear left at fork onto Bay View Road (unmarked), following the ocean on your right, and go ²/₁₀ mile to fork where Clark Road bears right. The land across the bay is the southern tip of Plum Island.

20. Bear right at fork, following the water, and go ⁸/₁₀ mile to crossroads

(Colby Road, unmarked). The large concrete building on the top of the hill is an Air Force installation.

21. Turn left uphill on Colby Road and go 1 mile to end (merge right at yield sign just past bottom of hill).

22. Bear right at end and go $2\frac{1}{10}$ miles to East Street on right . It's immediately after Spring Street on right. You'll pass the town wharf on the left shortly before the intersection.

23. Bear right on East Street and go $\frac{1}{2}$ mile until you come to a cemetery on your right, rising in terraces up a steep hillside. East Street becomes High Street, the heart of Old Ipswich, with most of the houses predating 1800.

24. At the cemetery make a U-turn and backtrack $\frac{3}{10}$ mile to North Main Street (unmarked) on right, at small brick traffic island. It's the third right.

25. Turn right on North Main Street and go $\frac{3}{10}$ mile to crossroads and stop sign at bottom of hill (Routes 1A and 133). Notice the varied old buildings lining both sides of the green. The modern church in the center of the green, clashing with all the architecture surrounding it, comes as a surprise. It was built to replace a classic New England church that burned to the ground in 1965 after being struck by lightning.

26. Turn right on Routes 1A and 133. Go $\frac{1}{10}$ mile to Hammatt Street on left.

27. Turn left on Hammatt Street. Parking lot is just ahead on left.

Directions for the ride: 11 miles (Crane Beach section)

1. Follow directions for the 21-mile ride through number 11.

2. Turn left on main road (Routes 1A and 133), and go $\frac{1}{2}$ mile to Hammatt Street on left, in center of town.

3. Turn left on Hammatt Street. Parking lot is just ahead on left.

Directions for the ride: 11 miles (Great Neck section)

1. Follow directions 1 and 2 for the 21-mile ride.

2. Go straight ahead onto Poplar Street at the intersection where Routes 1A and 133 curve 90 degrees right. Go $\frac{1}{10}$ mile to first left, Turkey Shore Road.

3. Follow directions for the 21-mile ride from number 13 to end.

Newburyport–Newbury–Rowley

Number of miles: 22 (17 without western loop)
Terrain: Gently rolling, with one hill.
Food: Grocery and snack bar in Rowley.
Start: Rupert A. Nock Middle School, corner of Low and Johnson streets in Newburyport.
How to get there: If you're coming from the south on Interstate 95, take the Scotland Road exit (exit 56). Turn right on Scotland Road and go 3 miles to end (Low Street). Turn left on Low Street and go ²/₁₀ mile to school on right. If you're coming from the north, exit east from Interstate 95 onto Route 113 (take exit 57). Go ³/₁₀ mile to Low Street on right at traffic light. Turn right on Low Street and go 1³/₁₀ miles to school on left.

This ride takes you exploring among the broad salt marshes, prosperous farmland, and gracious estates just inland from the coast south of New-buryport. You'll pass imposing mansions built by sea captains and mer-chants in Newburyport and also Governor Dummer Academy, one of the oldest preparatory schools in the country. The area abounds with coun-try roads that promise relaxed and delightful biking.

Situated at the mouth of the Merrimack River, Newburyport became a thriving shipbuilding community during the 1700s and then evolved as a commercial center. The most successful sea captains and merchants built elegant mansions along a 2-mile stretch of High Street, which you'll go along at the beginning of the ride.

The downtown and waterfront areas, lying just off the route between High Street and the river, have been restored and are worth exploring. Gracious brick buildings from the Federal era line State Street, the main downtown street. At the base of State Street, next to the river, is Market Square, where the old brick mercantile buildings have been recycled into a mini-mall of antique shops, galleries, and craft shops. The result is tasteful rather than touristy. The library, built in 1771, is an especially fine building, as is also the stately granite Custom House, built in 1835 and now a maritime museum. Adjoining the downtown are narrow streets lined with old wooden homes.

Just south of Newburyport is Newbury, a small town consisting mainly of salt marshes and farmland. In the village center are several historic homes from the 1600s and 1700s. Just outside of town you'll pass Old Town Hill, a small glacial drumlin rising 170 feet above the Parker River. Maintained by the Trustees of Reservations, it offers an outstanding view of the Parker River, Plum Island, and the broad estuary separating it from the mainland.

From Newbury you'll head along Route 1A past broad salt marshes and well-kept farms to Rowley, an attractive small town with several antiques shops and even an antiques flea market. As numbered routes go, Route 1A is one of the best in the state for bicycling—smooth, flat, not heavily traveled, and with a good shoulder. In Rowley you'll head inland, and after a few miles you'll go through the gracious campus of the Governor Dummer Academy, founded in 1763. The return to Newburyport leads along country lanes as you follow the Parker River a short distance, cross it, and proceed past stately old farmhouses and immaculate fields.

Directions for the ride: 22 miles 〰〰〰〰〰

1. Turn right on Low Street and go $^2/_{10}$ mile to crossroads (Hale Street on left, Toppans Lane on right).
2. Turn right at crossroads and go $^4/_{10}$ mile to end (Route 113).
3. Turn right on Route 113. After $^1/_2$ mile, at the Route 1 overpass, Route 113 becomes Route 1A. Continue straight on Route 1A for $1^2/_{10}$ miles to Green Street, which bears right at the Newbury town green. As you're going along, notice the numerous mansions built by the sea captains and merchants. Cushing House, at 98 High Street, is open to the public. Just beyond Route 1 you'll pass the stately Bulfinch-designed courthouse and the old granite jail. A few blocks to your left are the downtown and waterfront.
4. Bear right on Green Street and stay on the main road for $^2/_{10}$ mile to crossroads and stop sign. As you start down Green Street, notice the town hall on the left side of the green.
5. Go straight at crossroads for $^9/_{10}$ mile to end, at grassy traffic island.
6. Turn right at end (Hay) and go $^8/_{10}$ mile to Newman Road (unmarked) on left, just after small bridge.

7. Turn left on Newman Road, crossing a salt marsh, and go $1\frac{1}{10}$ miles to crossroads (Route 1A). **CAUTION:** Watch for bumps and potholes—parts of the road need to be repaved. Just before Route 1A you'll come to Old Town Hill on the left, maintained by the Trustees of Reservations. The view from the top is the scenic highlight of the ride.

8. Turn right on Route 1A and go $4\frac{1}{10}$ miles to traffic light and crossroads in the center of Rowley (Church Street, unmarked, on right). Here the short ride turns right and the long ride goes straight. You'll cross the Parker River just after you start down Route 1A.

9. Continue straight for $\frac{2}{10}$ mile to Summer Street (unmarked), which bears right at the town green.

10. Bear right on Summer Street and go $\frac{4}{10}$ mile to end. The graceful town hall is on your left at the intersection (Bradford Street).

11. Turn left at end and go $\frac{2}{10}$ mile to end, at yield sign (merge right on Route 133).

12. Bear right on Route 133 and go $1\frac{1}{10}$ miles to traffic light (Route 1).

13. Cross Route 1 and go $\frac{8}{10}$ mile to Daniels Road on right (sign may say ROWLEY COUNTRY CLUB). **CAUTION:** Bumps and potholes,

14. Turn right on Daniels Road and go $1\frac{1}{2}$ miles to Wethersfield Street on left, at traffic island. It's shortly after Long Hill Road, which turns sharply left.

15. Turn left on Wethersfield Street and go $\frac{4}{10}$ mile to the second right, Warren Street.

16. Turn right on Warren Street and go $\frac{9}{10}$ mile to end (merge right at yield sign).

17. Bear right at yield sign and go $1\frac{7}{10}$ miles to crossroads (Middle Road) on left, just before a footbridge across the road.

18. Turn left on Middle Road, passing through the campus of Governor Dummer Academy. Follow main road for 2 miles to fork where Boston Road (unmarked) bears right and the main road bears slightly left. **CAUTION:** The first $\frac{1}{2}$ mile of Middle Road is very bumpy and needs to be repaved.

19. Stay on main road for $\frac{8}{10}$ mile to Highfield Road on left.

20. Turn left on Highfield Road and go $\frac{7}{10}$ mile to end (Scotland Road, unmarked).

21. Turn right at end and go $1\frac{1}{10}$ miles to end (Low Street).

22. Turn left at end and go $\frac{2}{10}$ mile to school on right.

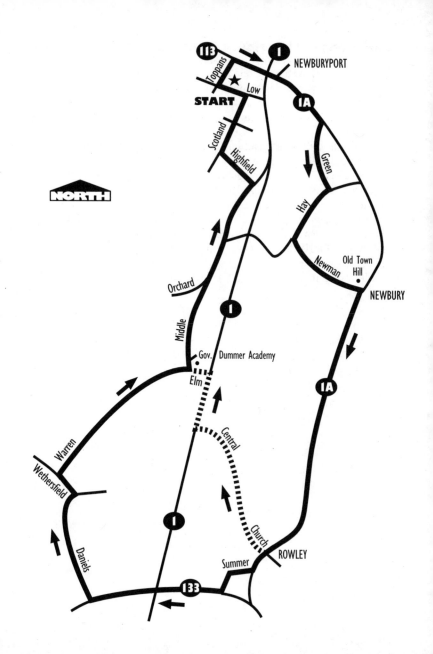

Directions for the ride: 17 miles

1. Follow directions for the long ride through number 8.
2. Turn right at traffic light onto 1A and go 100 yards to end (merge right at stop sign).
3. Bear right at end onto Church and go 2 miles to crossroads and stop sign (Route 1).
4. Turn right on Route 1 and go $^6/_{10}$ mile to Elm Street (unmarked) on left, at blinking light (sign may say GOVERNOR DUMMER ACADEMY).
5. Turn left on Elm Street and go $^2/_{10}$ mile to crossroads (Middle Road on right), just beyond the footbridge. The buildings of the Governor Dummer Academy are on both sides of the road.
6. Turn right on Middle Road. Stay on main road for 2 miles to fork where Boston Road (unmarked) bears right and the main road bears slightly left. **CAUTION:** The first $^1/_2$ mile of Middle Road is very bumpy and needs to be repaved.
7. Follow directions for the long ride from number 19 to the end.

14 Newburyport–Byfield– Georgetown–Groveland– West Newbury

Number of miles: 28 (18 without Byfield–Georgetown–Groveland extension)

Terrain: Rolling, with one tough hill. The long ride has an additional steep hill.

Food: Grocery in Byfield. Grocery and snack bar in Georgetown. Grocery in West Newbury.

Start: Rupert A. Nock Middle School, corner of Low and Johnson streets in Newburyport.

How to get there: Same as ride 13.

This is a tour of the delightfully rolling, prosperous farm country on the southern side of the Merrimack Valley along the river's lower reaches. The area has a succession of gently rounded hills with broad fields sweeping up and over them. Near the end you'll parallel the wide Merrimack River, curving between the hillsides with farms and estates on its banks, along a narrow rural lane. You will pass Maudslay State Park, one of the state's newest and most glorious. It was formerly the 476-acre estate of financial baron F. S. Moseley (Maudslay is the ancestral English spelling). The river is refreshingly undeveloped along its easternmost section between Haverhill and Newburyport. The long ride dips farther south into a more wooded area to the old town of Georgetown and then back north to the handsome village center of Groveland.

The ride starts from the elegant and historic small city of Newburyport, which became a prosperous shipbuilding and commercial center during Colonial times. In the first half of the 1800s, the most successful merchants and sea captains built mansions along High Street. The waterfront area and the graceful brick commercial buildings in the downtown section have been restored and are worth visiting after the ride.

Leaving Newburyport, you'll quickly get into open countryside, where large farms expand toward the horizon, and go along the undeveloped Upper Artichoke Reservoir. The road from here to West Newbury passes through inspiring rolling farmland reminiscent of Grant Wood's paintings. West Newbury is a handsome town on a hilltop overlooking the river, with two fine churches facing each other at the summit. From here you'll descend to the riverbank and enjoy a delightful run along its shore on a country lane. The return leg to Newburyport passes farms and estates. You'll go by a large school, formerly the Cardinal Cushing Academy, perched on a hilltop 200 feet above the river. The view from behind the building is outstanding. Maudslay State Park is just ahead.

The long ride heads farther south through woodland and small farms to the small village of Byfield and then on to the handsome crossroads town of Georgetown. Several antiques stores are in or just outside the center of town. Beyond Georgetown you'll pass through the old center of Groveland, where a white church and stately wooden homes cluster around a small green. After a few miles you'll pick up the short ride in West Newbury.

Directions for the ride: 28 miles ～～～～～～～

1. Turn right out of parking lot and go $^2/_{10}$ mile to crossroads (Toppans Lane on right, Hale Street on left).

2. Turn left at crossroads and go $1^8/_{10}$ miles to unmarked fork immediately after stop sign.

3. Bear right at fork and go $1^1/_{10}$ miles to crossroads and stop sign (Garden Street, unmarked). **CAUTION:** Bumps and potholes at end. You'll pass the Upper Artichoke Reservoir on your left.

4. Turn left on Garden Street and go $1^1/_{10}$ miles to end. Here the short ride turns right and the long ride turns left.

5. Turn left at end and go 1 mile to end (South Street, unmarked).

6. Turn right on South Street and go $^6/_{10}$ mile to fork where Moulton Street bears right and the main road bears left.

7. Bear left on main road and go $4^8/_{10}$ miles to traffic light (Route 97) in the center of Georgetown. You will pass through Byfield, which is part of Newbury.

8. Turn right on Route 97 and go $1^1/_{10}$ miles to King Street, which bears right.

9. Bear right on King Street and go $1^3/_{10}$ miles to crossroads and stop sign (Center Street).

10. Continue straight for $1^2/_{10}$ miles to end (Route 113), at a little green.

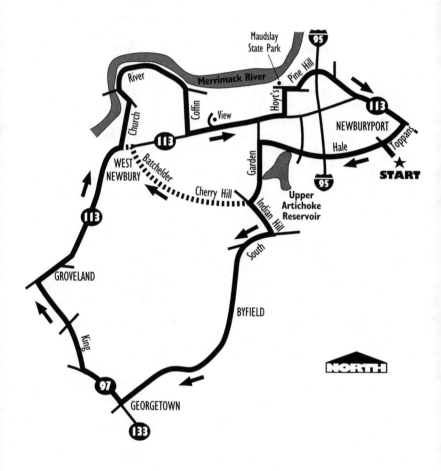

You'll have a steep climb followed by a fast descent. The old village center of Groveland is at the end.

11. Turn right on Route 113. Stay on main road for 2⁹/10 miles to Church Street on left, at top of hill just beyond traffic light. A sign may say TO ROUTE 110, MERRIMAC. Notice the two churches on your left at the intersection, one on each corner. This is West Newbury.

12. Turn left on Church Street and go 1 mile to end, at stop sign (merge left on Bridge Street, unmarked). You'll follow the Merrimack River on your left at the end.

13. Bear left at end and go 100 yards to River Road on right, just before the bridge over the Merrimack. River Road goes up a sharp hill, so shift into low gear as you approach it.

14. Turn right on River Road and go 2¹/10 miles to fork.

15. Bear right at fork, heading away from the river, and go ⁹/10 mile to end (Route 113). **CAUTION:** Watch out for bumpy spots.

16. Turn left on Route 113. After ½ mile, at top of hill, you'll see the John C. Page Elementary School and a water tower on your left. From behind the school there's a superb view of the valley that you shouldn't miss.

17. From the school, continue on Route 113 for 1⁷/10 miles to Hoyt's Lane or Gypsy Lane on left (the sign, visible from the opposite direction, says both names), just before top of hill.

18. Turn left on Hoyt's Lane and go ⁶/10 mile to end. At the end, Maudslay State Park is in front of you. It's legal to ride on the network of dirt paths that wind through the park, but it's safer and more relaxing to walk.

19. Turn right at end of Hoyt's Lane and go ³/10 mile to fork where the main road bears left.

20. Bear left at fork onto Pine Hill and go 1½ miles to end, at stop sign (merge head-on onto Route 113).

21. Go straight on Route 113 (**CAUTION** here) for ⁹/10 mile to Toppans Lane on right. It's immediately before the red-brick high school on right and just after house number 249 on right.

22. Turn right on Toppans Lane and go ⁴/10 mile to crossroads and stop sign.

23. Turn left at crossroads. The school is just ahead on left.

Directions for the ride: 18 miles

1. Follow directions for the long ride through number 4.

2. Turn right at end and go $\frac{1}{10}$ mile to Cherry Hill Street, which bears left.

3. Bear left on Cherry Hill Street and go $2\frac{4}{10}$ miles to end (Route 113). This is a beautiful run through rolling farmland.

4. Turn left on Route 113 and go $\frac{1}{2}$ mile to Church Street on right, just before traffic light. A sign may say TO ROUTE 110, MERRIMAC. You'll pass the dignified West Newbury town hall and then a graceful brick soldiers' and sailors' memorial hall, both on your left. When you get to Church Street, notice the two churches at the intersection, one at each corner. This is West Newbury.

5. Turn right on Church Street and go 1 mile to end, at stop sign (merge left on Bridge Street, unmarked). You'll follow the Merrimack River on your left at the end.

6. Follow directions for the long ride from number 13 to the end.

The Millyard, Amesbury

15 Whittier Country:
Amesbury–Merrimac–Newton, New Hampshire–Plaistow, New Hampshire–Haverhill

Number of miles: 29 (18 without Newton–Plaistow–Haverhill extension)

Terrain: Rolling, with several moderate hills.

Food: Grocery in Merrimac. Grocery in Newton, New Hampshire. Burger King ⁴⁄₁₀ mile west of starting point on Route 110.

Start: Cross Roads Plaza, Route 110 in Salisbury, just east of Interstate 95 at the Amesbury town line.

This is a tour of the rolling countryside along the north bank of the Merrimack River at the northern tip of the state and extending several miles into New Hampshire. At the end of the ride you'll parallel the river, a broad ribbon winding between gentle green hills, farms, estates, and gracious old homes overlooking its waters. The region is rural and excellent for biking, with a wealth of lightly traveled country roads. Unlike the stretch west of Haverhill, the river is surprisingly undeveloped along its lower reaches, paralleled by very pleasant secondary roads.

The ride starts by going through the lovely old town of Amesbury, with an unusual mixture of old mills and gracious, well-kept residential areas. The handsome nineteenth-century commercial area clusters around a central square. Amesbury is most famous as the longtime home of poet John Greenleaf Whittier, author of "Snowbound" and "Barefoot Boy." You'll bike past his house, which contains his original furnishings and is open to the public. Just outside of town is another historic landmark, the Rocky Hill Meetinghouse, a graceful yet simple wooden structure built in 1785. It is maintained by the Society for the Preservation of New England Antiquities and is open by appointment.

Leaving Amesbury, you'll crisscross the Massachusetts–New Hampshire border as you head on to Merrimac, passing between two ponds and then climbing onto an open ridge with a glorious view of the valley. Merrimac is another pleasant town with an ornate brick Victorian town hall, complete with clock tower. From here you'll parallel the river for 5 miles back to Amesbury in a beautiful, relaxing run.

The long ride heads farther west to the pretty little town of Newton, New Hampshire, typical of the many graceful small communities dotting the southernmost section of the state. A classic white church and ornate old town hall grace the center of town. Beyond Newton you'll wind through forested hills, small farms, and over a ridge with a fine view of the valley. You'll go by Whittier's birthplace in Haverhill and finally arrive at the Merrimack River. For the rest of the ride you'll parallel the river. At first the road is inland just a bit, rolling up and down past gracious estates and gentleman farms, with views of the river from the crest of the hills. After a while the road converges with the riverbank and follows it all the way back to Amesbury, passing through the attractive waterfront villages of Rocks Village and Merrimacport.

Directions for the ride: 29 miles

1. Turn right out of the west side of the parking lot, and just ahead turn left (west) at traffic light on Route 110. Go $4/10$ mile to traffic light just after the Interstate 95 interchange (Elm Street on right).

2. Turn right on Elm Street and go $1^7/10$ miles to end, at small rotary at top of short hill in the center of Amesbury. After $4/10$ mile, immediately before the Interstate 495 overpass, the Rocky Hill Meetinghouse is on your right.

3. Turn left at rotary and go 100 yards to Friend Street, which bears right. There's a small park called The Millyard behind the buildings on your right, with a stream tumbling over a dam and beneath a footbridge.

4. Bear right on Friend Street and go $3/10$ mile to Whitehall Road, which bears right. You'll pass the Whittier home on your left on the corner of Pickard Street.

5. Bear right on Whitehall Road and go $1^7/10$ miles to stop sign where the main road turns 90 degrees right and a smaller road turns left. You'll pass Lake Gardner on the right, with Powwow Hill rising sharply on the opposite shore.

6. Turn left at stop sign, crossing a small stream, and go $1^1/10$ miles to Newton Road on right (it's easy to miss). It is $3/10$ mile after the entrance to Tuxbury Pond Camping Area on the right.

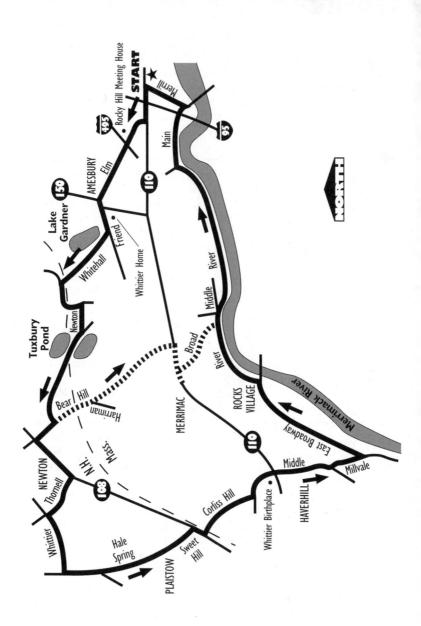

7. Turn right on Newton Road and go $7/10$ mile to end (merge right). Just before the end, there's a fine dam and millpond on your right.

8. Bear right at end and go $2^1/10$ miles to end (Bear Hill Road on left). Here the short ride turns left and the long ride turns right.

9. Turn right at end and go $3/10$ mile to crossroads and blinking light (Route 108 is straight ahead and also on left). This is Newton, New Hampshire. There's a grocery just beyond the intersection.

10. Turn left on Route 108 and go $1^3/10$ miles to Thornell Road (unmarked) on right. It's shortly after Tara Lane, a dead-end residential street on your right. Notice the old town hall on your left in the center of town.

11. Turn right on Thornell Road. Go 1 mile to stop sign where Peaslee Crossing Road turns left and the main road (West Main Street) bears slightly right.

12. Bear right on the main road and go $4/10$ mile to crossroads. An old church is on your right at the intersection.

13. Turn left at crossroads onto Whittier and go $1^8/10$ miles to end.

14. Turn left at end onto Hale Spring Road and go $8/10$ mile to fork just beyond railroad bridge (Hale Spring Road bears slightly left).

15. Bear left at fork and go $3/10$ mile to crossroads and stop sign (Smith Corner Road).

16. Go straight at crossroads for $1^7/10$ miles to end (Route 108).

17. Turn right on Route 108 and go less than $2/10$ mile to Corliss Hill Road on left. It's a narrow lane that goes up a steep hill.

18. Turn left on Corliss Hill Road and go $1^1/10$ miles to end. **CAUTION:** Watch for bumps and potholes at the beginning.

19. Turn left at end and go $4/10$ mile to crossroads and stop sign (Route 110). Just before the intersection, you'll pass the Whittier birthplace on the right. This old farmhouse is the locale for the poem "Snowbound."

20. Cross Route 110 and go $1^1/2$ miles to fork (Millvale Road, unmarked, bears slightly left). You'll pass a Jewish cemetery on your left and then a fine old church, dated 1744, on your right.

21. Bear slightly left on Millvale Road and go $7/10$ mile to end (merge right at stop sign). You will turn sharply left here onto East Broadway.

22. Turn sharply left at end. **CAUTION:** Watch for sand. Stay on the main road for $2^7/10$ miles to River Road (unmarked) on left, immediately before the bridge over the Merrimack. There's an old restored fire station on the far left corner. This is Rocks Village.

23. Turn left on River Road, paralleling the river on your right, and go $1^8/_{10}$ miles to fork where Middle Road goes straight and River Road (unmarked here) bears right.

24. Bear right at fork (still River Road), following the water, and go $3^1/_2$ miles to Main Street on right, at stop sign. It's $^1/_2$ mile beyond a Victorian mill on the riverbank, built in 1877.

25. Turn right on Main Street, still following the river. Go $1^1/_{10}$ miles to a road, Merrill, that turns sharply left at traffic light just after you go underneath Interstate 95 (sign may say TO ROUTE 110, SALISBURY).

26. Turn sharply left (**CAUTION** here) and go $^6/_{10}$ mile to shopping center on right.

Directions for the ride: 18 miles

1. Follow directions for the long ride through number 8.

2. Turn left on Bear Hill Road and stay on the main road for 3 miles to end (Route 110). After $^7/_{10}$ mile, at the state line, you'll see a granite marker on your left dated 1890. There's a glorious view from the top of the ridge, with glimpses of the Merrimack in the distance.

3. Turn right on Route 110 and go $^1/_2$ mile to Broad Street on left, at bottom of hill. The Landing School, a one-room schoolhouse built in 1857, is on your right at the intersection. Here the ride turns left, but if you continue straight for $^1/_{10}$ mile, you'll come to the center of Merrimac. There's a grocery in town.

4. Turn left on Broad Street and go 1 mile to end.

5. Turn left at end, paralleling the river on your right. Go $^1/_{10}$ mile to fork where Middle Road goes straight and River Road (unmarked) bears right.

6. Follow directions for the long ride from number 24 to the end.

16

Middleton–North Andover–Boxford–Topsfield

Number of miles: 26 (18 without Middleton–North Andover extension)
Terrain: Gently rolling, with a couple of short hills.
Road surface: 6/10 mile of dirt road in Middleton on the longer ride.
Food: Grocery and restaurant in Middleton. Country store in Boxford. Grocery and restaurant in Topsfield.
Start: Masconomet Regional High School, Endicott Road in Boxford, just east of Interstate 95. Take exit 51. Park at the tennis courts on the east side of the school.

This is a tour of the gently rolling, wooded, and well-to-do communities on the northern edge of the Boston metropolitan area, midway between the city and the New Hampshire border. The region is rural rather than suburban, with development limited to large, expensive homes on spacious wooded lots. The town centers of Boxford and Topsfield are New England classics.

At the beginning of the ride, you'll bike through Middleton, a relatively undeveloped town consisting primarily of forest and small farms, many with horse paddocks. You'll head along lovely Middleton Pond, completely surrounded by pine groves, and then go through the Harold Parker State Forest, which forms a large slice of the southern part of North Andover. You'll bike past two forest-rimmed ponds and then a pleasant mixture of small farms and attractive newer homes set back from the winding roads on large wooded lots. From North Andover you'll cross into Boxford, a gracious rural community that is one of the North Shore's most affluent suburbs and a paradise for bicycling. The town center is delightful, with a proud old church, a country store, and appealing, rambling wooden homes.

At the end of the ride, you'll pedal through Topsfield, another gracious, moneyed community where biking is a pleasure. The large green, with a stately white church and a marvelous Victorian town hall built in 1873, is one of the finest in the state. Just off the green is the Parson

Capen House, built in 1681 and open to visitors. Just outside of town you'll go along the Ipswich River and then through majestic estates with broad fields sloping down to the riverbank.

Directions for the ride: 26 miles

1. Turn left out of parking lot onto Endicott Road and go 1$\frac{1}{10}$ miles to Peabody Street on right. You'll cross the Ipswich River shortly before the intersection.

2. Turn right on Peabody Street and go 1$\frac{2}{10}$ miles to end (Liberty Street). Here the short ride turns right and the long ride turns left.

3. Turn left on Liberty Street and go 1$\frac{3}{10}$ miles to end (Route 62).

4. Turn right on Route 62 and go less than $\frac{7}{10}$ mile to Washington Street on right.

5. Turn right on Washington Street and go $\frac{1}{10}$ mile to end (Central Street).

6. Turn left at end and go $\frac{1}{10}$ mile to traffic light (Route 114), in the center of Middleton. Notice the attractive brick library, built in 1890, on the far left corner.

7. Continue straight onto Lake Street. Go $\frac{1}{2}$ mile to where road becomes dirt. You'll follow Middleton Pond on your left.

8. Continue straight on the dirt road. After $\frac{6}{10}$ mile the main road curves sharply left and becomes paved. Continue $\frac{2}{10}$ mile to crossroads at bottom of hill (**CAUTION** here).

9. Turn left at crossroads and go 1$\frac{3}{10}$ miles to Salem Street, a smaller road that turns right just after the North Reading town line (sign may say STATE FOREST).

10. Turn right on Salem Street and go $\frac{2}{10}$ mile to a bicycle path on your right. It comes up while you're going down a small hill. The path is blocked off to cars.

11. Turn right on the bike path and go $\frac{1}{2}$ mile to end. The path makes a little loop past Sudden Pond and comes back out on the main road. If you miss the path, or it doesn't look bikeable, it's no problem—just stay on the main road for 1 mile and resume with direction number 13.

12. Turn right at end of bike path and go $\frac{8}{10}$ mile to a road on your right shortly after the headquarters for the Harold Parker State Forest.

13. Turn right after forest headquarters and go 1$\frac{1}{10}$ miles to crossroads and stop sign (Route 114). You'll pass Stearns Pond on your right.

14. Turn left on Route 114 and go 1$\frac{7}{10}$ miles to Brook Street on right.

15. Turn right on Brook Street and go $^3/_{10}$ mile to end (Farnum Street, unmarked).

16. Turn left on Farnum Street and go $^6/_{10}$ mile to Summer Street (unmarked), which turns sharply right at yield sign.

17. Make a sharp right on Summer Street and go $1^1/_{10}$ miles to end (Salem Street).

18. Turn right on Salem Street. After $^6/_{10}$ mile there's a crossroads. Continue straight for $^2/_{10}$ mile to Forest Street on right.

19. Turn right on Forest Street and go $1^6/_{10}$ miles to fork (Lacy Street bears left).

20. Bear left on Lacy Street and go $1^7/_{10}$ miles to end (merge right).

21. Bear right at end and go $^4/_{10}$ mile to end (merge to the right on Main Street, unmarked, at a little traffic island).

22. Bear right at end and go $^9/_{10}$ mile to crossroads and stop sign (Middleton Road).

23. Turn left at crossroads and go $^4/_{10}$ mile to another crossroads and stop sign. This is the center of Boxford. Here the ride goes straight, but if you turn right a country store is just ahead on your right.

24. Go straight at crossroads onto Depot Road for $1^2/_{10}$ miles to Bare Hill Road on right. It is immediately past a small pond on left.

25. Turn right on Bare Hill Road and go $2^4/_{10}$ miles to end (Haverhill Road, Route 97).

26. Turn right on Route 97 and go $^8/_{10}$ mile to the Topsfield town green. When you get to the green, the Parson Capen House is to your left just around the corner.

27. At the green go straight on Main Street (unmarked); don't bear left on Route 97. Go $^9/_{10}$ mile to Salem Road on right, just before Route 1.

28. Turn right on Salem Road and go $^1/_{10}$ mile to River Road on right.

29. Turn right on River Road and go $1^3/_{10}$ miles to crossroads and stop sign. This is a magnificent run along the Ipswich River and then past broad fields and estates.

30. Turn left at crossroads and go $^1/_2$ mile to school on left.

Directions for the ride: 18 miles ～～～～～～

1. Follow directions 1 and 2 for the long ride.
2. Turn right at end onto Liberty Street and go $^4/_{10}$ mile to School Street on left.

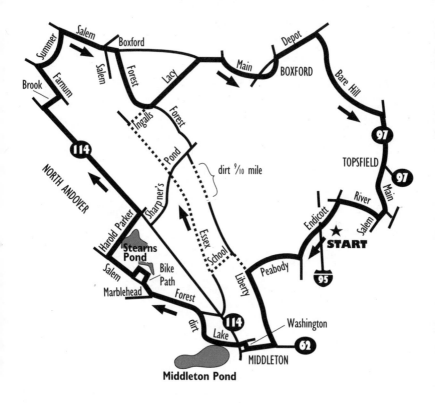

NORTH

Summer
Salem
Boxford
Depot
Salem
Forest
Lacy
Main
BOXFORD
Bare Hill
Brook
Farnum
Ingalls
Forest
Pond
114
dirt 9/10 mile
97
NORTH ANDOVER
Sharpner's
TOPSFIELD
97
River
Main
Harold Parker
Endicott
Salem
Stearns
Pond
Essex
School
★
START
Bike
Path
95
Salem
Marblehead
Forest
Liberty
Peabody
dirt
114
Washington
Lake
62
MIDDLETON
Middleton Pond

3. Turn left on School Street and go $^8/_{10}$ mile to end (Essex Street).

4. Turn right on Essex Street and go $1^9/_{10}$ miles to crossroads and stop sign (Sharpner's Pond Road).

5. Go straight at crossroads for $1^2/_{10}$ miles to Ingalls Street on right. There's a traffic island with a rock in the middle at the intersection.

6. Turn right on Ingalls Street and go $^4/_{10}$ mile to end (Forest Street).

7. Turn right on Forest Street and go $^2/_{10}$ mile to fork (Lacy Street bears left).

8. Follow directions for the long ride from number 20 to the end.

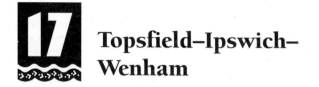

Topsfield–Ipswich–Wenham

Number of miles: 24 (12 without Ipswich extension)
Terrain: Gently rolling.
Food: Groceries and snack bars in the towns. The local specialty in Ipswich is clams.
Start: Topsfield Village shopping center, Main Street in Topsfield, just south of the green.
How to get there: Take I-95 to the Topsfield Road exit (exit 52). Turn right on Topsfield Road and go 1⁴/₁₀ miles (1⁶/₁₀ if you're coming from the north) to High Street Extension, which bears right just before white church. Bear right, and just ahead turn right at the crossroads and stop sign. Shopping center is just ahead on right.

This is a tour exploring three elegant old North Shore communities connected by delightful secondary roads winding past horse farms, country estates, and ponds and along the Ipswich River. You start from Topsfield, a handsome town with one of the finest traditional New England centers in the state. The large green is framed by an exceptionally fine classic white church and a marvelous Victorian town hall built in 1873. Adjoining the green is the Parson Capen House, built in 1681 and open to visitors. Topsfield is best known for its two giant annual fairs, the American Crafts Exposition in July and the Topsfield Fair in October. The latter is one of the country's oldest agricultural fairs, running since 1818. Surrounding the town are gentleman farms and estates spreading up rolling hills and the marshes of the Ipswich River, along which is the state's largest Audubon sanctuary.

From Topsfield you'll head through gently rolling farmland to Ipswich, a jewel of a town both geographically and architecturally. It boasts more pre-Revolutionary houses, some going back to the 1600s, than any other place in America north of Colonial Williamsburg. With the continuing efforts of a preservation-conscious citizenry, these buildings have been painstakingly restored and maintained. The center of town lies between a north green and a south green and contains a wonderful mixture of buildings of every architectural style from the early Colonial period to the turn of the century. Many of these houses are open to visitors; if you're a historic-house enthusiast, you can spend the entire day in town. If you want to see just one house, the one to visit is the John Whipple House, built in 1640. It has an herb garden and period furnishings.

The Ipswich River courses through town and passes underneath the graceful stone-arched Choate Bridge, built in 1764 and one of the oldest original bridges in the country. East of town are vast expanses of salt marsh, the steep-ridged Great Neck Peninsula, and magnificent Crane Beach and Castle Hill, all of which you can explore on the Ipswich ride.

A couple of miles out of town is another splendid North Shore landmark, the LaSallette Shrine and Seminary. Formerly an estate, it is everything that a shrine should be, complete with spreading, elaborately landscaped grounds, sunken gardens with squared-off hedges and trees pruned into parabolas, an ornate red-brick mansion, and Stations of the Cross with a flight of stairs to be climbed on your knees. Beyond the Shrine, you'll parallel the Ipswich River and wind through carefully maintained horse farms and estates to Wenham, another gracious and moneyed town with a stately white church and old town hall. Shortly before Wenham you'll pass Asbury Grove, a Methodist campground containing small Gothic-style cottages and a central tabernacle. It is similar to Oak Bluffs in Martha's Vineyard, but not as extensive or ornamented. Asbury Grove was founded in 1858.

Next to the Wenham town hall is the Claflin-Richards House, built in 1664. It adjoins the Wenham Historical Association and Museum, which maintains a fascinating display of dolls, toys, and games from the 1800s. It's open in the afternoon every day except Saturday. From Wenham it's a short ride back to Topsfield, passing Wenham Lake and rolling, open hillsides.

Directions for the ride: 24 miles

1. Turn left (north) out of parking lot onto Main Street. Just ahead you'll merge head-on into Route 97 at the green. The Parson Capen House is on Howlett Street, the side street on your right running parallel to Route 97, just north of the green. It's a small building with a steeply pitched roof.

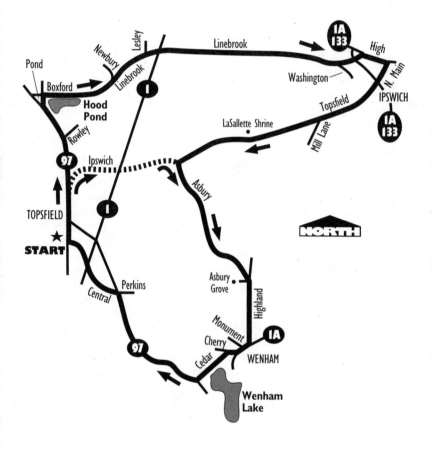

2. At the green, go straight on Route 97 for $^4/_{10}$ mile to fork where Route 97 bears left and Ipswich Road bears right. Here the short ride bears right and the long ride bears left.

3. Bear left on Route 97 and go $1^7/_{10}$ miles to Pond Street (unmarked), a narrow lane that bears right at bottom of hill. It comes up $^8/_{10}$ mile beyond Rowley Road, which also bears right.

4. Bear right on Pond Street and go less than $^2/_{10}$ mile to end (Boxford Road). Hood Pond is on your right.

5. Turn right at end onto Boxford Road and go $2^6/_{10}$ miles to stop sign and blinking light (Route 1), staying on main road. Two smaller roads bear left, but curve right on the main road at both intersections.

6. Cross Route 1 and go $3^6/_{10}$ miles to a large modern church on right. Continue past the church for $^2/_{10}$ mile to fork where the main road bears slightly left.

7. Bear left (almost straight) at fork and go $^2/_{10}$ mile to stop sign (merge left on Route 1A).

8. Bear left at stop sign (**CAUTION:** busy intersection). Go 100 yards to end, where Route 1A turns left and High Street (unmarked) turns right.

9. Turn right at end on High Street, passing a cemetery on your left. Notice how it rises up the steep hillside in terraces. Go $^4/_{10}$ mile to the third right, North Main Street (unmarked), at small brick traffic island. It's the third right. High Street is the heart of old Ipswich, and most of the houses on the street date back to the 1700s.

10. Turn right on North Main Street and go $^3/_{10}$ mile to crossroads and stop sign at bottom of hill (Routes 1A and 133). You'll go along Meeting House Green. The modern church in the center, clashing with the early buildings surrounding it, was built to replace the splendid traditional church that burned to the ground in 1965 after it was struck by lightning. It's surprising that this preservation-minded and history-conscious town did not rebuild the church to resemble the old one.

11. Cross Routes 1A and 133. **CAUTION:** Busy intersection. Stay on the main road $4^4/_{10}$ miles to Asbury Street on left (sign may say BRADLEY PALMER STATE PARK after you turn left). **CAUTION:** Diagonal railroad tracks at the beginning.

You'll pass the LaSallette Shrine and Seminary, which is worth visiting, on your right after $2^7/_{10}$ miles. Beyond the shrine you'll parallel the Ipswich River on your left. There's a fine dam 1 mile beyond the shrine.

12. Turn left on Asbury Street and go $2^7/_{10}$ miles to end (merge to right

at stop sign). This is a pleasant stretch past horse farms and estates.

13. Bear right at stop sign onto Highland and go 1⁴/10 miles to crossroads and stop sign (Route 1A, Main Street), in the center of Wenham. At the beginning you'll pass Asbury Grove on the right. The center of the campground is set back ¼ mile from the road.

14. Turn right on Route 1A and go ¹/10 mile to Cherry Street (unmarked), your second right. On your left you'll pass the town hall and the doll museum.

15. Turn right on Cherry Street and go ²/10 mile to Cedar Street on left.

16. Turn left on Cedar Street and go ⁹/10 mile to end (Route 97). You'll pass Wenham Lake on your left.

17. Turn right onto Route 97 and continue for 3¹/10 miles to diagonal crossroads where Perkins Row turns sharply right and Central Street bears left.

18. Bear left on Central Street and go ⁴/10 mile to crossroads and stop sign (Route 1). The Topsfield Fairgrounds are to your left on Route 1.

19. Cross Route 1 and go ½ mile to end (Main Street, unmarked).

20. Turn right at end and go 100 yards to shopping center on left.

Direction for the ride: 12 miles

1. Follow directions 1 and 2 for the long ride.

2. Bear right at fork on Ipswich Road and go ⁸/10 mile to traffic light (Route 1).

3. Cross Route 1 and go 1²/10 miles to Asbury Street on right. A sign may say TO BRADLEY PALMER STATE PARK after you turn right.

4. Turn right on Asbury Street and go 2⁷/10 miles to end (merge to your right at stop sign). This is a pleasant stretch past horse farms and estates.

5. Follow directions for the long ride from number 13 to the end.

Church, North Andover

Pedaler's Paradise:
North Andover–Boxford

Number of miles: 32 (16 without Boxford extension)
Terrain: Delightfully rolling, with lots of little ups and downs. There's one hill on the long ride.
Food: Country store in South Groveland. Country store in Boxford. Country store in West Boxford.
Start: Salem Street, Andover, just east of Route 28, adjacent to Phillips Academy. It's 1 mile south of the center of town.
How to get there: If you're heading north on Interstate 93, exit north onto Route 125, and then exit north onto Route 28. Go about 3 miles to Salem Street on right, at traffic light. There's a tall brick tower at the intersection.

If someone asked you to describe the ideal bike ride, with the limitation that it be in the eastern half of Massachusetts, you'd probably end up describing a ride like this one. Just southeast of Lawrence, on the wealthy, woodsy fringe of Boston suburbia, is a bicyclist's paradise of untraveled and well-paved country lanes, gentleman farms, lakeside runs with manicured estates sloping down to the shore, and a couple of graceful, unspoiled New England town centers with stately old homes and picket fences. You might also have mentioned oceanfront runs with crashing surf, but, sorry—you can't have everything.

The ride starts next to Phillips Academy, the classic New England preparatory school. Its large, impressive campus equals that of any college for elegance. You'll quickly cross the town line into North Andover, a double-faced town. The section closest to Lawrence (which you won't see on the ride) is a congested area of housing developments and industrial parks; everything else is a beautiful mixture of estates, woods, and large, well-landscaped newer homes on good-sized wooded lots. The old center of town is a gem, with a stately old church and a green framed by gracious Colonial-style homes. The centerpiece of the town is Lake Cochichewick, a large, refreshingly unspoiled lake surrounded by estates and wooded hills. You'll parallel the shore and then bike past the Brooks School, another preparatory school with a magnificent campus of graceful white wooden buildings and broad fields sweeping down to the lakefront. The rest of the ride brings you through the better of the town's two faces back to Phillips Academy.

The long ride makes a long loop through Boxford, which is even nicer than North Andover. Boxford epitomizes the gracious, well-to-do suburb that is rural rather than suburban, like the setting for the movie *Ordinary People.* (Funny how those ordinary people didn't have ordinary incomes.) Silk-smooth roads curve past woodlots, horse farms with pastures crisscrossed by rustic white wooden fences, rambling old homes, and impressive new ones harmoniously integrated with the landscape on two- and three-acre forested lots. The center of town is another New England classic, with a fine old church, a country store, and stately old homes. After looping through Boxford you'll pick up the route of the short ride back in North Andover in time to bike along the estate-lined southern shore of Lake Cochichewick.

Directions for the ride: 32 miles

1. Head east on Salem Street and go ¹⁄₁₀ mile to crossroads (Highland Road).
2. Turn left on Highland Road and go 1³⁄₁₀ miles to diagonal crossroads and stop sign (Route 125).
3. Cross Route 125 onto a dead-end road. **CAUTION** crossing Route 125. Go less than ²⁄₁₀ mile to the dead end. At the end Route 114 is in front of you, on the far side of a small grassy field.
4. Walk your bike about 100 feet across the field to Route 114. Hillside Road is in front of you on the opposite side of Route 114.
5. Cross Route 114 onto Hillside Road. **CAUTION** crossing Route 114. Go 1²⁄₁₀ miles to end (merge right at stop sign). When you get to the end, Stevens-Coolidge Place, an early nineteenth-century house with lovely gardens open to the public, is on the far side of the intersection. It's maintained by the Trustees of Reservations.
6. Bear right at end and go ¹⁄₁₀ mile to fork.
7. Bear right at fork, passing a large green on your left. Go ²⁄₁₀ mile to stop sign, at a five-way intersection. This is the lovely village of North Andover Center.
8. Go straight at stop sign, passing the church on left, and go one block

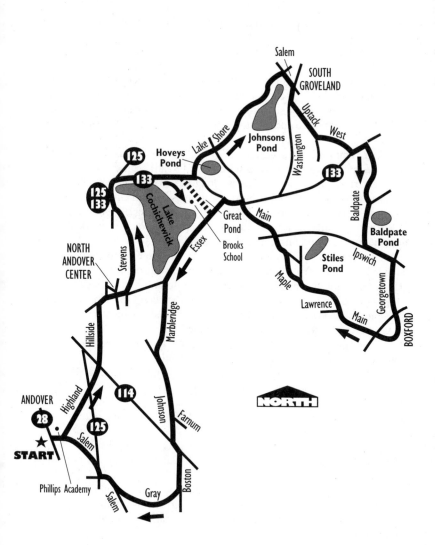

to diagonal crossroads (Stevens Street bears left; the sign is after the intersection).

9. Bear left on Stevens Street and go ⁴/₁₀ mile to fork (Pleasant Street bears left).

10. Bear right at fork (still Stevens Street), passing a picturesque pond on your right and hideous condominiums on your left. After ½ mile you'll merge head-on at stop sign into Osgood Street (unmarked). Continue straight for ½ mile to end, at stop sign (merge right on Routes 125 and 133).

11. Bear right on Routes 125 and 133. Go ⁶/₁₀ mile to fork where Route 125 goes straight and Route 133 (Great Pond Road) bears right.

12. Bear right on Route 133, going along Lake Cochichewick. Go 1⁴/₁₀ miles to crossroads where Bradford Street turns left and Great Pond Road bears right. Here the short ride bears right and the long ride goes straight.

13. Continue straight for ³/₁₀ mile to Lake Shore Road (unmarked) on left, at a traffic island immediately after crest of hill.

14. Turn left on Lake Shore Road and go ⁹/₁₀ mile to crossroads and stop sign (Main Street). You'll pass Hovey's Pond on your right.

15. Go straight at crossroads for 2¹/₁₀ miles to another crossroads and stop sign (Salem Street, unmarked). Toward the end of this stretch you'll go along Johnson's Pond. **CAUTION:** The second half of this stretch needs to be repaved; watch for bumps and potholes.

16. Turn right on Salem Street and go ³/₁₀ mile to crossroads (Washington Street). This is the village of South Groveland.

17. Turn right on Washington Street and go ³/₁₀ mile to Uptack Road, a smaller road that bears left.

18. Bear left on Uptack Road and go 1³/₁₀ miles to fork. You'll climb a tough hill, the worst one on the ride. **CAUTION:** Watch for bumps and potholes. The road needs repaving.

19. Bear left at fork onto West and go 1 mile to end (Route 133).

20. Turn left on Route 133 and go ⁴/₁₀ mile to Baldpate Road on right.

21. Turn right on Baldpate Road and go 1⁴/₁₀ miles to end, at small traffic island. Shortly before the end, at top of hill, you'll see a rambling Victorian mansion on the right. This is Baldpate, a private psychiatric hospital.

22. Turn right at end (still Baldpate Road, unmarked) and go 1 mile to end. You'll pass Baldpate Pond on the left.

23. Turn left at end onto Ipswich and go ⁸/₁₀ mile to crossroads (Georgetown Road). It's just after a small pond on right.

24. Bear right at crossroads and go 1⁷/₁₀ miles to end (merge right at yield sign). Just before the end you'll go through the center of Boxford and pass a country store on the right.

25. Bear slightly right at yield sign. Go 1³/₁₀ miles to fork where Lawrence Road bears left and the main road bears slightly right.

26. Bear slightly right on main road and go 2 miles to another fork where the main road goes straight and Maple Avenue bears left. It's shortly after Foster Street on left.

27. Bear left on Maple Avenue and go ⁴/₁₀ mile to end (merge left at stop sign).

28. Bear left at end and go ⁸/₁₀ mile to crossroads and stop sign (Ipswich Road).

29. Go straight at crossroads for 1 mile to another crossroads and stop sign (Route 133, Washington Street). This is the village of West Boxford.

30. Turn left on Route 133 and go ⁴/₁₀ mile to Essex Street on left, at traffic island. There is a good ice cream spot on the right as soon as you turn onto Washington Street.

31. Turn left on Essex Street and go ⁴/₁₀ mile to end, at stop sign (merge left at bottom of hill).

32. Bear left at end and go 1⁶/₁₀ miles to unmarked fork where Great Pond Road bears right and Marbleridge Road bears slightly left. You'll catch glimpses of Lake Cochichewick on your right.

33. Bear slightly left on Marbleridge Road and go 1¹/₁₀ miles to end, going straight at three crossroads.

34. Turn left at end and go 1 mile to fork where Farnum Street bears left and Johnson Street (unmarked) bears right.

35. Bear right on Johnson Street and go ⁶/₁₀ mile to end, at stop sign (merge left on Salem Turnpike, Route 114).

36. Bear left on Salem Turnpike and go ³/₁₀ mile to Boston Street, which bears right uphill.

37. Bear right on Boston Street and go ½ mile to fork (Gray Street bears right).

38. Bear right on Gray Street and go 1½ miles to end, at yield sign (merge right on Salem Street, unmarked).

39. Bear right on Salem Street and go ⁴/₁₀ mile to crossroads and stop sign (Route 125).

40. Turn right on Route 125 and go 100 yards to Salem Street on left, at blinking light.

41. Turn left on Salem Street and go 1 mile back to starting point. **CAUTION:** Bumpy spots.

Directions for the ride: 16 miles

1. Follow directions for the long ride through number 12.
2. Bear right on Great Pond Road and go 2⁶/₁₀ miles to unmarked fork where Great Pond Road bears right and Marbleridge Road bears slightly left. You'll pass the Brooks School on your right near the beginning. **CAUTION:** Potholes on the second ½ mile of this stretch.
3. Follow directions for the long ride from number 33 to the end.

America's Stonehenge Ride:
Haverhill–Salem, New Hampshire–
Hampstead, New Hampshire–Atkinson,
New Hampshire

Number of miles: 27 (12 without America's Stonehenge extension)
Terrain: Rolling, with one tough hill near the beginning.
Food: None en route for the short ride. Grocery and snack bar in Hampstead. Country store in Atkinson.
Start: Haverhill High School, at the corner of Monument Street and North Broadway. If you're coming from the south on Interstate 495, take the Route 97–Broadway exit (exit 50). At the end of the exit ramp, go straight onto Monument Street and go ⁴/₁₀ mile to school on right. If you're coming from the north on Interstate 495, get off at the same exit, turn left at end of ramp onto Route 97 South, cross over highway, and take your first left on Monument Street. The school is ⁴/₁₀ mile ahead on right.

Just northwest of Haverhill, extending several miles into New Hampshire, is a delightful area for bicycling with gentle wooded hills, several lakes, some open hillsides with fine views, and unspoiled small towns. The long ride is highlighted by a visit to America's Stonehenge, formerly called Mystery Hill, a complex of prehistoric stone ruins and monoliths of unknown origin. It is one of the major archaeological sites in the Northeast.

The ride starts on the outskirts of Haverhill, a congested nineteenth-century mill city sloping up the hills on both sides of the Merrimack River. You quickly get into rural countryside as you head into Salem, New Hampshire, and ride along the twisting shore of Arlington Mill Reservoir, lined with older summer cottages nestled among pine groves. In the last thirty years, Salem has become a bedroom suburb of Boston, only forty-five minutes away along Interstate 93, which runs through the middle of the town. The ride sticks to the section farthest from the highway, still mostly undeveloped.

Shortly beyond the reservoir you'll come to America's Stonehenge. The complex consists of an elaborate pattern of walls, tomblike buildings, wells, drains, remains of buildings, and rocks carved with mysterious inscriptions. Radiocarbon dating has shown the site to be more than 2,000 years old, eliminating the possibility that Indians, colonists, or early European explorers could have constructed it. Around the perimeter of the site, various stones are placed to serve as a giant astronomical calendar, lining up with the North Star, the cycles of the moon, sunrise and sunset on the longest and shortest days of the year, and other celestial phenomena. Some of the inscriptions match those of ancient Celtic tribes, raising the possibility that Europeans may have visited North America even before the Vikings. The most distinctive artifact in the site is a massive grooved stone slab supported on legs, most likely to have been used for sacrifices. America's Stonehenge is privately owned and is the scene of continuing research.

From America's Stonehenge you'll head to Hampstead and Atkinson, two unspoiled little New England towns. At the village crossroads in Hampstead stand the handsome Victorian town hall and a classic white church. Atkinson boasts the Atkinson Academy, a graceful schoolhouse dated 1803. Leaving Atkinson, you'll enjoy a soaring downhill run. The homestretch back to Haverhill leads along broad, open ridges with sweeping views of the valley.

Directions for the ride: 27 miles

1. Turn left out of parking lot on Monument Street. Just ahead is a crossroads and blinking light (North Broadway). Continue straight for $3/10$ mile to Route 97, at stop sign.
2. Turn right on Route 97 and go $6/10$ mile to Forest Street (unmarked) on left. There's a long, grassy traffic island at the intersection.
3. Turn left on Forest Street and go $1/2$ mile to crossroads and stop sign midway down sharp hill (West Lowell Avenue, unmarked).
4. Turn right at crossroads. Stay on the main road for 1 mile to fork. **CAUTION:** Potholes at the beginning. The last $6/10$ mile is a steep climb. This is the toughest hill of the ride—don't get discouraged.
5. Bear left at fork and go $3/10$ mile to another fork where a smaller road (North) bears right.
6. Bear right at fork onto North and go $12/10$ miles to crossroads and stop sign (Hampstead Road, unmarked).

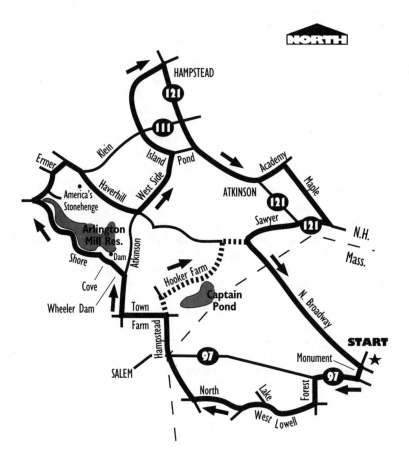

7. Turn right at crossroads and go 1²/10 miles to traffic light (Route 97, Ayers Village Road). You cross into Salem, New Hampshire, 100 yards before the light.

8. Cross Route 97 and go ⁶/10 mile to another crossroads (Liberty Street on right, Town Farm Road on left). Here the short ride goes straight and the long ride turns left.

9. Turn left at crossroads onto Town Farm Road. Stay on the main road for ⁸/10 mile to crossroads and stop sign.

10. Turn right at crossroads and go ⁶/10 mile to Wheeler Dam Road, which bears left. **CAUTION:** Watch for potholes. You'll pass a grocery on the right.

11. Bear left on Wheeler Dam Road and go ³/10 mile to fork (Cove Road bears left). **CAUTION:** Bumps and potholes. Here the ride bears left, but if you bear right and go 200 yards you'll come to Wheeler Dam at the end of the Arlington Mill Reservoir. It's a great spot for a picnic and worth looking over.

12. Bear left on Cove Road and go ¹/10 mile to another fork at top of hill (Shore Drive bears left).

13. Bear left on Shore Drive and go 2⁶/10 miles to end, following the shore of the Arlington Mill Reservoir. **CAUTION:** This road is very curvy with potholes, bumps, and sandy spots; take it easy.

14. Turn right at end and go ²/10 mile to fork (Millpond Road bears right). This is the village of North Salem, New Hampshire.

15. Bear left at fork and go ⁶/10 mile to another fork where the main road curves right and Ermer Road bears left. **CAUTION:** Watch for potholes.

16. Stay on main road for ⁴/10 mile to end (Haverhill Road).

17. Turn right at end and go ²/10 mile to fork where Klein Drive bears left and Haverhill Road bears slightly right.

18. Bear slightly right on Haverhill Road. After ³/10 mile, America's Stonehenge is on your right. Continue 1 mile to crossroads (Atkinson Road on right, West Side Road on left).

19. Turn left at crossroads onto West Side Road. Stay on main road for 1½ miles to end (Island Pond Road).

20. Turn left at end and go ⁸/10 mile to wide crossroads and stop sign (Route 111).

21. Cross Route 111 and go 1⁶/10 miles to crossroads and blinking light (Main Street, Route 121) in the center of Hampstead. Here the ride turns right, but there's a pharmacy selling snacks 50 yards to your left on

Route 121. The graceful Victorian town hall is across the road from the pharmacy.

22. Turn right on Route 121 and go $1\frac{1}{10}$ miles to Route 111, at traffic light.

23. Cross Route 111 and go $2\frac{1}{10}$ miles to Academy Avenue, which bears left at top of hill. There's a country store on the far left side of the intersection. This is the village of Atkinson.

24. Bear left on Academy Avenue and go $\frac{1}{2}$ mile to crossroads (Maple Avenue). You'll pass the graceful Atkinson Academy on your left.

25. Turn right at crossroads onto Maple Avenue and go $1\frac{1}{2}$ miles to end (merge into Route 121 at bottom of little hill). There's a splendid downhill run on this stretch—enjoy it! At the end the road merges left, but you will turn sharply right.

26. Turn sharply right on Route 121 and go $\frac{1}{2}$ mile to fork where Sawyer Avenue bears left downhill.

27. Bear left on Sawyer Avenue and go $1\frac{1}{10}$ miles to North Broadway on left. (North Broadway also goes straight at the intersection.)

28. Turn left on North Broadway and go $3\frac{1}{2}$ miles to crossroads and blinking light (Monument Street). **CAUTION:** Potholes and cracks on the first half of this section.

29. Turn left on Monument Street. The school is just ahead on right.

Directions for the ride: 12 miles

1. Follow directions for the long ride through number 8.

2. Go straight at crossroads for almost $\frac{4}{10}$ mile to Hooker Farm Road on right.

3. Turn right on Hooker Farm Road and go $1\frac{8}{10}$ miles to end (Providence Hill Road on left). **CAUTION:** Watch for potholes for the first mile. You'll pass Captain Pond on your right.

4. Turn right at end and go $\frac{3}{10}$ mile to where North Broadway turns right.

5. Turn right on North Broadway and go $3\frac{1}{2}$ miles to crossroads and blinking light (Monument Street). **CAUTION:** Potholes and cracks for the first half of this section.

6. Turn left on Monument Street. The school is just ahead on right.

20 Middlesex Canal Ride:
Burlington–Billerica–Wilmington

Number of miles: 24 (16 without Billerica extension)
Terrain: Rolling, with several short hills and one tough one.
Food: Groceries and snack bars in the towns.
Start: Vinebrook Plaza, a small shopping center on Middlesex Turnpike in Burlington, just north of Burlington Mall. It's ⁶/₁₀ mile north of Route 128. Take exit 32B.

On this ride you'll explore three pleasant middle-class communities midway between Boston and Lowell. The region is primarily suburban, interspersed with some wooded stretches and a few small farms. Biking in this area is pleasant if you stick to the secondary roads. This ride features fascinating traces of the Middlesex Canal, which was completed in 1803 to connect Boston with the Merrimack River in Lowell. The canal was the first in the country and sparked the growth of Lowell as an early industrial center. A massive feat of civil engineering for its time, the canal had twenty locks, eight aqueducts, and forty-eight bridges. Today only traces remain, most notably the Shawsheen River Aqueduct, which you'll see on the longer ride. The canal suffered an early death with the completion of the Boston and Lowell Railroad in 1835. It took all day for the small-capacity, horse-drawn towboats to run the length of the waterway, but the railroad could carry a much larger payload from Lowell to Boston in an hour. By 1850 the canal was virtually unused.

The ride starts by heading north along the ramrod-straight Middlesex Turnpike, sprouting with new, boldly architectured high-technology firms. After crossing Nutting Lake you'll come to the center of Billerica, which is surprisingly attractive for a populous bedroom suburb. The large, well-landscaped green, with a monument in the middle, is framed by a traditional white New England church and an ornate brick Victorian library. A couple of miles ahead is North Billerica, an old mill village with a row of identical houses, two grim but ornate Victorian mills, and a fine dam spanning the Concord River. Here the Middlesex Canal crossed the river at water level. To enable the horsemen pulling towboats to get across the river, the engineers built a floating bridge. The bridge could be opened to allow traffic on the river itself to pass through.

From here you'll parallel the remains of the Middlesex Canal, which is noticeable only as a slight depression running in a straight line across the land. When you cross the Shawsheen River into Wilmington, the three stone abutments of the aqueduct, one on each bank of the river and one in the middle, remain intact. The canal was built across the top of the river, fitting into the U-shaped slot visible in the center abutment. The canal couldn't have simply been built at ground level or its waters would have been diverted by the river. The only solution was to build an aqueduct above the river. These aqueducts severely limited the size of the boats that the canal could accommodate.

From the aqueduct, the return trip to Burlington leads through some surprisingly rural stretches. You'll pass two wooden schoolhouses from the 1800s and a monument to the Baldwin apple, which was first grown in the vicinity.

Directions for the ride: 24 miles ~~~~~~~~

1. Turn right from the parking lot on Middlesex Turnpike, heading north, and go 1²/₁₀ miles to Route 62 (unmarked), at second traffic light. Here the short ride turns right and the long ride goes straight.
2. Continue straight for 4²/₁₀ miles to end, at traffic light (Concord Road). You'll cross Nutting Lake 1 mile before the end.
3. Turn right at end onto Concord Road. Go ⁷/₁₀ mile to fork where the main road curves left and Charnstaffe Lane, a smaller road, goes straight.
4. Stay on main road for ³/₁₀ mile to end (Route 3A, Boston Road). You'll go alongside the Billerica town green on your left. Notice the fine white church and Victorian library on the far side of the green.
5. Turn left on Route 3A and go 1 mile to traffic light where Route 129 turns 90 degrees right and another road (Pollard Street) bears slightly right.
6. Bear slightly right on Pollard Street immediately before the traffic light. Go 1²/₁₀ miles to a three-way fork immediately after you cross the Concord River.
7. At the three-way fork, take the middle road, passing the church on your left. Go ³/₁₀ mile to fork, at a grassy, triangular traffic island. It's just

after a large oval green. This is North Billerica, also called Talbot Mills.

8. Bear right at fork, passing factory on left. Go $^4/_{10}$ mile to another fork where Rogers Street bears right and Mount Pleasant Street bears left. The dam spanning the Concord River on your right is impressive.

9. Bear left at fork, going under railroad bridge, and go $^4/_{10}$ mile to end.

10. Turn right at end and go $^2/_{10}$ mile to fork (High Street bears right, Sheldon Street bears left).

11. Bear left at fork and go $^3/_{10}$ mile to your second right, Oak Street, which bears right up a tiny hill.

12. Bear right on Oak Street and go $^8/_{10}$ mile to stop sign (merge head-on into Pond Street).

13. Continue straight for $^2/_{10}$ mile to fork where Pond Street bears left and Pine Street bears right. You'll see Long Pond on your left just before the fork.

14. Bear right at fork and go $^3/_{10}$ mile to crossroads and stop sign (Whipple Road).

15. Turn right on Whipple Road and go $^4/_{10}$ mile to fork just after stop sign (Chandler Street, unmarked, bears slightly right).

16. Bear slightly right on Chandler Street and go $1^1/_{10}$ miles to crossroads and stop sign (Route 129, Salem Road). Currently a railroad bridge on this section is under construction and may be impassable. If so, turn left just before the bridge on Patten Road (unmarked) and go almost $^4/_{10}$ mile to crossroads and stop sign (Whipple Road). Turn right and go $^3/_{10}$ mile to another crossroads and stop sign. Turn right and go almost $^1/_2$ mile to traffic island. Turn sharp left at traffic island onto Route 129, Salem Road. Go almost $^1/_2$ mile to fork where Route 129 bears left. Resume with direction number 19.

17. Turn left on Route 129. Just ahead merge left at stop sign. Bear left and go $^3/_{10}$ mile to fork where Route 129 (Salem Street) bears right.

18. Bear right at fork (still Route 129) and go $^1/_2$ mile to another fork where Route 129 bears left.

19. Bear left at fork (still Route 129). After $^7/_{10}$ mile, the remains of the Shawsheen River aqueduct of the Middlesex Canal are on your left. Continue on Route 129 for $^8/_{10}$ mile to traffic light (Lake Street on left, Hopkins Street on right).

20. Continue straight at light for $^8/_{10}$ mile to Aldrich Road (unmarked) on right. There is a little red schoolhouse, built in 1875, on your left at the intersection.

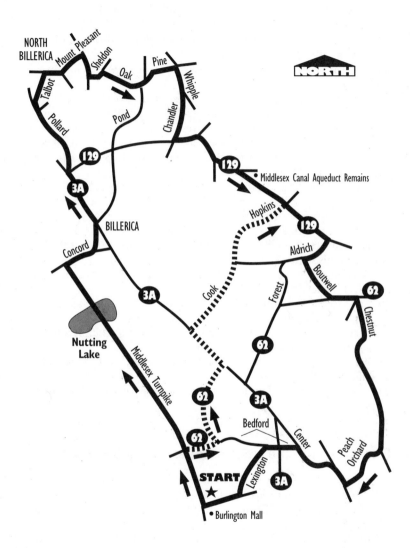

21. Turn right on Aldrich Road and go ½ mile on Boutwell Street on left. It is just after Mozart Avenue on left.

22. Turn left on Boutwell Street and go ⁸/₁₀ mile to end (merge left on Route 62 at stop sign).

23. Bear left on Route 62 and go ⁴/₁₀ mile to Chestnut Street on right, at traffic light.

24. Turn 90 degrees right on Chestnut Street (don't turn sharply right on Marion Street) and go 2⁷/₁₀ miles to Peach Orchard Road, which turns right up a steep hill. The main road curves left at the intersection.

You'll pass another little red schoolhouse, built in 1894, on the left after ⁷/₁₀ mile. The Baldwin apple monument, dated 1895, is on your right ¹/₁₀ mile after the schoolhouse.

25. Turn right on Peach Orchard Road and go ⁹/₁₀ mile to end.

26. Turn right at end and go ²/₁₀ mile to fork at far end of school on left (Center Street bears left uphill).

27. Bear left at fork and go ⁶/₁₀ mile to Bedford Street, which bears left immediately before the Burlington green. There's a tough hill at the beginning of this stretch.

28. Bear left on Bedford Street and go ²/₁₀ mile to Route 3A (Cambridge Street), at traffic light.

29. Cross Route 3A (**CAUTION:** busy intersection). Go ¹/₁₀ mile to Lexington Street, which bears left.

30. Bear left on Lexington Street and go 1⁷/₁₀ miles to end. Burlington Mall is on the far side of the intersection.

31. Turn right at end and go less than ²/₁₀ mile to Meadow Road on right, at traffic light.

32. Turn right on Meadow Road and immediately left into Vinebrook Plaza.

Directions for the ride: 16 miles

1. Turn right from the parking lot onto Middlesex Turnpike and go 1²/₁₀ miles to Route 62 (unmarked), at second traffic light.

2. Turn right on Route 62 and go ⁶/₁₀ mile to where Route 62 (Francis Wyman Road) turns left.

3. Turn left on Route 62 and go 1½ miles to end (Route 3A, Cambridge Street). There's a tough hill at the end.

4. Turn left on Route 3A and go $9/10$ mile to Cook Street on right, at the third traffic light.

5. Turn right on Cook Street and go $1^2/10$ miles to crossroads where the main road curves sharply left (there's a large school on the left at the intersection).

6. Stay on the main road for $1^4/10$ miles to traffic light (Shawsheen Avenue, Route 129). **CAUTION:** Watch for bumps and potholes. Here the ride turns right, but if you turn left and go $8/10$ mile, you'll come to the Shawsheen River aqueduct of the Middlesex Canal on your right.

7. Turn right on Route 129 and go $8/10$ mile to Aldrich Road (unmarked) on right. At the intersection, on the left, you will see a little red schoolhouse, built in 1875.

8. Follow directions for the long ride from number 21 to the end.

21

Reading–Wilmington–
North Reading–
Lynnfield–Wakefield

Number of miles: 26 (16 without Wilmington–North Reading extension)
Terrain: Gently rolling, with a couple of moderate hills.
Food: Groceries and snack bars in the towns.
Start: Lord Wakefield Hotel or the adjacent Lakeside Office Park, North Avenue, Wakefield, just south of Route 128. Take exit 39.

This ride loops through a cluster of attractive middle-class to affluent communities midway between Boston and Lawrence. The region is semisuburban and semirural, with large expanses of greenspace in the northern sections of the ride as you head through the Harold Parker State Forest. The town centers are New England classics, with well-tended greens framed by old churches and town halls, unspoiled even though there may be residential and commercial development close by.

At the beginning of the ride you'll pass through the graceful town center of Reading, where six roads radiate symmetrically from the green and a stately white church stands proudly above the town. From here you'll proceed to Wilmington, with an old cemetery and church marking the original center of town, and then head north into more wooded, less-developed landscape. You'll pass unspoiled Fosters Pond and Field Pond as you wind through the Harold Parker State Forest. From here it's a smooth run to North Reading, a charming town with a large triangular green, an old clock-towered church, and a striking white Victorian building that was formerly the town hall. From North Reading you'll parallel the upper reaches of the Ipswich River for a couple of miles and then turn south to Lynnfield, the most affluent of the five communities along the route. The town center is a New England classic, with a handsome white church and a slender triangle of a green surrounding a meeting-house built in 1715. From here it's not far to Wakefield, one of the most visually appealing of the suburbs inside the Route 128 semicircle. The focal point of the community is Lake Quannapowitt, with the center of town at its southern end. In good weather the lakeshore is a giant outdoor health club, with a constant flow of walkers, joggers, in-line skaters, and cyclists. You'll enjoy a mile-long ride along the lakefront. At the far end of the lake is a beautifully landscaped park with an old bandstand overlooking the water. Across from the park is the town green, framed by a classic white church, an impressive stone church, and fine old homes. From here, ride a short distance up the other side of the lake back to the start.

Directions for the ride: 26 miles

1. Turn right onto North Avenue and go underneath Route 128. Continue $^4/_{10}$ mile to John Street (unmarked) on right. It's immediately after Lakeview Avenue on right.

2. Turn right on John Street and go $^1/_2$ mile to end (Route 129). Here the short ride turns left and then right on Route 28, and the long ride turns left but stays on Route 129.

3. Turn left at end and then immediately bear right on Route 129, passing the Reading town green on your left and the fine white church on your right. Follow Route 129 for 2$^6/_{10}$ miles to traffic light (Woburn Street). It is the second traffic light after the Interstate 93 interchange.

4. Turn right on Woburn Street and go 1$^4/_{10}$ miles to traffic light (Concord Street). **CAUTION:** Diagonal railroad tracks after 1 mile.

5. Continue straight for 8/10 mile to Woburn Street (unmarked) on left, immediately after the bridge over Interstate 93.

6. Turn left on Woburn Street and go $^7/_{10}$ mile to crossroads and stop sign (Route 62, Salem Street).

7. Cross Route 62 and go $^9/_{10}$ mile to traffic light (Route 125).

8. Cross Route 125 and go 1$^4/_{10}$ miles to fork, at traffic island (Rattlesnake Hill Road, unmarked, bears right).

9. Bear right at fork. After $^2/_{10}$ mile the main road bears slightly left at traffic island. Bear left and go $^6/_{10}$ mile to end (Rattlesnake Hill Road on left, Old County Road on right). You'll pass a little dam on the right at bottom of hill.

10. Turn right at end and go $^1/_{10}$ mile to fork where Glenwood Road (unmarked), a newer road, bears right.

11. Bear left at fork and go $^1/_2$ mile to Route 28, at stop sign.

12. Cross Route 28 and go $^3/_{10}$ mile to Route 125, at stop sign.

13. Cross Route 125, continuing straight ahead through a pair of stone pillars into the Harold Parker State Forest (don't bear right on Gould Road past police station). Go 1½ miles to crossroads and stop sign (Jenkins Road, unmarked). **CAUTION:** Watch for bumps and potholes. You'll pass Field Pond on your right.

14. Turn right at crossroads onto Haverhill and go 2⁷⁄₁₀ miles to fork at the North Reading town green. There's a clock-towered church, built in 1829, in the middle of the fork.

15. Bear right at fork and go ¹⁄₁₀ mile to crossroads and stop sign (Route 62).

16. Turn left on Route 62 and go ³⁄₁₀ mile to fork where Park Street bears right and Route 62 (unmarked here) bears left. You'll pass the Victorian former town hall, now a library, on your left. It was built in 1875.

17. Bear left on Route 62 and go 2½ miles to grassy traffic island where Route 62 bears left and another road bears right. This stretch parallels the Ipswich River, visible from a few spots on your right.

18. Bear right at this intersection and go ²⁄₁₀ mile to fork immediately after you cross the river (Russell Street bears left).

19. Bear right at fork and go 4½ miles to traffic light (Lowell Street). It's ⁶⁄₁₀ mile after you go underneath Route 128.

You'll just nick a corner of Peabody for about 50 feet, ⁴⁄₁₀ mile from the fork. Immediately after the PEABODY-MIDDLETON TOWN LINE sign, if you follow the stone wall to your right about 50 feet, you'll see an old granite marker indicating the point where Peabody, Lynnfield, and Middleton meet. Two miles farther on you'll go through the center of Lynnfield.

20. Turn right on Lowell Street and go ⁷⁄₁₀ mile to Route 129 East (Main Street) on left, immediately before Lake Quannapowitt on left.

21. Turn left on Main Street, going along the lake on your right. Go 1¹⁄₁₀ miles to Church Street, which bears right at traffic light at the Wakefield town green. Notice the fine church at far end of green.

22. Bear right on Church Street and go ⁴⁄₁₀ mile to traffic light (North Avenue).

23. Turn right on North Avenue and go ⁷⁄₁₀ mile to hotel on right.

Directions for the ride: I6 miles

1. Follow directions 1 and 2 for the long ride.
2. Turn left at end and immediately bear right on Route 129. Then im-

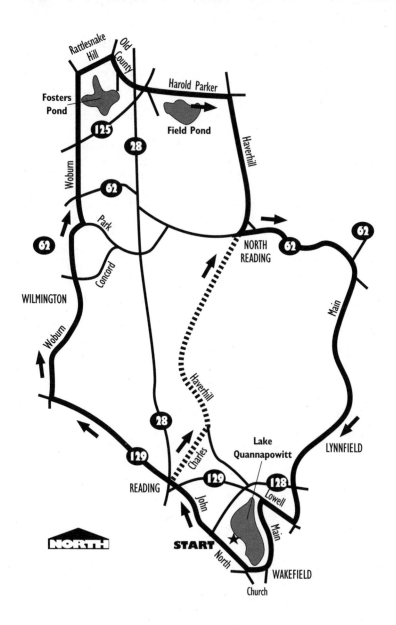

mediately turn right on Route 28 at traffic light. Go less than $2/10$ mile to Charles Street, which bears right.

3. Bear right on Charles Street and go $2/10$ mile to end (merge left at round, grassy traffic island).

4. Bear left at end. Just ahead the main road bears right at a fork. Bear right (still Charles Street, unmarked) and go 1 mile to end, at stop sign (merge left on Haverhill Street).

5. Bear left on Haverhill Street and go 2.4 miles to crossroads and stop sign (Route 62) in the center of North Reading.

6. Turn right on Route 62 and go $3/10$ mile to fork where Park Street bears right and Route 62 (unmarked here) bears left. You'll pass the Victorian former town hall, now a library, on your left. It was built in 1875.

7. Follow the directions for the long ride from number 17 to the end.

Chapter 3:
The Closer Western Suburbs

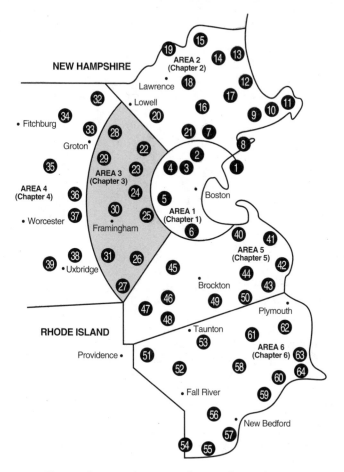

The numbers on this map refer to rides in this book.

Minutemen and Muskets:
Concord–Carlisle–Bedford–Lexington

Number of miles: 24 (18 without Carlisle extension, 11 with Concord–Carlisle loop only)

Terrain: Gently rolling, with one tough hill.

Food: Grocery stores or snack bars in the towns.

Start: The 24- and 18-mile rides start at Minute Man National Park, Battle Road Visitor Information Center in Lexington, off Route 2A, ⁹/₁₀ mile west of Route 128. Exit west from Route 128 onto Route 2A and follow the signs to the visitor center.

The 11-mile ride starts from the Old North Bridge parking lot on Monument Street in Concord. To get there, exit west from Route 128 onto Route 2A. Go about 5½ miles into the center of Concord, where Route 62 East turns right at a small rotary. Continue straight for 1 block to end (Monument Street). Turn right and go ½ mile to parking lot on right.

This is a tour of four affluent communities northwest of Boston, passing several historic sites related to the battles of Lexington and Concord, the first skirmishes of the Revolution. Between the town centers lies a gently rolling landscape of gentleman farms, some estates surrounded by acres of open land, and gracious Colonial-style homes and farmhouses. The long ride heads along an open ridge to Carlisle, the closest completely unspoiled, classic New England town to Boston.

At the beginning of the ride, you'll skirt Hanscom Field, an Air Force base incongruously dropped in the midst of wealthy suburbs, with jet fighters poised for action in the same spot where musket-armed colonists waited two centuries ago. You'll pass several high-technology firms adjoining the base; then, in a flash, you enter a delightful landscape of horse farms, rolling meadows, and old clapboard homes.

From here it's a couple of miles into Concord, a town unique as both a historic and literary center. Nearly a century after the Revolution, Concord was the home at one time or another of the Alcotts, Hawthorne, Emerson, and Thoreau. They are all buried in Sleepy Hollow Cemetery, just outside of town. Coming into Concord, you'll pass the Wayside, where the Alcotts and Hawthorne once lived; the Orchard House, another Alcott home; and the Emerson House. Just north of town, ½ mile off the route, is Concord's most famous landmark, the Old North Bridge. It's a lovely spot despite the daily onslaught of hundreds of sightseers and schoolchildren on field trips—a simple, gently bowed wooden bridge over the lazy Concord River, replaced several times since the Revolution. Adjacent to the bridge is the Old Manse, built in 1770 by Emerson's grandfather and the residence of both Hawthorne and Emerson, and the North Bridge Visitor Center, housed in an elegant brick mansion.

From Concord it's not far to Bedford, a pleasant residential community with an unusually large and elegant white church in the center of town. The run from Bedford to Lexington passes through gracious, well-to-do residential areas, going past an appealing mixture of tastefully designed newer homes and fine older ones set off by shade trees and broad lawns. Finally you arrive at famed Lexington Green, also called Battle Green, scene of the first American casualties of the Revolution. The large, triangular, tree-shaded green, with a stately white church at its head, is a delightful place to rest. At one corner of the green is a fine old statue in honor of the Minutemen, built in 1799. Across the street from the green is the Buckman Tavern, where the Minutemen assembled to await the British, a superbly restored and maintained old tavern with its original furnishings intact.

The long ride heads north from Concord past the Old North Bridge and the visitor center to the elegant, unspoiled rural town of Carlisle. You'll go along a ridge with fine views across broad, open meadows, and then pass the gracious campus of the Middlesex School, an exclusive preparatory school with broad lawns and handsome red-brick buildings. The center of town is a jewel, with a stately white church standing over the green, an old wooden schoolhouse on top of the hill, a fine brick Victorian library, and a delightful country store. From Carlisle it's a smooth run to Bedford, where you'll pick up the route of the short ride.

Directions for the ride: 24 miles

1. Go to the far end of the parking lot, where you'll see a service road with a DO NOT ENTER sign. Follow the service road 50 yards to end (Route 2A). Walk your bike around a gate at the end.

2. Turn right (west) on Route 2A and go almost $^9/_{10}$ mile to Virginia Road, a narrow lane that bears right (sign says BATTLE ROAD, 1775). It's $^2/_{10}$ mile after the road leading to Hanscom Field on right. The restored William Smith House, which is typical of homes from the Revolutionary era, is on your right at Virginia Road.

3. Bear right on Virginia Road and go $^1/_2$ mile to a dirt road, blocked off to cars, on the right that passes through a pair of stone pillars. It comes up just as you start to go downhill. You'll pass the Samuel Hartwell House (only the chimney remains) and the Ephriam Hartwell Tavern, a typical house-plus-tavern from the mid-1700s.

4. Turn right on the dirt road and go $^1/_{10}$ mile to paved road. **CAUTION:** Walk along the rough, rocky dirt road.

5. Bear slightly left on paved road (still Virginia Road, unmarked), and go $1^9/_{10}$ miles to end. You'll pass Hanscom Field on your right.

6. Turn left at end and go $^1/_2$ mile to end, at stop sign (merge right on Old Route 2A, unmarked).

7. Bear right on Old Route 2A and go $1^3/_{10}$ miles to Route 62 East, in the center of Concord. It's immediately after a small rotary. You'll pass the Wayside, the Orchard House, and the Emerson House. When you get to Route 62 East, the 18-mile ride turns right and the longer ride goes straight. To visit the Sleepy Hollow Cemetery, turn right on Route 62 East and go $^1/_4$ mile to cemetery on left..

8. Continue straight for 1 block to end (Monument Street).

9. Turn right on Monument Street. After $^1/_2$ mile you'll see the Old Manse on your left. Immediately after the Manse a path on the left leads to the Old North Bridge.

10. Continue on Monument Street $^3/_{10}$ mile to Liberty Street on left (sign says TO MINUTEMAN VISITOR CENTER). Here the ride turns left, but if you go straight for $^7/_{10}$ mile, you'll come to a hillside with an idyllic view of gracious estates and rolling, open meadows.

11. Turn left on Liberty Street and go $^2/_{10}$ mile to end, at traffic island (Estabrook Road on right). Just before the intersection, the visitor information center is on your left.

12. Turn right on Estabrook Road and go $^3/_{10}$ mile to fork (Estabrook Road bears right).

13. Bear slightly left at fork and go $^4/_{10}$ mile to crossroads and blinking light (Lowell Road).

14. Turn right on Lowell Road and go $4^3/_{10}$ miles to the center of

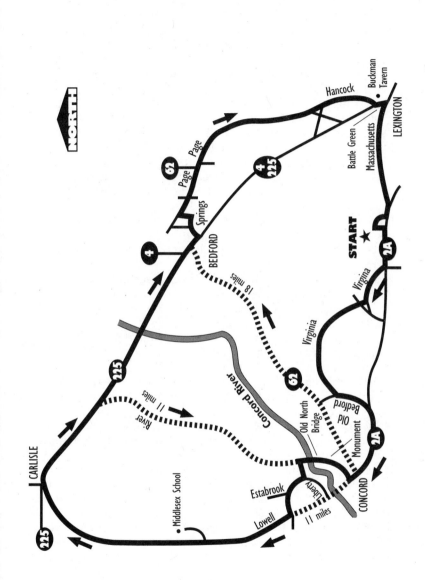

Carlisle, where you merge right on Route 225 (no stop sign). You'll pass the Middlesex School, which is worth a look, on the right after 1⁴/₁₀ miles. It's just before a smaller road bears left. The school is set back ³/₁₀ mile from the road.

When you come to Route 225 in Carlisle, notice the graceful white church on your right.

15. Bear right on Route 225 and go 4²/₁₀ miles to fork where Route 62 West bears right and Routes 4, 62, and 225 bear left. The fork is just after a yield sign. After ⁶/₁₀ mile you'll pass Kimball Farm Ice Cream, an excellent spot for a treat, on the left.

16. Bear left at fork onto Routes 4, 62, and 225 (sign may say TO BED-FORD, LEXINGTON). Go ³/₁₀ mile to traffic light just after an impressive church on right (South Road on right, Springs Road on left). This is the center of Bedford.

17. Turn left on Springs Road (**CAUTION:** busy intersection) and go ¹/₁₀ mile to fork.

18. Bear right at fork (still Springs Road) and go less than ²/₁₀ mile to end (merge left at stop sign).

19. Bear left at stop sign and go ¼ mile to crossroads and stop sign (Pine Hill Road on left, Page Road on right).

20. Turn right on Page Road and go ⁷/₁₀ mile to stop sign (merge head-on into Route 62).

21. Go straight on Route 62 for ²/₁₀ mile to where Route 62 curves sharply left and Page Road goes straight.

22. Go straight on Page Road for ¹/₁₀ mile to fork.

23. Bear left at fork (still Page Road) and go 2⁸/₁₀ miles to rotary. You'll climb a long, steady grade, the only real hill on the ride, and enjoy a fast, smooth descent.

24. Go two-thirds of the way around the rotary onto Hancock Street (un-marked), passing a garden store on left. Go ½ mile to traffic island where Adams Street turns left and the main road bears right.

25. Bear right on main road and go ½ mile to another traffic island oppo-site Lexington Green. **CAUTION:** Bumps and potholes. Shortly before the green you'll pass the Hancock-Clarke house on your right, built in 1698. You'll cross the Minuteman Bikeway immediately before the end.

26. Bear left at traffic island and stop sign, following the green on your right. Go 1 block to the tip of the green. The Buckman Tavern is on your left opposite the green.

Battle Green, Lexington

27. At the tip of the green, turn sharply right on Massachusetts Avenue (unmarked). At the far end of the green, notice the statue honoring the Minutemen. From the end of the green, go ^{2}/10 mile to traffic light (Worthen Road).

28. Continue straight on Massachusetts Avenue for 1^6/10 miles to crossroads and stop sign (Route 2A).

29. Turn right on Route 2A and go ^{2}/10 mile to Airport Road on right (it's unmarked; sign says TO BATTLE ROAD VISITOR CENTER).

30. Turn right on Airport Road and go ^{1}/4 mile to the entrance road to the visitor center, which bears left (sign says BATTLE ROAD, 1775).

Directions for the ride: 18 miles

1. Follow directions for the long ride through number 7, to Route 62 East in the center of Concord. Here the ride turns right, but if you want to visit the Old North Bridge, continue straight for 1 block to end (Monument Street). Turn right on Monument Street and go ^{1}/2 mile.

2. Turn right on Route 62 (Bedford Street) and go 4^1/2 miles to traffic light in center of Bedford just after an impressive church on the right. At the light, South Road turns right and Springs Road turns left.

You'll pass Sleepy Hollow Cemetery on your left after ^{1}/4 mile.

3. Follow directions for the 24-mile ride from direction number 17 to the end.

Directions for the ride: 11 miles

Here's a short, easy ride passing entirely through an idyllic landscape of estates, gentleman farms, and rolling, open meadows and hillsides. On the way to Carlisle you'll pass the Middlesex School, a preparatory school with beautiful grounds and elegant brick buildings that is worth visiting.

Start: Old North Bridge parking lot on Monument Street in Concord.

1. Turn left out of parking lot and go ^{1}/2 mile to end (Lowell Road), in center of Concord.

2. Turn right on Lowell Road and go 5^1/2 miles to end, where you merge right on Route 225 in the center of Carlisle (no stop sign).

The entrance to Middlesex School is on your right after 2^6/10 miles, just before a smaller road bears left. The school is set back $3/10$ mile from the road.

When you come to Route 225 in Carlisle, notice the graceful white church on your right.

3. Bear right on Route 225 and go $1^7/10$ miles to River Road, which bears right. After $6/10$ mile you'll pass Kimball Farm Ice Cream, an excellent snack spot, on your left.

4. Bear right on River Road and go $3^8/10$ miles to Old North Bridge parking lot on left.

Lincoln–Sudbury–
Wayland–Weston

Number of miles: 27 (14 without Sudbury–Wayland–Weston extension)
Terrain: Gently rolling, with one moderate hill.
Food: Groceries and restaurants in all the towns except Lincoln.
Start: DoubleTree Guest Suites, Winter Street in Waltham, just west of Route 128. Take exit 27B.

This is a tour of the gracious, wealthy communities west of Boston outside the Route 128 semicircle. Bicycling in this area is pure joy as you wind through a neat landscape of horse farms; estates; broad, gently rolling fields; unspoiled ponds; and classic New England town centers along a network of smooth, well-maintained country roads. Walden Pond, where Thoreau built his cabin, is ½ mile off the route.

You start off by pedaling along the shore of the Cambridge Reservoir, a blur when you brush past it on Route 128, delightful when you cruise along it on a bicycle. From here it's a short ride to the center of Lincoln, one of Boston's most elegant and old-moneyed suburbs. The town center is unusual for its lack of commercial establishments. The business section is a mile southwest. Gracing the town center is an old brick library, a stately white church on the hillside, and the old burying ground across the street from it. Just ahead is the DeCordova Museum, an impressive, castlelike brick building on top of a hill overlooking Sandy Pond. Surrounding the building are twenty-five acres of finely landscaped grounds. The museum offers changing exhibits of local artists, special programs and events, and outdoor concerts on Sunday afternoons.

From the museum you'll head past estates and gentleman farms to the Codman House, a majestic Federal-era mansion maintained by the Society for the Preservation of New England Antiquities. Just ahead is Drumlin Farm, a 200-acre farm with a full contingent of barnyard animals and fowl, run by the Massachusetts Audubon Society. There's an inspiring view from the top of Hathaway Hill on the grounds.

152

The long ride heads farther west across the Sudbury River into the beautiful rural town of Sudbury. In the center of town are two fine old churches facing each other across the road and a handsome, pillared town hall. Sudbury is best known for the Wayside Inn, celebrated in Longfellow's *Tales of a Wayside Inn*. It is in the southwestern corner of the town, several miles off the route. You can visit it on the Wayside Inn Ride, ride 30 in this book. After you leave Sudbury, you'll head past unspoiled Heard Pond on country lanes to Wayland, another attractive town with a large, graceful white church and a fine brick library. From Wayland it's a short ride to Weston, a community as affluent as Lincoln, with a similar landscape of estates on spacious grounds and large homes nestled amid five-acre wooded lots. The center of town is elegant, with an attractive row of shops, two handsome stone churches, and a large, football-shaped green with the impressive, pillared town hall standing over it.

Directions for the ride: 27 miles

1. Turn right onto Winter Street and immediately make a U-turn, heading west (away from Route 128). Go $1^7/_{10}$ miles to fork where Winter Street bears left uphill and Old County Road bears right. You'll follow the Cambridge Reservoir on your right.
2. Bear right on Old County Road and go $^7/_{10}$ mile to crossroads and stop sign (Trapelo Road, unmarked).
3. Turn left on Trapelo Road and go $1^7/_{10}$ miles to a crossroads and stop sign where five roads come together. This is the center of Lincoln. Notice the library on your right and the church just up the hill from the library.
4. Go straight at crossroads onto Sandy Pond Road. After $^6/_{10}$ mile the entrance to the DeCordova Museum is on your right. Continue $^2/_{10}$ mile to Baker Bridge Road on left. Here the ride turns left, but if you go straight for $^1/_{10}$ mile you'll come to unspoiled Sandy Pond.
5. Turn left on Baker Bridge Road and go $1^2/_{10}$ miles to end (Route 126). After $^6/_{10}$ mile you'll pass a stark, square house on the left designed by Walter Gropius in 1938. When you come to Route 126 the ride turns left, but if you turn right and go $^6/_{10}$ mile you will come to famed Walden Pond in Concord, where Thoreau built his cabin. There's a beach, and a footpath circles the pond.

6. Turn left on Route 126 and go $8/10$ mile to first left, Codman Road (sign may say TO LINCOLN CENTER).

7. Turn left on Codman Road and go $6/10$ mile to crossroads and stop sign (Lincoln Road). You'll pass the Codman House on left, set back $1/10$ mile from the road.

8. Turn right at crossroads and go $3/10$ mile to another crossroads and stop sign (Route 117). Immediately before the intersection is a traffic island; bear left when you come to it. Here the short ride turns left and the long ride goes straight. If you turn left you'll come to Drumlin Farm just ahead on your right.

9. Cross Route 117 and go $7/10$ mile to another crossroads and stop sign.

10. Turn right at crossroads and go $2/10$ mile to end (Route 126).

11. Turn left on Route 126 and go $1/2$ mile to Sherman Bridge Road on right. It's immediately after Tally Ho Road on right.

12. Turn right on Sherman Bridge Road and go $1\,9/10$ miles to Water Row Road on left, at traffic island with a stone milepost on it. You will see several similar mileposts farther along the ride. You'll cross a rustic wooden bridge over the Sudbury River. A half mile beyond the bridge, Weir Hill Road on the right leads to a state wildlife refuge.

13. Turn left on Water Row Road and go $1\,4/10$ miles to Plympton Road, your second right.

14. Turn right on Plympton Road and go $8/10$ mile to fork (Candy Hill Road bears left).

15. Bear slightly right at fork (still Plympton Road) and go $2/10$ mile to end.

16. Turn left at end and go $1/2$ mile to traffic light (Route 27), in the center of Sudbury.

17. Cross Route 27 and go $1/10$ mile to Goodmans Hill Road on left.

18. Turn left on Goodmans Hill Road and go $1\,6/10$ miles to end (Route 20).

19. Turn right on Route 20 and go $2/10$ mile to Landham Road on left (sign may say TO FRAMINGHAM).

20. Turn left on Landham Road and go $6/10$ mile to Pelham Island Road on left, immediately after church on left.

21. Turn left on Pelham Island Road and go $2\frac{1}{2}$ miles to diagonal crossroads (Route 20). You'll pass Heard Pond on your right and cross the Sudbury River.

22. Cross Route 20 diagonally and go 100 yards to Route 126. This is the

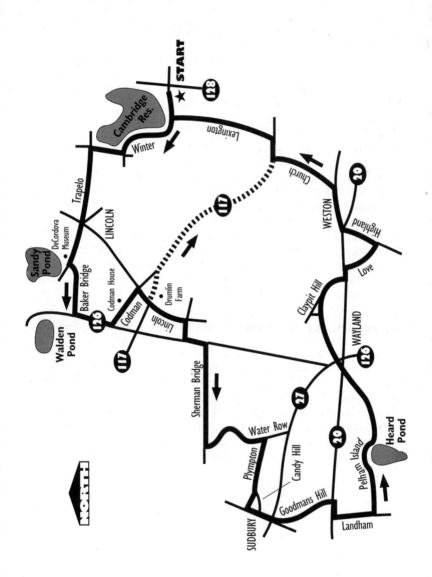

center of Wayland. Notice the church at the corner of Routes 20 and 126 and the pillared house on your left.

23. Cross Route 126 and stay on main road for $1^8/10$ miles to end (Route 20).

24. Turn left on Route 20 and go $3/10$ mile to fourth right, Love Lane. (The second and third rights are both Buckskin Drive.)

25. Turn right on Love Lane and go $7/10$ mile to end. This is a steady climb, but a fast descent follows.

26. Turn left at end onto Highland and go $6/10$ mile to crossroads and stop sign (Route 20 again).

27. Cross Route 20 onto Boston Post Road. Go $9/10$ mile to a fork with a stone church in the middle (Church Street, unmarked, bears left). You'll go through the center of Weston. At the fork, notice the pillared town hall on your left on the far side of the green.

28. Bear left at fork and go $1^2/10$ miles to end (Route 117, North Avenue). You'll pass the old train station, now vacant, on your right after $2/10$ mile.

29. Turn right on Route 117 and go $2/10$ mile to Lexington Street on left.

30. Turn left on Lexington Street and go $1^4/10$ miles to end.

31. Turn right at end and go $1/10$ mile to hotel on right.

Directions for the ride: 14 miles

1. Follow directions for the long ride through number 8.

2. Turn left on Route 117 and go 4 miles to Lexington Street on left. It comes up $2/10$ mile after you pass Church Street on your right. **CAUTION:** Bad diagonal railroad tracks after $8/10$ mile; please walk across them. Shortly after you turn onto Route 117, you'll come to Drumlin Farm on the right. There's a good snack bar on your left 2 miles after the tracks.

3. Turn left on Lexington Street and go $1^4/10$ miles to end.

4. Turn right at end and go $1/10$ mile to hotel on right.

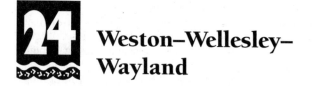

Weston–Wellesley–Wayland

Number of miles: 29 (22 without Wellesley extension)
Terrain: Gently rolling.
Food: Grocery stores and restaurants in the towns.
Start: M.D.C. Duck Feeding Area parking lot in Weston, on the west bank of the Charles River. It's immediately north of Route 30 and immediately east of Route 128.
How to get there: Getting there by car is a little tricky because the access road is on the *west* side of Route 128.

If you're heading south on Route 128, take the Route 30 exit (exit 24). At the end of the ramp, cross Route 30 at traffic light. Go ¹/₁₀ mile to the first right after the entrance to the Massachusetts Turnpike. Turn right and just ahead turn right again into the parking lot.

If you're heading north on Route 128, take the Route 30 exit (exit 24). Turn left (west) at end of ramp on Route 30 and go to traffic light on the far side of Route 128. Turn right and go ¹/₁₀ mile to your first right after the entrance ramp to the Massachusetts Turnpike. Turn right and just ahead turn right again into parking lot.

From the Massachusetts Turnpike, follow the signs to Interstate 95 North and Route 30. Turn left (west) at end of ramp onto Route 30 and follow directions for heading north on Route 128.

If you're coming from Newton on Commonwealth Avenue, turn right onto the entrance ramp to Route 128 North. Just ahead, bear right (don't get on Route 128) and then turn right into parking lot.

This is a tour of three wealthy, gracious communities west of Boston just outside the Route 128 semicircle. The region is a pleasure for bicycling, with smooth roads winding past seminaries, colleges, and stately older brick and wooden homes. Highlights of the ride are two colleges in Wellesley—Babson College, where you'll visit the largest revolving globe in the world and a giant relief map of the country, and Wellesley College, which has one of the most beautiful campuses in the state.

You'll start by going through Weston, one of Boston's most affluent suburbs, with estates on spacious grounds and large homes, each surrounded by five acres of trees and lawn. You'll pass Regis College, a Catholic women's school with a handsome stone and brick main building, a tall stone tower on a hilltop, and a postal museum on the campus. The town center is a New England jewel, with an attractive row of shops, two handsome stone churches, and an impressive, pillared town hall standing over the large elliptical green. From Weston you'll ride through Wayland, the next town to the west. Wayland is a little more rural, with some extensive sections of woods and rolling pastureland. The center of town boasts a dignified white church and a fine brick library. The return trip brings you back through another section of Weston, passing the Weston Observatory (part of Boston College), where there are rocks containing the imprint of fossils and dinosaur feet.

The long ride heads south into Wellesley, a more densely populated but equally elegant suburb. You'll visit Babson College, a top-rated business school with a fascinating attraction—a relief map of the United States, 65 feet long and 40 feet wide, which you view from a balcony above. The map was built from 1937 to 1940 with painstaking attention to detail, including the curvature of the earth. Outside the building where the map is housed is the largest revolving globe in the world, 28 feet in diameter. There is no admission charge. From Babson you'll go through the center of Wellesley, with its ornate, clock-towered, Gothic-style town hall and an attractive row of smart shops. Just ahead is the centerpiece of the town, Wellesley College. The rolling, elm-shaded campus, bordering the shore of Lake Waban, is a delight to bike through as you pass its dignified ivy-covered buildings in a wide variety of architectural styles. After leaving the college you'll join the route of the short ride, going through Wayland and then back through Weston.

Directions for the ride: 29 miles

1. Head out of the parking lot and go 100 yards to your first left (sign says TO ROUTES 30 AND 95).
2. Turn left, going underneath the highway, and continue $1/10$ mile to end.
3. Turn left at end and go less than $2/10$ mile to end, at yield sign (merge right on Route 30).

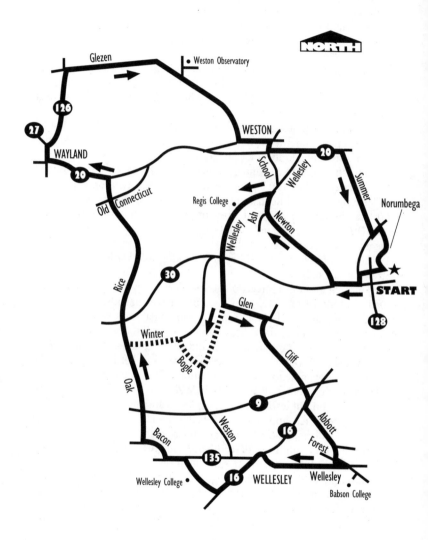

4. Bear right on Route 30 and go $4/10$ mile to Newton Street, which bears right at second traffic light.

5. Bear right on Newton Street and go $1^8/10$ miles to Wellesley Street, which turns sharply left at traffic island. It's just after Ash Street, which also turns sharply left.

6. Turn sharply left on Wellesley Street and go $1\frac{1}{2}$ miles to traffic light (Route 30). You'll pass the Case Estate of Arnold Arboretum, 112 acres of nurseries and cultivated plants, on your right. Then you'll pass Regis College.

7. Cross Route 30 and go $8/10$ mile to Glen Road on left. It is the first left after you pass underneath the Massachusetts Turnpike. Here the short ride goes straight and the long ride turns left.

8. Turn left on Glen Road and go 1 mile to crossroads (Oak Street on left, Cliff Road on right). You'll pass the Norumbega Reservoir on your left.

9. Turn right on Cliff Road and go $1^7/10$ miles to end (Route 16).

10. At end, turn right and then immediately left on Abbot Road (**CAUTION** here). Go $7/10$ mile to fork where Inverness Road bears left and the main road bears right uphill.

11. Bear right at fork (still Abbot Road) and go 100 yards to end (Forest Street, unmarked).

12. Turn left on Forest Street and go less than $2/10$ mile to diagonal crossroads and stop sign (Wellesley Avenue). Here the ride turns sharply right, but if you would like to visit the map at Babson College, continue straight for $2/10$ mile to the college entrance on right. The map is in Coleman Hall. Turn right into the college and take second left to end.

13. Turn sharply right on Wellesley Avenue (bear left if you visited the map) and go $8/10$ mile to stop sign at bottom of hill. Continue straight for $6/10$ mile to end (Routes 16 and 135), in Wellesley.

14. Turn left on Routes 16 and 135. Go less than $2/10$ mile to a fork where Route 16 bears left and Route 135 bears right. You'll pass the ornate stone town hall, with a clock tower, on the right.

15. Bear left on Route 16 (**CAUTION** here) and go $6/10$ mile to the entrance to Wellesley College on right, at traffic light.

16. Turn right into the college and go $8/10$ mile to end (Route 135). You'll see Lake Waban on your left as soon as you enter the college. Side roads on the left lead down to the lakeshore.

17. Turn left on Route 135 and go $4/10$ mile to Bacon Street on right.

18. Turn right on Bacon Street and go ½ mile to Oak Street on right, at blinking light.

19. Turn right on Oak Street and go 7/10 mile to Route 9, at traffic light.

20. Cross Route 9 (**CAUTION:** The intersection is very busy) and go 1 6/10 miles to crossroads and stop sign (Route 30).

21. Cross Route 30 onto Rice Road and go 2½ miles to end.

22. Jog right and immediately left (almost straight) onto Pine Brook Road. It is one-way in the wrong direction; walk your bike. Go 3/10 mile to end (Route 20).

23. Turn left on Route 20 and go 1 mile to traffic light (Routes 27 and 126) in the center of Wayland.

24. Turn right on Routes 126 and 27. Go 1/10 mile to a fork where Route 27 bears left and Route 126 bears right. Notice the white, pillared house on your left.

25. Bear right on Route 126 and go 1 3/10 miles to Glezen Lane, which is your second crossroads. As soon as you bear right, notice the graceful library on the right.

26. Turn right on Glezen Lane and stay on the main road for 3 6/10 miles to end, at a T-intersection in Weston. After 2 miles you'll pass the Campion Center, an impressive domed building, on your left. It is a Jesuit spiritual center and retirement home. Just north of it is the Weston Observatory, in front of which are rocks with fossils and dinosaur footprints. To get there, turn sharply left on Concord Street (unmarked) just before the Campion Center and then immediately right.

27. Turn left at end and go 4/10 mile, through the center of Weston, to School Street on right. It's opposite a stone church on the left. Notice the pillared town hall to the left on the far side of the green.

28. Turn right on School Street and go 1/10 mile to traffic light (Route 20).

29. Turn left on Route 20 and go 1 mile to Summer Street on right, just after the Gifford School on left.

30. Turn right on Summer Street and go 1 4/10 miles to a yield sign where you can merge head-on into a larger road. You will turn sharply left here.

31. Turn sharply left at yield sign and go 2/10 mile to crossroads (Gate House Road on left, Norumbega Road on right). You come to it while you're going downhill.

32. Turn right at crossroads onto Norumbega and go 8/10 mile to Duck

Wellesley College

Feeding Area parking lot. You'll pass a stone tower on the left at the beginning (don't bother going into it—there's no view from the top and the odor is foul). Then you'll follow the Charles River on your left.

Directions for the ride: 22 miles

1. Follow directions for the long ride through number 7.
2. Continue straight for $1\frac{1}{10}$ miles to Bogle Street on right, at bottom of hill (sign may say RIVERS SCHOOL).
3. Turn right on Bogle Street and go $\frac{6}{10}$ mile to end (Winter Street, unmarked).
4. Turn left on Winter Street and stay on the main road for 1 mile to end (Oak Street). After $\frac{6}{10}$ mile a dead-end road (Frost Street) is on your right, but curve left here on the main road.
5. Turn right on Oak Street and go $\frac{1}{2}$ mile to crossroads and stop sign (Route 30).
6. Follow directions for the long ride from number 21 to the end.

25 Charles River Tour:
Westwood–Dover–South Natick–
Needham–Dedham

Number of miles: 31 (20 without South Natick extension, 14 with short-cut bypassing Dover)
Terrain: Gently rolling.
Food: None on two shorter rides until near end. Grocery store in South Natick.
Start: Holiday Inn, Route 1 in Dedham, just north of Route 128. Park at west side of the lot near Route 1A.

The valley of the Charles River upstream from Newton provides relaxed and scenic cycling. The river flows peacefully past landed estates with broad meadows sloping gently to its banks and graceful old communities as it follows a west-to-east course from South Natick to Dedham. A fine network of country roads crisscrosses the region, winding past country estates, gentleman farms where horses graze in pastures set off by stone walls and white wooden fences, and stately old homes.

The ride starts off by heading through Westwood, an affluent mansion-dotted community, and then into Dover, one of Boston's most old-moneyed enclaves. Dover is the closest really rural and undeveloped town to Boston and is a paradise for biking. After paralleling the Charles through Dover, you'll cross the river into Needham. Most of Needham is a bedroom suburb, but the southern rim of the town along the river has the same gracious landscape you rode through on the south bank. From Needham you'll go into Dedham, a handsome town with a distinguished cluster of public buildings gracing its center. Approaching downtown you'll pass fine old Colonial-style homes and two graceful white churches facing each other across the road. Just ahead are a trio of stately granite courthouses and the handsome stone public library, a New England classic built in 1873. After passing one more impressive, Gothic-style stone church, it's a short ride back to the starting point.

The long ride heads farther upriver through more elegantly rural countryside to the delightful old community of South Natick. Like Needham, most of Natick is an uninspiring bedroom community along the dreadful Route 9 commercial strip, but the southern part of the town near the Charles is beautiful and quite rural. Gracing the village of South Natick are a pair of handsome churches, an ornate Victorian library, and a dam across the Charles.

Directions for the ride: 31 miles

1. Turn left out of the west side of the parking lot onto Route 1A, heading south, and go $3/10$ mile to Gay Street (unmarked) on right, at the Westwood town line.

2. Turn right on Gay Street and go $16/10$ miles to Fox Hill Street, which bears right up a gradual hill. **CAUTION:** Watch for potholes.

3. Bear right on Fox Hill Street and go $9/10$ mile to end (Route 109).

4. Turn right on Route 109 and go $4/10$ mile to Summer Street on left (sign may say TO DOVER, 4 MILES).

5. Turn left on Summer Street (**CAUTION** here) and go $12/10$ miles to end (Westfield Street, unmarked).

6. Turn left on Westfield Street and go $2/10$ mile to Wilsondale Street, a narrow lane that bears left.

7. Bear left on Wilsondale Street and go $12/10$ miles to where the main road turns right and a dead-end, private road is on the left.

8. Turn right on the main road and go $4/10$ mile to end.

9. Turn left at end. Go $4/10$ mile to Mill Street on right, at top of little hill.

10. Turn right on Mill Street and go $4/10$ mile to end. The road runs along the Charles River on your right.

11. Turn right at end. Go less than $2/10$ mile to Fisher Street on left, immediately after the bridge over the Charles River. Here the 14-mile ride goes straight and the two longer rides turn left. You'll pass a beautiful little dam on your right.

12. Turn left on Fisher Street and go $4/10$ mile to end. (**CAUTION:** Bad diagonal railroad tracks after $1/10$ mile.)

13. Turn left at end and go $3/10$ mile to Claybrook Road on right, just after recrossing the Charles. You are now in Dover.

14. Turn right on Claybrook Road and go $16/10$ miles to crossroads and stop sign. You can catch glimpses of the Charles on your right.

15. Go straight at crossroads for $4/10$ mile to end (merge to your right on Pleasant Street).

16. Bear right on Pleasant Street and go ½ mile to Dover Road on right. Here the 20-mile ride turns right and the long ride goes straight. You'll pass Lookout Farm, an excellent fruit and vegetable stand, on your left.

17. Continue straight for ¹/₁₀ mile to Glen Street on left (street sign visible only from opposite direction).

18. Turn left on Glen Street and go 2⁴/₁₀ miles to end (merge to your right at bottom of hill, at stop sign).

19. Bear right at end onto Farm and go ½ mile to fork where Bridge Street bears right at the traffic island.

20. Bear right on Bridge Street and go 1³/₁₀ miles to South Street on right, at top of hill. You will cross the Charles into Sherborn and pass a magnificent old dairy farm on the right shortly before the intersection.

21. Turn right on South Street and go 1⁷/₁₀ miles to a stop sign where the road merges right on Route 16 (you will turn sharply left here). You'll pass an Audubon sanctuary on your right.

22. Turn sharply left on Route 16 and go ½ mile to fork where Everett Street bears right uphill.

23. Bear right on Everett Street. Go ⁸/₁₀ mile to Rockland Street (unmarked) on right, just past the condominiums on right at top of hill.

24. Turn right on Rockland Street and go ⁶/₁₀ mile to fork (Farwell Street bears right). Just after you turn onto Rockland Street you'll see a cider mill on your left. It's a great rest stop during apple season.

25. Bear right on Farwell Street and go ½ mile to end (Fay Way, unmarked).

26. Turn right at end and go 50 yards to end.

27. Turn left at end and then immediately right on Woodland Street. Go 1³/₁₀ miles to end. **CAUTION:** The end comes up suddenly at bottom of sharp hill.

28. Turn right at end onto Union and go ½ mile to traffic light (Route 16). This is South Natick.

29. Cross Route 16 onto Pleasant Street. Notice the ornate Victorian library on the far right-hand corner. Just ahead you'll cross the Charles, with a little dam on your right. Continue ³/₁₀ mile to Dover Road on left, just after Phillips Street on left.

30. Turn left on Dover Road and go 2³/₁₀ miles to crossroads and stop sign (Central Avenue). After ⁶/₁₀ mile you'll cross the Charles again into Needham.

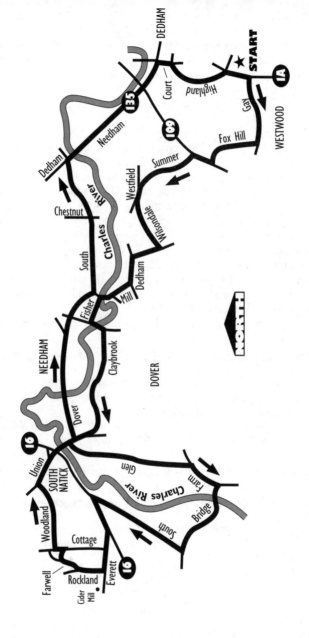

31. Go straight at crossroads for 6/10 mile to end (South Street). **CAUTION:** Diagonal railroad tracks just before end.

32. Turn left on South Street and go 1³/10 miles to stop sign and blinking light (Chestnut Street).

33. Cross Chestnut Street and go 1 mile to traffic light (Dedham Avenue, Route 135).

34. Turn right on Dedham Avenue and go 2³/10 miles to traffic light (Route 109), at the Dedham green. At the beginning of this section, you will cross the Charles once more, into Dedham.

35. Cross Route 109 and go 4/10 mile to another light (Court Street, unmarked). This is the center of Dedham. The granite buildings on the far side of the intersection are courthouses.

36. Turn right on Court Street and go 2/10 mile to crossroads where School Street turns left and Highland Street turns right. Notice the classic white church on your right just after you turn right, and the magnificent stone church just before Highland Street.

37. Turn right on Highland Street. After 7/10 mile Sandy Valley Road bears right, but bear slightly left on main road and go 4/10 mile to end, at stop sign (merge right on Route 1A).

38. Bear right on Route 1A. The Holiday Inn is 1/10 mile ahead on left.

Directions for the ride: 20 miles ⚓⚓⚓⚓⚓⚓

1. Follow directions for the 31-mile ride through number 16 to Dover Road. Here the ride turns right, but if you go straight for 3/10 mile you'll come to the dam in South Natick.

2. Turn right on Dover Road and go 2³/10 miles to crossroads and stop sign (Central Avenue). After 6/10 mile you'll cross the Charles into Needham.

3. Follow directions for the 31-mile ride from number 31 to the end.

Directions for the ride: 14 miles ⚓⚓⚓⚓⚓⚓

1. Follow directions for the 31-mile ride through number 11.

2. Continue straight on South for 1⁴/10 miles to stop sign and blinking light (Chestnut Street).

3. Follow directions for the 31-mile ride from number 33 to the end.

26 The Upper Charles River:
Walpole–Millis–Medfield–Sherborn–Dover

Number of miles: 28 (16 without Millis–Sherborn–Dover extension)
Terrain: Delightfully rolling, with lots of little ups and downs.
Food: Grocery store and restaurants in Medfield. Lunch counter in Dover.
Start: Main Street Shopping Center, Route 1A in Walpole, immediately north of Route 27.

The wealthy, woodsy suburbs southwest of Boston, halfway between the city and the northeastern corner of Rhode Island, provide ideal cycling on an impressive network of well-maintained, winding country lanes. The region is far enough from Boston to be rural rather than suburban. The landscape has a trim, prosperous look to it, with stone walls; old, well-maintained farmhouses framed by shade trees; spacious homes nestled on five-acre, pine-studded lots; and some estates in Dover. Coursing through the region are the upper reaches of the Charles River, a favorite canoeing run.

You'll start from Walpole, an attractive residential community with a brick Victorian town hall framing its green. You'll quickly head into undeveloped countryside as you cross the Charles into Millis and recross it into Medfield, both well-scrubbed, upper-middle-class communities. The return leg to Walpole brings you through forests with a few well-designed, spacious homes set back from the road among the trees.

The long ride heads farther north into Sherborn, one of Boston's most unspoiled suburbs and a paradise for bicycling. You'll ride beside pretty Farm Pond, pass a sweeping dairy farm, and cross the Charles again into Dover, the closest truly rural and unspoiled town to Boston and one of the city's most upper-crust, old-moneyed suburbs. You'll pass several estates with mansions surrounded by acres of rolling meadows. The return run to Walpole brings you through a large stretch of open farmland and then along beautiful Willett Pond.

Directions for the ride: 28 miles

1. Turn right out of parking lot onto Route 1A. You'll immediately cross Route 27. Go $\frac{1}{10}$ mile to fork at the green (there is a traffic light here). Notice the Victorian town hall on the left just before the fork.

2. Bear right on West Street (unmarked). After $\frac{2}{10}$ mile the main road bears right under a railroad bridge. Continue $\frac{9}{10}$ mile to crossroads, at yield sign.

3. Turn right at crossroads (still West Street) and go $\frac{2}{10}$ mile to Lincoln Road on right, immediately after railroad overpass.

4. Turn right on Lincoln Road. After $\frac{3}{10}$ mile Granite Street turns right, but curve left on the main road. Go $1\frac{7}{10}$ miles to fork where the main road bears slightly left.

5. Bear left at fork and go $\frac{2}{10}$ mile to end.

6. Turn right at end onto Seekonk and go $\frac{6}{10}$ mile to Fruit Street, which bears left up a little hill.

7. Bear left on Fruit Street and go $\frac{1}{4}$ mile to crossroads and stop sign.

8. Go straight for $2\frac{3}{10}$ miles to fork where Birch Street bears right and the main road curves left. You'll cross the Charles River after $1\frac{6}{10}$ miles.

9. Curve left on the main road and go $\frac{2}{10}$ mile to crossroads and stop sign (Village Street). Here the short ride turns right and the long ride turns left.

10. Turn left at crossroads and go $\frac{2}{10}$ mile to your first right, Spring Street.

11. Turn right. Just ahead is a crossroads and stop sign (Route 115). Continue straight for $\frac{7}{10}$ mile to another crossroads and stop sign (Route 109).

12. Cross Route 109 onto Auburn Road. After $\frac{4}{10}$ mile, Curve Street bears right, but go straight onto Ridge Street for $\frac{1}{2}$ mile to end (merge left at stop sign; Union Street is on right).

13. Bear slightly left at stop sign (still Ridge Street) and go $\frac{6}{10}$ mile to crossroads and stop sign (Orchard Street).

14. Cross Orchard Street and go $\frac{3}{10}$ mile to another crossroads and stop sign (Middlesex Street). Continue straight for $2\frac{1}{10}$ miles to end (merge to right into Mill Street).

15. Bear right on Mill Street and go $\frac{6}{10}$ mile to fork where Woodland Street bears right and West Goulding Street bears left.

16. Bear left at fork and go $\frac{1}{2}$ mile to crossroads and stop sign (Route 27).

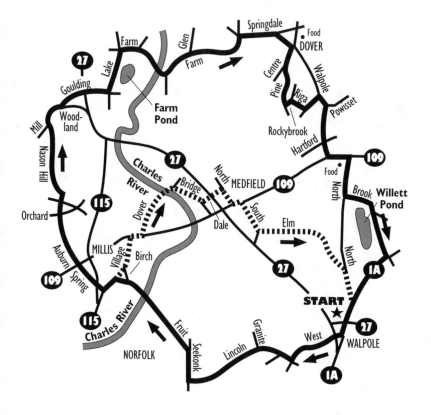

17. Cross Route 27 onto East Goulding Street and go $6/10$ mile to Lake Street, which turns sharply left at top of hill. **CAUTION:** Diagonal railroad tracks after $1/4$ mile.

18. Turn sharply left on Lake Street and go $1\,1/10$ miles to crossroads and stop sign (Farm Road). You'll pass Farm Pond.

19. Turn right on Farm Road and go $1\,7/10$ miles to end (Farm Street). You'll cross the Charles near the end.

20. Turn left on Farm Street. After $1/2$ mile, Glen Street bears left, but continue straight for $1\,1/2$ miles to crossroads (Pegan Lane on left, Springdale Avenue on right. A sign may point right TO DOVER, NEEDHAM).

21. Turn right on Springdale Avenue and go $8/10$ mile to fork just before railroad tracks.

22. Bear right at fork and go $2/10$ mile to traffic light in the center of Dover. There's a lunch counter at the Dover Pharmacy, on the far side of the intersection.

23. Turn right at light on Centre Street and go $4/10$ mile to Pine Street, a smaller road that bears left.

24. Bear left on Pine Street and go $1\,1/10$ miles to Rockybrook Road on left. It's just after a dirt road on the right that leads to a fire tower. (The tower is closed to the public.)

25. Turn left on Rockybrook Road and go $1/10$ mile to fork (Riga Road bears right).

26. Bear right on Riga Road and go $3/10$ mile to end (Cedarhill Road, unmarked).

27. Turn left at end and go $4/10$ mile to end.

28. Turn right at end and stay on the main road for 1 mile to crossroads and stop sign (Hartford Street).

29. Cross Hartford Street and go $1/2$ mile to end (County Street, Route 109).

30. Turn left on Route 109 and go $1/2$ mile to North Street on right. The Bubbling Brook, a great spot for ice cream, is on your right at the intersection.

31. Turn right on North Street and go 1 mile to Brook Street on left. The farmland on your right belongs to the Norfolk County Agricultural Laboratory.

32. Turn left downhill on Brook Street and go $8/10$ mile to rotary. You will go along Willett Pond on your right.

33. Bear slightly right at rotary, following the shore of Willet Pond, and go 1$\frac{1}{10}$ miles to Route 1A (Main Street), at crossroads and stop sign.

34. Turn right on Route 1A and go 1$\frac{8}{10}$ miles to shopping center on right. **CAUTION:** Route 1A is very busy.

Directions for the ride: 16 miles

1. Follow directions for the long ride through number 9.

2. Turn right at crossroads and go $\frac{8}{10}$ mile to end, at stop sign (merge right on Route 109).

3. Bear right on Route 109 and go $\frac{3}{10}$ mile to Dover Road on left.

4. Turn left on Dover Road and go 1$\frac{2}{10}$ miles to Bridge Street on right, just after you cross the Charles River. (Ignore another Bridge Street on right before you cross the river.)

5. Turn right on Bridge Street and go $\frac{6}{10}$ mile to Dale Street (unmarked) on left. It's your fourth left, opposite house number 20 on right.

6. Turn left on Dale Street and go $\frac{4}{10}$ mile to traffic light (Route 27, North Meadows Road).

7. Go straight at light for $\frac{3}{10}$ mile to end (North Street, unmarked).

8. Turn right on North Street and go $\frac{4}{10}$ mile to end (Route 109), in the center of Medfield.

9. Turn left on Route 109 and go 100 yards to South Street on right, at traffic light. Notice the small church on right with unusual Gothic architecture.

10. Turn right on South Street and go $\frac{8}{10}$ mile to Elm Street on left, just before railroad tracks.

11. Turn left on Elm Street and go 1$\frac{1}{2}$ miles to fork where Homeward Lane bears left and the main road bears right.

12. Bear right on main road (North) and go 1$\frac{4}{10}$ miles to end (merge right at stop sign).

13. Bear right at end and go $\frac{4}{10}$ mile to fork where Gill Street (unmarked) bears left and main road bears right.

14. Bear right on the main road and go $\frac{2}{10}$ mile to end (Route 1A).

15. Turn right on Route 1A and go $\frac{4}{10}$ mile to shopping center on right. **CAUTION:** Route 1A is very busy.

Horse farm, Wrentham

27 Plainville–Cumberland, Rhode Island–Wrentham

Number of miles: 28 (11 without Cumberland–Wrentham loop)
Terrain: Rolling to hilly. There's a tough climb at the beginning and some exhilarating descents.
Food: Country store in Cumberland. Country store in Wrentham. Burger King at end.
Start: Burger King, junction of Routes 106 and 152 in Plainville.
How to get there: From the north, take Interstate 95 to the Route 140 South exit. Go about a mile to Route 106, at third traffic light. Turn right on Route 106 and go about 4 miles to Route 152, at traffic light. Burger King is on the far left corner. From the south, take Interstate 95 to the Route 152 exit (exit 5). Turn left at end of ramp and just ahead turn left at end (Route 152). Go 3 miles to Burger King on left, just before Route 106.

This ride explores the rural, largely wooded area surrounding the northeastern corner of Rhode Island. You can amble along at a leisurely pace to savor the beauty of the narrow, twisting back roads. The long ride includes an enjoyable spin along the Diamond Hill Reservoir, a large pond just across the Rhode Island border.

The ride starts from Plainville, a pleasantly rural town consisting mainly of woods, farmland, and orchards. The short ride stays almost entirely within the town's boundaries, following small roads with very little traffic. A steep climb at the beginning is counterbalanced by a long, steady descent to Whiting Pond. You'll climb again, more gradually this time, past horse farms and onto a ridge with a fine view, and enjoy a swooping descent to Route 1A.

The long ride heads farther west into Cumberland, Rhode Island, a lovely rural town in the northeast corner of that state. As you pedal along a narrow lane, you'll descend a short hill, and suddenly the Diamond Hill Reservoir will unfold before you. The reservoir, which provides water for the city of Pawtucket, is completely undeveloped and surrounded by low, wooded hills. The road hugs the shore and crosses a causeway with water on both sides. After leaving the watershed the route ascends gradually onto a ridge with fine views and descends to the Wrentham, Massachusetts, border.

Wrentham is a gracious community on the outer fringe of the Boston metropolitan area, far enough away from the city to be nearly undeveloped. Spring Street, a narrow winding lane, bobs up and over several sharp hills, none long enough to be discouraging. Horse pastures and fine wooden houses greet you at each bend. Soon you'll arrive in Sheldonville, a village within Wrentham with an old church and a good country store. Just ahead you'll climb sharply onto a ridge and rejoin the short ride just before the exhilarating downhill run to Route 1A.

Directions for the ride: 28 miles 🐛🐛🐛🐛🐛🐛

1. Turn left from the side entrance onto Route 106 (not Route 152) and go $3/10$ mile to crossroads (George Street).
2. Turn left on George Street and go $1/10$ mile to end (Messenger Street, unmarked).
3. Turn right at end (onto Elmwood) and go $1\frac{1}{2}$ miles to traffic light (Routes 1 and 1A). There's a steep hill at the beginning. At the top you'll pass World War I Memorial Park on your left; there's a small zoo here and a good view from the base of a fire tower.
4. Go straight across Route 1 at traffic light and immediately turn right on Route 1A. Be sure you're on Route 1A and not Route 1. Go 100 yards to Whiting Street on left.
5. Turn left on Whiting Street and go $1\frac{1}{10}$ miles to end. The road turns sharply and changes its name several times, but stay on it to the end. You'll pass a small dam and Whiting Pond on your left at the beginning.
6. Turn right at end and go $3/10$ mile to Warren Street (unmarked) on left. It's just after the Heather Hills Country Club on left.
7. Turn left on Warren Street and go $1^2/10$ miles to end (High Street, unmarked). This stretch is a steady climb, with a steep pitch at the beginning.
8. Turn right on High Street and go $3/10$ mile to Rhodes Street on left, at bottom of little hill. Here the short ride goes straight and the long ride turns left.
9. Turn left on Rhodes Street and go $1^3/10$ miles to end (Burnt Swamp Road, unmarked). Most of this section is downhill. You'll pass a branch

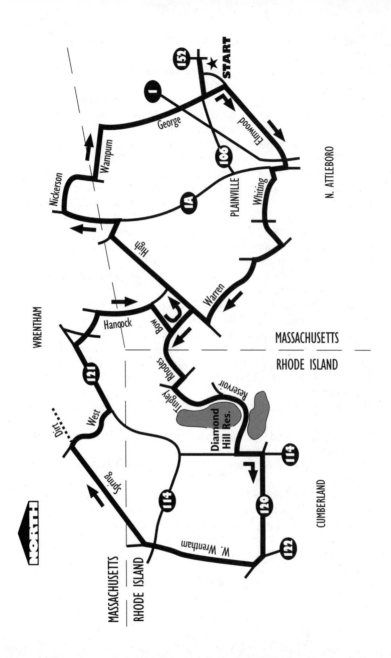

of the Wentworth Institute, an engineering school with its main campus in Boston. At the end you're in Cumberland, Rhode Island.

10. Turn right on Burnt Swamp Road and go $3/10$ mile to end (Reservoir Road on left).

11. Turn left at end. Stay on main road for $2\frac{1}{2}$ miles to end (Route 114). You'll ride along the Diamond Hill Reservoir. At the end, there's a country store on the far side of the intersection.

12. Turn left on Route 114 and go $6/10$ mile to traffic light (Route 120, Nate Whipple Highway).

13. Turn right on Route 120 and go $2\frac{1}{2}$ miles to end (Route 122, Mendon Road). You'll pass Sneech Pond on your right near the end.

14. Turn right on Route 122 and go $2/10$ mile to West Wrentham Road on right, at traffic light.

15. Turn right on West Wrentham Road and go $2^4/10$ miles to traffic light (Route 114, Pine Swamp Road). There's a tough hill on the first half of this section and a relaxing descent at the end.

16. Cross Route 114 and go $1/10$ mile to fork where Jencks Road bears left and West Wrentham Road bears right.

17. Bear right at fork and go 2 miles to crossroads and stop sign (West Street, unmarked). **CAUTION:** Watch for sandy spots. West Wrentham Road becomes Spring Street at the Massachusetts state line, after $1/2$ mile.

18. Turn right on West Street and go $9/10$ mile to end (Route 121).

19. Turn left on Route 121 and go $1^2/10$ miles to Hancock Street on right. There's a country store at the intersection. This is Sheldonville, a village in Wrentham.

20. Turn right on Hancock Street and go $7/10$ mile to end, at top of steep hill.

21. Turn right at end (still Hancock Street, unmarked) and go $1^1/10$ miles to Bow Street on right (sign may say TO WENTWORTH).

22. Turn right on Bow Street and go $1/2$ mile to end (Rhodes Street, unmarked).

23. Turn left on Rhodes Street and go $6/10$ mile to end (High Street, unmarked). You'll climb steadily, but you will be rewarded for your efforts.

24. Turn left on High Street and go $1^4/10$ miles to end, at stop sign. There's a fine view to your left at the beginning; then you'll enjoy a fast downhill run. **CAUTION:** Take it easy on the descent—watch for potholes and cracks.

25. Turn right at end and go $2/10$ mile to end (Route 1A).

26. Turn left on Route 1A and go $^7/_{10}$ mile to Nickerson Street on right, just before Interstate 495.

27. Turn right on Nickerson Street and go $^7/_{10}$ mile to Wampum Street on left.

28. Turn left on Wampum Street. After $^6/_{10}$ mile the main road (George) turns 90 degrees right. Stay on the main road for $1^4/_{10}$ miles to Route 1, at stop sign.

29. Cross Route 1 (**CAUTION** here) and go $^1/_2$ mile to crossroads and stop sign (Route 106).

30. Turn left on Route 106 and go $^3/_{10}$ mile to Burger King on right, immediately before traffic light. The Burger King is set back from the road.

Directions for the ride: II miles 🪱🪱🪱🪱🪱🪱

1. Follow directions for the long ride through number 8.

2. Continue straight on High Street for $1^4/_{10}$ miles to end, at stop sign. There's a fine view to your left at the beginning; then you'll enjoy a fast downhill run. **CAUTION:** Take it easy on the descent—watch for potholes and cracks.

3. Follow directions for the long ride from number 25 to the end.

28 Chelmsford–Carlisle–Westford

Number of miles: 25 (14 without Westford extension)

Terrain: Rolling, with a few moderate hills and one tough one.

Food: Grocery in Carlisle. Grocery and pizza parlor in Westford. Friendly's Ice Cream at end. Ice cream shops in Carlisle and Westford, each ⁶/₁₀ mile off the route.

Start: Friendly Ice Cream, Route 4, Chelmsford, just south of the center of town. If you're coming from the south on Route 3, exit west onto Route 129 and go into the center of Chelmsford. Turn left on Route 4 South and make a U-turn to your left at the first opportunity (a sign says ROUTE 4 NORTH). Friendly's is on your right as you complete the U-turn.

This ride takes you exploring in three attractive towns on the outer edge of suburban Boston. You start from Chelmsford, a pleasant, middle-class suburb of Lowell with an attractive town center. Several churches, an old cemetery with slate tombstones from the early 1800s, and the Victorian town hall frame the green with a monument in the middle. The first few miles go through residential areas and pass several industrial parks, but fortunately the landscape changes 100 percent as you cross the town line into Carlisle. Carlisle is one of the closest truly unspoiled towns to Boston, with a strict no-growth policy. Narrow lanes weaving past farms, estates, and woodland provide a paradise for biking. The center of town is a jewel, with a magnificent old church fronting the green, a fine brick Victorian library, and an old wooden schoolhouse on top of a hill.

From Carlisle to Westford the rural landscape of gentleman farms, woodland, and an occasional orchard continues. Westford is an unspoiled hilltop town with a large green framed by a classic white church, a fine turn-of-the-century library, and gracious old homes. Just off the route on the edge of town sits the Westford Knight, one of New England's unsolved mysteries. It is an outline of a medieval knight, complete with shield and sword, drawn on a rock. It was noticed by the earliest settlers, and its origin remains unknown. One theory is presented on a nearby stone marker. The return to Chelmsford passes farms and orchards and then becomes more residential but remains pleasant after you cross the Chelmsford town line.

The short ride bypasses Westford, taking a more direct route from Carlisle back to Chelmsford along a rolling secondary road. You'll pass Great Brook Farm State Park, an extensive natural area with woods, fields, a working dairy farm, an ice cream stand, and 10 miles of trails suitable for mountain biking.

Directions for the ride: 25 miles 〰️〰️〰️

1. Turn right out of the parking lot and go $^2/_{10}$ mile to Route 129, in the center of town. Notice the handsome brick library across the road as you leave the parking lot.

2. Turn right on Route 129. As soon as you turn, notice the splendid stone church on your left. Continue ½ mile to Turnpike Road, a smaller road that bears right at blinking light.

3. Bear right on Turnpike Road and go $1^6/_{10}$ miles to end, at bottom of steep hill (**CAUTION** here). Unfortunately, the land on your left has been despoiled by industrial parks. Twenty years ago it was woods and orchards.

4. Turn left at end and go $^7/_{10}$ mile to end (Route 129), at traffic light.

5. Turn right on Route 129 and go $1^1/_{10}$ miles to crossroads (Rangeway Road).

6. Turn right on Rangeway Road and go $2^1/_{10}$ miles to crossroads and stop sign (Route 4). **CAUTION:** Big sandy spot near end.

7. Cross Route 4 and go $1^6/_{10}$ miles to end, at stop sign (merge right on East Street). **CAUTION:** Watch for potholes at the beginning.

8. Bear right at stop sign and go $1^1/_{10}$ miles to end, at stop sign (merge right on Route 225). Here the ride bears right, but if you turn sharply left and go $^6/_{10}$ mile you'll come to Kimball Farm Ice Cream, a great spot for a snack, on your left.

9. Bear right on Route 225 and go $^1/_{10}$ mile to rotary in the center of Carlisle. Notice the handsome brick library on your left, built in 1895. At the rotary, on your right, there's a country store. When you get to the rotary, the short ride turns right and the long ride goes straight and then left.

10. Go straight at the rotary and then immediately bear left uphill on

School Street, passing the magnificent white church on your left, built in 1811. (Don't bear left on Concord Street, which is immediately after School Street.) Go 2 miles to end. Just past the church there's a fine old wooden school on your left, at the top of the hill.

11. Turn left at end and go $^1/_{10}$ mile to South Street on right.

12. Turn right on South Street and go $^3/_{10}$ mile to fork (Cross Street bears right).

13. Bear left at fork (still South Street) and go 1 mile to end, at traffic island (West Street). Here the road merges left, but you will turn sharply right.

14. Turn sharply right on West Street. Go $1^1/_2$ miles to fork where Acton Street bears right and West Street bears slightly left.

15. Bear slightly left at fork and go $^7/_{10}$ mile to end, at stop sign (merge left on Route 225).

16. Bear left on Route 225. Immediately ahead is a traffic light (Route 27). Stay on Route 225 for $2^1/_2$ miles to a diagonal crossroads and stop sign (Power Road).

17. Continue straight on Route 225 for $^3/_{10}$ mile to end, at stop sign (merge left on Route 110).

18. Bear left on Routes 110 and 225. Go $^3/_{10}$ mile to where Route 225 (Concord Road) turns right and Route 110 goes straight. Here the ride turns right, but if you go straight for $^6/_{10}$ mile you'll come to Kimball Farm Ice Cream on your left.

19. Turn right on Route 225 and go $^7/_{10}$ mile to Hildreth Street (unmarked) on right, at a small traffic island. It's shortly after Tallard Road on left.

20. Turn right on Hildreth Street and go $1^6/_{10}$ miles to the traffic island with a monument in the middle at the top of the hill, in the center of Westford.

21. Bear right at traffic island and immediately go straight at crossroads onto Lincoln Street, passing the green on your left. Go $^3/_{10}$ mile to fork where Depot Street bears left and Main Street bears right. Notice the elegant white church and the handsome beige-brick library on the far side of the green. Just beyond the green on your right is the town hall and a wooden Victorian schoolhouse, now a community center.

When you get to the fork the ride bears right on Main Street, but if you bear left and go $^2/_{10}$ mile you'll come to the Westford Knight on your right just as you start to go downhill—watch for a stone marker and five

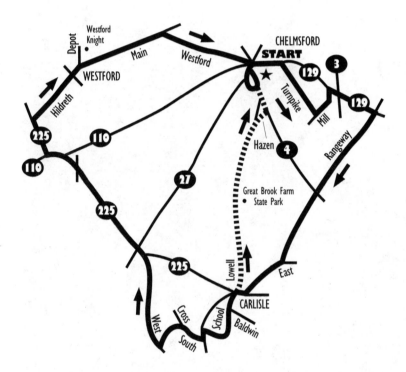

Farm in Carlisle

small stone pillars connected by chains. If you come to Abbott School, you've gone $\frac{1}{10}$ mile too far.

22. Bear right on Main Street and go $2\frac{9}{10}$ miles to Westford Street (unmarked), which bears right just beyond a ballfield and fire station on your right. There's a fast downhill run out of Westford. At the bottom of the hill there's a grocery and pizza parlor on your right.

23. Bear right on Westford Street and go $2\frac{1}{10}$ miles to stop sign in the center of Chelmsford. Two smaller roads bear left on this stretch, but stay on the main road. Just before the green you'll pass an unusual Gothic church on your left and then an old cemetery with weathered slate tombstones on your right. Notice the fine Victorian town hall and the monument in the center of the green.

24. Bear slightly right at the stop sign onto Route 4 South. **CAUTION:** Busy intersection. Go $\frac{1}{4}$ mile to Route 4 North on left.

25. Make a U-turn to the left onto Route 4 North (**CAUTION** here). As soon as you turn, Friendly's is on your right.

Directions for the ride: 14 miles 〰️〰️〰️

1. Follow the long ride through direction number 9.

2. Turn right at rotary onto Lowell Street (unmarked) and go $3\frac{4}{10}$ miles to fork where the main road bears left and Hazen Road bears right. As soon as you turn onto Lowell Street, there's a country store on your right. To visit Great Brook Farm State Park, turn right after $1\frac{8}{10}$ miles on North Road. Go $\frac{3}{10}$ mile to park entrance on left.

3. Bear right on Hazen Road and go $\frac{3}{10}$ mile to end (Route 4).

4. Turn left on Route 4 and go $1\frac{1}{10}$ miles to Friendly's on right.

29 Nashoba Valley Tour:
Littleton–Boxboro–Harvard–
Bolton–Stow–Acton

Number of miles: 33 (18 without Harvard–Bolton–Stow extension)
Terrain: Very rolling, with one long, gradual hill and several shorter ones on the longer ride.
Food: Groceries or restaurants in all the towns except Boxboro.
Start: Nagog Park, a shopping center on Route 119 in Acton, at the Littleton town line. It's between Routes 27 and 110, and it's about 3 miles east of Interstate 495.

The Nashoba Valley is the nickname for the rolling, rural, apple-growing country northwest of Boston near Interstate 495. The Nashua Valley would be a more accurate name because the Nashua River flows along the region's western edge. The area is just far enough away from Boston to be rural rather than suburban, and it is dotted with graceful, unspoiled New England towns. Abounding with narrow lanes twisting past orchards and old farmhouses, the Nashoba Valley provides superb biking that is a bit challenging because of the numerous ups and downs in the landscape. On the longer ride, a scenic and historic highlight are the Fruitlands Museums, set on a broad hillside with an outstanding view.

At the start of the ride you'll immediately head into Littleton along the shore of undeveloped Nagog Pond and then get into rolling orchard country. Once through the tiny center of Littleton, you'll ascend onto a long, high ridge capped with orchards that leads into Harvard. At the highest point is an astronomical observatory belonging to Harvard University (the names of the town and the university are coincidental and confusing to newcomers) and a fire tower.

Harvard is one of the most graceful and classically elegant of the outer Boston suburbs, and strict zoning laws will keep it that way for the foreseeable future. No tract housing mars the landscape; instead you'll find only gentleman farms with broad fields, orchards, weathered barns, and widely spaced newer homes tastefully integrated with the wooded landscape on large lots. The town center is a jewel, with a fine old brick library, a general store, a large sloping green, and a classic white church on a little hill at the head of the green.

Just outside of town you'll ascend Prospect Hill, a magnificent open ridge with a spectacular view to the west. On a clear day you can see Mount Wachusett and even Mount Monadnock, 40 miles away. At the top of the ridge are the Fruitland Museums, a group of buildings with an eighteenth-century farmhouse, a Shaker house, a museum of American Indian relics, and a gallery of early American portraits and landscape paintings. The farmhouse contains a museum of the Transcendentalist movement, with memorabilia of the Alcott family, Emerson, Thoreau, and its other leaders, along with period furnishings and early farm implements. The Shaker house was moved several miles from a smaller Shaker village built during the 1790s. The rest of the village is 2 miles off the route.

From Harvard you'll proceed on winding lanes to Bolton, another delightful rural town with a cluster of antique shops and an ornate stone library, and then east to Stow, another unspoiled community consisting mainly of orchards, wooded hills, and farms along the Assabet River, a favorite of canoeists. From Stow you'll return to the start through the length of Acton, the most populous of the towns on the ride but still essentially rural. The center of town is another New England classic, with a fine, white, clock-towered town hall, graceful old church, and a small green with a tall obelisk honoring the leader of the Acton Minutemen. The homestretch takes you through woods, old farms, and back along the shore of Nagog Pond.

The short ride bypasses Harvard, Bolton, and Stow by cutting across Boxboro, which was circled by the long ride but never actually touched. Boxboro, a rural wooded town like Bolton and Stow, is unique in that it has no distinct town center.

Directions for the ride: 33 miles

1. Turn right out of parking lot on Route 119 and immediately left onto Nashoba Road. Go 1²/10 miles to crossroads and stop sign (Nagog Hill Road). You'll go along Nagog Pond on the left.
2. Go straight at crossroads for ⁶/10 mile to end (merge left at stop sign).
3. Bear left at end and go ¹/10 mile to Harwood Avenue, which bears right.

4. Bear right on Harwood Avenue and go $^6/_{10}$ mile to fork where Tahatawan Road bears right and the main road goes straight.

5. Continue straight for $^9/_{10}$ mile to crossroads and stop sign (Foster Street, unmarked).

6. Cross Foster Street and go $1^2/_{10}$ miles to end. This is Littleton. Notice the old railroad station on your left at the intersection. The commercial center of town, Littleton Common, is 2 miles east at the junction of Routes 110 and 27.

7. Turn left at end, crossing railroad tracks, and go less than $^2/_{10}$ mile to fork where Oak Hill Road bears right. The short ride turns left immediately after the tracks instead of going straight.

8. Bear right on Oak Hill Road, which climbs gradually up a long hill. Go $2^9/_{10}$ miles to fork where Old Schoolhouse Hill Road bears left and the main road (Old Littleton Road, unmarked) bears right.

9. Bear right on main road and go $^4/_{10}$ mile to crossroads and stop sign (Pinnacle Road).

10. Cross Pinnacle Road and go $1^4/_{10}$ miles to Route 111, at blinking light, in the center of Harvard. Notice the stately brick library on right.

11. Turn right on Route 111 and go $^3/_{10}$ mile to Depot Road, which bears left while you're going downhill.

12. Bear left on Depot Road and go $^7/_{10}$ mile to fork where Craggs Road bears right and the main road bears left.

13. Bear left on main road and go $^1/_2$ mile to end, at stop sign (merge left onto Prospect Hill Road; Old Shirley Road is on right).

14. Bear left on Prospect Hill Road and go $1^9/_{10}$ miles to end (Route 110). Fruitlands is on your right just past the top of the hill.

15. Turn right on Route 110 and go $1^3/_{10}$ miles to West Bare Hill Road on left. It comes up while you're going downhill.

16. Turn left on West Bare Hill Road, passing a big old weathered barn on right. Go $^4/_{10}$ mile to fork where West Bare Hill Road bears left and Scott Road bears right.

17. Bear right on Scott Road and go $1^3/_{10}$ miles to end (merge right at stop sign). Scott Road becomes Bare Hill Road at the Bolton town line.

18. Bear right at end and go $^3/_{10}$ mile to Nourse Road on left.

19. Turn left on Nourse Road and go 1 mile to end (Route 117).

20. Turn left on Route 117 and go $2^1/_{10}$ miles to Long Hill Road, which bears right shortly after you pass Route 85 on your right. You'll go through the center of Bolton. Notice the ornate stone library on your

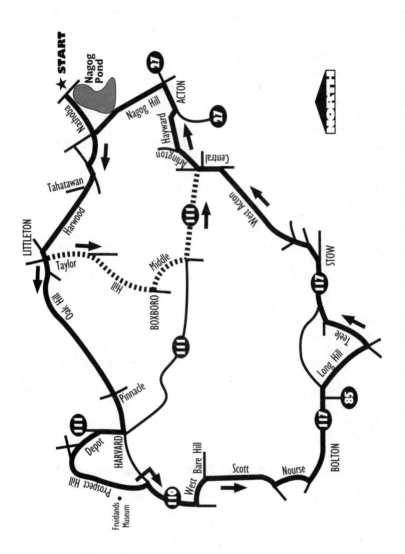

right as you come into town.

21. Bear right on Long Hill Road. Stay on the main road for 1½ miles to diagonal crossroads (Teele Road). It comes up while you're going downhill.

22. Turn sharply left on Teele Road and go 1½ miles to end, at traffic island (Old Bolton Road).

23. Turn right at end and go ⁴/₁₀ mile to end, at stop sign (merge right on Route 117).

24. Bear right on Route 117 and go 1⁷/₁₀ miles to a road that bears left at the Stow town hall (sign may say TO ACTON).

25. Bear left here and go ³/₁₀ mile to fork where Crescent Street bears right and West Acton Road bears left. As soon as you leave Route 117, notice the fine church and library on your right.

26. Bear left on West Acton Road (sign may say TO ROUTE 2, ACTON) and go ²/₁₀ mile to a three-way fork.

27. Continue straight for 2³/₁₀ miles to end (merge left at stop sign on Central Street).

28. Bear left at end onto Central and go ²/₁₀ mile to traffic light (Route 111, Massachusetts Avenue). This is West Acton.

29. Cross Route 111 and immediately turn right on Arlington Street. Go ½ mile to Hayward Road, which turns right uphill.

30. Turn right on Hayward Road and go 1³/₁₀ miles to end (Route 27).

31. Turn left on Route 27 and go ⁷/₁₀ mile to crossroads just beyond the center of Acton (Nagog Hill Road).

32. Turn left on Nagog Hill Road and go 2⁴/₁₀ miles to crossroads and stop sign at top of hill (Nashoba Road). There's a fast downhill to Nagog Pond.

33. Turn right at crossroads and go 1²/₁₀ miles to end (Route 119). You'll go along Nagog Pond on your right.

34. Turn right on Route 119 and immediately left into shopping center at traffic light.

Directions for the ride: 18 miles

1. Follow directions for the long ride through number 6.
2. Turn left at end across railroad tracks, and then immediately turn left again at crossroads onto Taylor Street. Go 1⁹/₁₀ miles to Hill Road, which bears right at a small green. It's just past the top of a long, steady hill.

3. Bear right on Hill Road and go $1^8/_{10}$ miles to Middle Road on left, just before you go downhill.

4. Turn left on Middle Road and go $1^1/_{10}$ miles to crossroads and stop sign (Route 111). There's a fast descent at the beginning. Just before the intersection, the Boxboro town hall is on your left.

5. Turn left on Route 111 and go $2^1/_{10}$ miles to traffic light at bottom of hill (Central Street). This is West Acton.

6. Turn left on Central Street and immediately right on Arlington Street. Go $1/_2$ mile to Hayward Road, which turns right uphill.

7. Follow directions for the long ride from number 30 to the end.

The gristmill next to the Wayside Inn, Sudbury

Wayside Inn Ride:
Framingham–Southboro–Sudbury

Number of miles: 22
Terrain: Gently rolling.
Food: Grocery and pizza place just off the route in Southboro. Snack bars on Route 20 in Marlboro.
Start: Shopping center at corner of Franklin Street and Mount Wayte Avenue in Framingham, about a mile south of Route 9.
How to get there: From Route 9, if you're coming from the east, take the Route 30 West exit and turn left at light on Main Street. Go ²/₁₀ mile to second right, Franklin Street. Turn right and go ⁶/₁₀ mile to Mount Wayte Avenue, at traffic light. The shopping center is on the right on the far side of the intersection. If you're coming from the west on Route 9, take the Edgell Road–Main Street exit and turn right at traffic light on Main Street. Go ²/₁₀ mile to second right, Franklin Street. Turn right and go ⁶/₁₀ mile to Mount Wayte Avenue, at traffic light.

From the junction of Routes 135 and 126, go north on Route 126 and just ahead bear left on Union Avenue. Go 1 mile to Mount Wayte Avenue, at traffic light. Turn left, and just ahead is another light (Franklin Street). Shopping center is on left on the far side of the intersection.

Midway between Boston and Worcester, delightful bicycling abounds in the region lying around the Sudbury Reservoirs, a long chain of lakes surrounded by rolling hills, orchards, and open farmland. The landscape is rural in a prosperous, well-scrubbed sort of way, with gentleman farms, horse paddocks, and rambling, well-maintained old New England farmhouses set off by spreading shade trees and stone walls. A network of smooth secondary roads, many going along the lakeshores, gets you away from the traffic. A historic highlight of the ride is the Wayside Inn in Sudbury, the oldest continually operating inn in the country, built around 1700 and visited by Longfellow during the mid-1800s. The poet was fascinated and celebrated it in his famed poems, *Tales of a Wayside*

Inn. Sixty years later another captivated visitor, Henry Ford, decided to construct elements of a New England village next to the Inn, so he added an operating gristmill, a little red schoolhouse, and a classic white church.

The ride starts from Framingham, one of Boston's most populous suburbs, with 65,000 residents. Framingham is a city of three faces: partly an old industrial town with dreary rows of old wooden houses, partly a bedroom suburb with tract houses and modern apartment complexes, and partly a gracious rural town with lakes, horse farms, and a classic New England green. This ride goes through the third face. At the beginning you'll head along two ponds and pass Macomber Farm, formerly an estate and now an educational farm (with a variety of barnyard creatures) run by the Massachusetts Society for the Prevention of Cruelty to Animals (MSPCA). Its rather steep admission fee is, a staff member explained to me with blunt honesty, a forced contribution to the MSPCA. From here you'll head into Southboro, a gracious, well-to-do community with gentleman farms spreading across rolling hillsides, the prestigious St. Mark's preparatory school, and a classic New England village center. The school and center of town are about a mile off the route. After two delightful runs along the lake, it's not far to the Wayside Inn.

Approaching the Inn you first come to the gristmill, a masterpiece of historical reconstruction built for Henry Ford in 1929. It is an authentic, working reproduction of an eighteenth-century stone mill, with a massive water wheel 18 feet in diameter. Just past the mill is the Martha-Mary Chapel, a replica of a New England church that somehow looks more sterile than the real one. It is now used only for weddings. Next to the chapel is the Redstone School, an actual one-room little red schoolhouse that was moved in 1926 from Sterling, 20 miles to the west, and used as a public school until 1951. This is the school that Mary and her little lamb went to. Just past the school is the Inn itself, a graceful gambrel-roofed building all but overshadowed by the attractions leading up to it.

The return to Framingham takes you back through the city's third face, passing horse farms and gracious old Colonial-style homes. At the end you'll go by the handsome green, framed by two stately brick churches facing each other across the road and an ornate, steep-gabled Victorian library.

Directions for the ride

1. Turn left out of parking lot onto Mount Wayte Avenue and go $1^1/_{10}$ miles to end (Fountain Street). You'll pass Farm Pond on your left.

2. Turn right on Fountain Street and go $^4/_{10}$ mile to traffic light (Winter Street).

3. Continue straight at light for $^1/_2$ mile to Jodie Road on right, just after bridge.

4. Turn right on Jodie Road and go $^2/_{10}$ mile to Singletary Lane on right, halfway up the hill.

5. Turn right on Singletary Lane and go $1^4/_{10}$ miles to end (Salem End Road, unmarked). On your right is one of the several lakes composing the Sudbury Reservoir system.

6. Turn left on Salem End Road and go $^4/_{10}$ mile to fork where Gates Street bears right. You'll pass Macomber Farm on the left. **CAUTION:** Watch for potholes.

7. Bear right on Gates Street and go $^1/_{10}$ mile to another fork where Gates Street bears right and Parker Road bears slightly left.

8. Bear left on Parker Road and go $1^3/_{10}$ miles to end, at stop sign (merge to your right on Oregon Road, unmarked).

9. Bear right on Oregon Road and go $^6/_{10}$ mile to crossroads and stop sign (Oak Street, unmarked).

10. Go straight at crossroads. You'll immediately come to a fork. Bear slightly left, staying on the main road, and go 1 mile to end, at stop sign (merge to your right on Woodland Road, unmarked).

11. Bear right at end, passing underneath the Massachusetts Turnpike. Go 100 yards to fork on the far side of the underpass (Woodland Road bears right, Breakneck Hill Road bears left).

12. Bear left on Breakneck Hill Road and go $^9/_{10}$ mile to another fork (Mount Vickery Road bears left).

13. Bear right at fork (still Breakneck Hill Road) and go $^1/_{10}$ mile to Route 9, at traffic light.

14. Cross Route 9 and go $^4/_{10}$ mile to fork where Latisquama Road bears left and White Bagley Road bears right. **CAUTION:** Be very careful crossing Route 9. You'll follow the shore of the Sudbury Reservoir on your right.

15. Bear right at fork, following the Reservoir, and go $^1/_2$ mile to crossroads and stop sign (Route 30).

16. Cross Route 30 and, just ahead, merge head-on into a larger road.

Continue 1⁶⁄₁₀ miles to Acre Bridge Road, which bears right.

17. Bear right on Acre Bridge Road and go ⁷⁄₁₀ mile to stop sign where the main road bears left and Farm Road (unmarked) turns right.

18. Turn right at end onto Farm Road and go 1½ miles to fork where Broad Meadow Road bears right and the main road curves left.

19. Curve left and go ½ mile to traffic light where you merge head-on into Route 20. You'll pass Marlboro Airport, the oldest commercial airport in Massachusetts, on your right.

20. Go straight onto Route 20 for 1²⁄₁₀ miles to Wayside Inn Road, at second traffic light. Here you will turn left by making a jug-handle turn—you bear right just before the light and cross Route 20 at right angles. **CAUTION:** Route 20 is very busy.

21. Make a jug-handle left turn at traffic light. After ⁷⁄₁₀ mile you'll pass the gristmill, the chapel, the little red schoolhouse, and finally the Wayside Inn itself. From the inn, continue ³⁄₁₀ mile to end (Route 20).

22. Turn sharply right on Route 20 and go ⁴⁄₁₀ mile to your second left, Bowditch Road.

23. Turn left on Bowditch Road. After ¼ mile a smaller road bears right, but curve left on the main road. Go 1¹⁄₁₀ miles to end (Edmands Road). You'll climb and then descend steeply. **CAUTION:** The end comes up suddenly at bottom of steep hill.

24. Turn left at end onto Edmands Road and then immediately bear right on Grove Street. Go ⁹⁄₁₀ mile to fork where Winch Street bears left uphill.

25. Bear right at fork (still Grove Street) and go 1¹⁄₁₀ miles to crossroads and stop sign (Belknap Road).

26. Continue straight for ⁹⁄₁₀ mile to end (Vernon Street), opposite the Framingham town green.

27. Turn left at end, going alongside the green on your right, and go ¹⁄₁₀ mile to end (Edgell Road). Notice the two impressive brick churches facing each other across the road at the head of the green.

28. Turn right on Edgell Road. After ²⁄₁₀ mile you'll cross the overpass above Route 9. (**CAUTION** here—busy intersections.) Continue ²⁄₁₀ mile to second right, Franklin Street.

29. Turn right on Franklin Street and go ⁶⁄₁₀ mile to Mount Wayte Avenue, at traffic light. The shopping center is just past light on right.

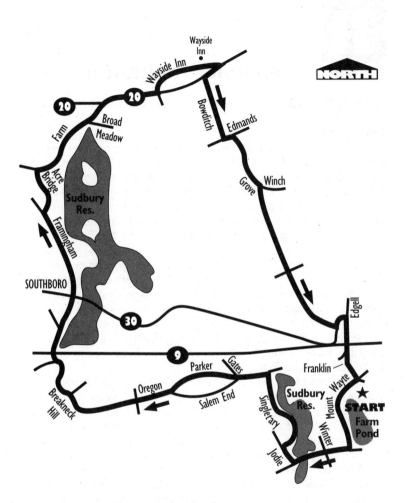

NORTH

Wayside Inn

Wayside Inn

20

20

Broad Meadow

Farm

Bowditch

Edmands

Acre Bridge

Sudbury Res.

Grove

Winch

Framingham

SOUTHBORO

30

Edgell

9

Parker

Gates

Franklin

Oregon

Salem End

Singletary

Sudbury Res.

Wayte

Mount

Breakneck Hill

★ START

Winter

Farm Pond

Jodie

Holliston–Hopkinton

Number of miles: 29 (19 without western loop, 10 if you do the western loop only)
Terrain: Rolling, with several hills.
Food: Grocery store and restaurant in Hopkinton. Burger King at end.
Start: Radisson Hotel, on Beaver Street in Milford. It's ²/₁₀ mile north of Route 109 and just west of Interstate 495. To do just the western loop, start at the junction of Routes 135 and 85 in the center of Hopkinton.
How to get there: To get to the hotel from Interstate 495, take exit 19 (Route 109). Follow Route 109 West to traffic light just ahead (Beaver Street). Turn right and go ²/₁₀ mile to hotel on left.

This ride will take you exploring two wooded, wealthy communities on the outer edge of Boston's suburbia, midway between Boston and Worcester and a little south of both. The landscape is rural rather than suburban, consisting mainly of wooded hills, some open farmland and orchards, and several unspoiled lakes. A wide-ranging network of narrow country roads provides superb bicycling if you're willing to tackle a few hills. The ride consists of a figure-eight with Hopkinton at the center. You can do either loop or both.

The eastern loop heads through woods and past small farms to the center of Hopkinton, located on a broad hilltop. Hopkinton becomes known to the world on Patriot's Day, in April, when the Boston Marathon starts here at noon. In recent years the number of contestants has far surpassed that of the town's 6,000 residents. From Hopkinton you'll traverse large expanses of farmland and pass the undeveloped Ashland Reservoir. Then you'll ascend onto a long ridge with orchards on the top and fine views of the surrounding hills and valleys. The return leg brings you through a rural landscape along winding lanes through woods, past old barns and farmhouses, and along Weston Pond.

The western loop passes through a landscape that is similar but a little more wooded. You'll ride through the well-kept villages of Woodville and Southville and then along the Hopkinton Reservoir, adjoining Hopkinton State Park. The reservoir is surrounded by round, green hills.

Directions for the ride: 29 miles

1. Turn left out of parking lot and go $^2/_{10}$ mile to traffic light (Route 16).
2. Turn right on Route 16 and go $^9/_{10}$ mile to Adams Street (unmarked), a small road that bears left.
3. Bear left on Adams Street and go $^9/_{10}$ mile to fork where Marshall Street (unmarked) bears right and the main road goes straight.
4. Continue straight on main road for 1 mile to end (Hanlon Road).
5. Turn left on Hanlon Road and go $^9/_{10}$ mile to end (Route 85).
6. Turn right on Route 85. After $1^7/_{10}$ miles, Route 85 curves sharply to the left at blinking light. Continue on Route 85 for $^6/_{10}$ mile to traffic light (Route 135, Main Street). This is the center of Hopkinton. Here the 19-mile ride turns right and the 33-mile ride turns left.
7. Turn left on Route 135 and go $^4/_{10}$ mile to traffic light where Route 135 bears right. You'll pass the former brick high school, built in 1894, on the left.
8. Bear right on Route 135 and go $2^1/_2$ miles to Fruit Street, which bears right. After 2 miles you'll go through the gracious village of Woodville (part of Hopkinton) and pass a small dam on your left. The Whitehall Reservoir is just past Fruit Street on the left.
9. Bear right on Fruit Street and go $^3/_{10}$ mile to fork (Cunningham Street bears left).
10. Bear right at fork (still Fruit Street) and go $2^3/_{10}$ miles to end, at grassy traffic island.
11. Turn right at end and go $1^1/_2$ miles to Route 85, at traffic light. You'll go through the tiny village of Southville, a part of Southboro. An old-fashioned country store is on the right, just before the light.
12. Turn right on Route 85 and go $2^9/_{10}$ miles to traffic light (Route 135, Main Street), back in the center of Hopkinton. You'll pass Hopkinton State Park and the Hopkinton Reservoir on your left. There's a tough hill leading into town.
13. Turn left on Route 135 and go $1^7/_{10}$ miles to Clinton Street on right (sign may say LABORERS TRAINING CENTER). Notice the handsome stone library on your right at the beginning.

14. Turn right on Clinton Street and go $^6/_{10}$ mile to traffic island with a crossroads immediately after it (Front Street on right, Olive Street on left).

15. Turn left at traffic island and go $^2/_{10}$ mile to Spring Street on right.

16. Turn right on Spring Street and go $^9/_{10}$ mile to South Street (unmarked) on left, shortly after you pass the Ashland Reservoir on left. It comes up while you're climbing a steep hill.

17. Turn left on South Street and go $^4/_{10}$ mile to end.

18. Turn right at end onto Highland and go 2 miles to Prentice Street on right.

19. Turn right on Prentice Street and go $1^6/_{10}$ miles to Marshall Street on left.

20. Turn left on Marshall Street and go $1^7/_{10}$ miles to fork where Marshall Street bears right and Courtland Street bears left. **CAUTION:** Watch for bumps and potholes.

21. Bear left on Courtland Street and go $^7/_{10}$ mile to crossroads and stop sign (Route 16, Washington Street). Just before the intersection you'll pass Weston Pond on your left.

22. Cross Route 16 onto South Street and go $1^8/_{10}$ miles to end (Route 109).

23. Turn right on Route 109 and go $^7/_{10}$ mile to traffic light (Beaver Street, unmarked, on right).

24. Turn right on Beaver Street and go $^2/_{10}$ mile to hotel on left.

Directions for the ride: 19 miles ～～～～～～～

1. Follow directions for the long ride through number 6.

2. Turn right on Route 135 and go $1^7/_{10}$ miles to Clinton Street on right (sign may say LABORERS TRAINING CENTER). Notice the handsome stone library on your right at the beginning.

3. Follow directions for the long ride from number 14 to the end.

Directions for the ride: 10 miles ～～～～～～～

(Start from junction of Routes 135 and 85 in the center of Hopkinton.)

1. Head west on Route 135 and go $^4/_{10}$ mile to fork where Route 135 bears right and West Main Street bears slightly left.

2. Follow directions for the 29-mile ride from numbers 8 through 12.

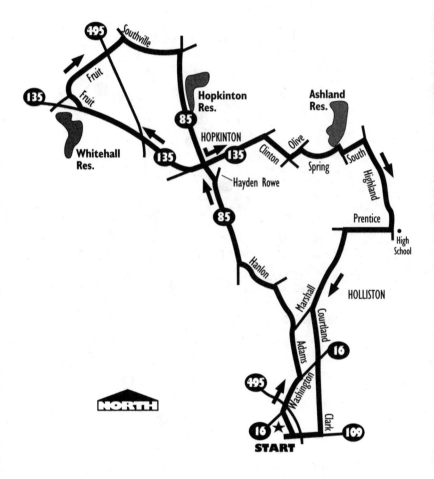

495

Southville

Fruit

Fruit

135

Whitehall
Res.

85

Hopkinton
Res.

HOPKINTON

135

Hayden Rowe

85

Clinton

Olive

Spring

Ashland
Res.

South

Highland

Prentice

High
School

Hanlon

Marshall

HOLLISTON

Courtland

Adams

16

495

Washington

Clark

16 ★

START

109

NORTH

Chapter 4:
The Outer Western Suburbs

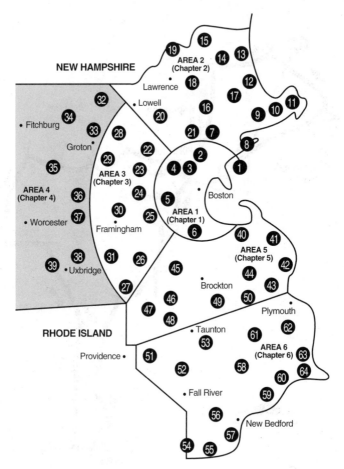

The numbers on this map refer to rides in this book.

32 Westford–Dunstable–Tyngsborough

Number of miles: 26 (13 without Dunstable–Tyngsborough extension)
Terrain: Rolling, with two tough hills.
Food: Groceries and snack bars in the towns. Burger King and McDonald's near end, on Route 110 just east of Boston Road.
Start: Westford town green, about a mile northwest of Interstate 495. Park on Lincoln Street, or in the public parking lot behind the town hall (also on Lincoln Street) if there is no on-street parking.
How to get there: From Interstate 495, take the Boston Road exit (exit 32). Turn left at the end of the ramp if you were heading north on Interstate 495; turn right if you were heading south. Go about a mile to Licoln Street on right, at the green, and turn right.

Just west of Lowell, along the west bank of the Merrimack River, is a delightful biking area of gentle wooded hills, small farms, and unspoiled small towns. As you head west of Lowell, the countryside quickly becomes rural because you're just far enough from Boston to make commuting impractical. Westford actually lies on the fringe of the metropolitan area, but it is a well-to-do community with a no-growth policy and is very much a small town.

The ride starts from Westford, one of the many gracious, still-unspoiled towns that dot the countryside northwest of Boston along Interstate 495. The hilltop village center is exceptionally appealing, with a large tree-studded green framed by a graceful white church, the stately white wooden town hall, and a turn-of-the-century beige-brick library. Just beyond the green is an ornate wooden Victorian schoolhouse, now a community center. On the edge of town sits the Westford Knight, one of New England's unsolved mysteries. It is an outline of a medieval knight, complete with shield and sword, drawn on a rock. It was noticed by the earliest settlers and its origin remains unknown. One theory is presented on a nearby stone marker.

From Westford you'll enjoy a long downhill run and then proceed on wooded backroads to Dunstable, a graceful picture-postcard town with a traditional old church, little village green, and a fine brick library. From Dunstable you'll hug the Massachusetts–New Hampshire border to Tyngsborough, another small town lying directly along the west bank of the Merrimack. Its major landmark is the graceful steel-arched bridge across the Merrimack. Until 1960, Tyngsborough sat on the main road from Boston to New Hampshire; then Route 3 was built, bypassing the town, and it became nearly forgotten. Most people prefer to live and shop a few miles north in New Hampshire, which has no sales or income tax.

From Tyngsborough you'll return to Westford along winding lanes through the handsome mill village of Graniteville, which is part of Westford. Graniteville is accurately named, with a handsome bell-towered granite mill standing above a delightful little millpond. Since Westford sits on top of a hill, you'll have a climb at the end of the ride.

Directions for the ride: 26 miles

1. Follow Lincoln Street for ¼ mile to fork where Main Street bears right and Depot Street bears left.
2. Bear left on Depot Street and stay on the main road for 1 mile to fork immediately after railroad tracks (Plain Road bears right). The Westford Knight will be on your right after ²⁄10 mile, just as you start to go downhill. Watch for a stone marker and five small stone pillars connected by chains. If you come to Abbott School, you've gone ¹⁄10 mile too far. Beyond the Knight there's a magnificent downhill run.
3. Bear left at fork (still Depot Street). After ⁸⁄10 mile there'll be a small crossroads (Nutting Road). Continue straight for ³⁄10 mile to fork (Dunstable Road bears left).
4. Bear left on Dunstable Road and go ½ mile to crossroads and stop sign (Groton Road, Route 40).
5. Cross Route 40 and go ⁸⁄10 mile to crossroads (Long-Sought-for Pond Road). It's immediately after the pond with the same name on your right.
6. Go straight at crossroads for ³⁄10 mile to another crossroads (Tenney Road).
7. Go straight at crossroads. Stay on the main road for the 1⁷⁄10 miles to Chestnut Road on right, at bottom of hill. Here the short ride turns right and the long ride goes straight.

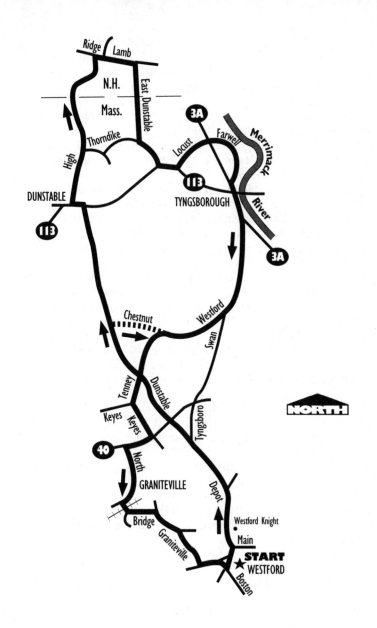

8. Continue straight for 1⁹/₁₀ miles to end (Route 113).

9. Turn left on Route 113 and go ²/₁₀ mile to High Street on right, opposite the church in the center of Dunstable. Notice the fine brick library on your right. Here the ride turns right, but there's a country store just ahead on Route 113.

10. Turn right on High Street and go ⁸/₁₀ mile to fork where Thorndike Street bears right and High Street bears left.

11. Bear left at fork and go 1⁸/₁₀ miles to end (Ridge Road). At the end you're in Nashua, New Hampshire, a city promoting the development of condominiums and subdivisions.

12. Turn right on Ridge Road and go 1 mile to East Dunstable Road on right. There's a tough hill midway along this stretch.

13. Turn right on East Dunstable Road and go 1⁴/₁₀ miles to end.

14. Turn left at end and go ⁶/₁₀ mile to end (Route 113).

15. Turn left on Route 113 and go ½ mile to Locust Avenue on left, shortly before the Route 3 overpass.

16. Turn left on Locust Avenue. Just ahead Old Kendall Road bears right, but continue straight for ⁸/₁₀ mile to crossroads and stop sign (Route 3A, Middlesex Road). You'll pass Locust Pond on your right.

17. Cross Route 3A and go 1⁴/₁₀ miles to end (merge left on Route 3A). Notice the fine brick library on the far side of the intersection.

18. Bear left on Route 3A. Just ahead, at the junction of Route 113, is the center of Tyngsborough. There's a small dam on your right at the intersection. Continue on Route 3A for ³/₁₀ mile to Westford Road, which bears right at traffic light.

19. Bear right on Westford Road and go 1⁷/₁₀ miles to fork (Swan Road bears slightly left, Westford Road bears right).

20. Bear right at fork and go ⁹/₁₀ mile to another fork (Chestnut Road bears slightly right, Westford Road bears left).

21. Bear left at fork (still Westford Road) and go 1½ miles to crossroads (Dunstable Road, unmarked).

22. Cross Dunstable Road onto Tenney Road. Go ⁷/₁₀ mile to fork, at traffic island (Keyes Road bears both right and left).

23. Bear left at fork and go ⁶/₁₀ mile to end (Route 40). You'll pass Keyes Pond on your right.

24. Turn right on Route 40 and go ⁶/₁₀ mile to North Street on left (sign may say TO FORGE VILLAGE).

25. Turn left on North Street and go 1¹/₁₀ miles to a small road that turns

left underneath a narrow railroad bridge. It's just after a millpond on the left. Notice the turreted Victorian mansion on your right opposite the pond. This is Graniteville, a village in Westford.

26. Turn left under the railroad bridge and then immediately turn left again on Bridge Street. Go ½ mile to end (merge to your right at stop sign).

27. Bear right at end and go $^4/_{10}$ mile to fork where Cold Spring Road bears left and Graniteville Road (unmarked) bears right.

28. Bear right at fork and go $^8/_{10}$ mile to end, at top of long hill.

29. Turn left at end and go $^1/_{10}$ mile to fork at the Westford green (Boston Road, unmarked, bears right).

30. Bear right on Boston Road and go 100 yards to crossroads (Lincoln Street). The starting point is to your left.

Directions for the ride: 13 miles

1. Follow directions for the long ride through number 7.

2. Turn right on Chestnut Road and go 1$^2/_{10}$ miles to end, at stop sign (Westford Road). Here the road merges left, but you will turn sharply right. **CAUTION:** Watch for potholes and cracks.

3. Turn sharply right on Westford Road and go 1½ miles to crossroads (Dunstable Road, unmarked).

4. Follow directions for the long ride from number 22 to the end.

33 Covered-Bridge Ride:
Groton–Pepperell–
Hollis, New Hampshire–Ayer

Number of miles: 30 (20 without Hollis extension)
Terrain: Rolling.
Food: Grocery stores and snack bars in the towns.
Start: Victory Super Market on Route 2A, Ayer, 8/10 mile north of the center of town. It's just north of the fork of Routes 2A and 111.

The valley of the Nashua River, midway between Fitchburg and Lowell, is a bicyclist's paradise of country roads traversing broad farms and orchards and winding through rolling hills. The region is one of the major apple-growing areas of the state. Adding variety to this refreshingly rural landscape are the three gracious New England towns of Groton, Pepperell, and Hollis, New Hampshire. In Pepperell you'll bike over the only original-style covered bridge in the eastern half of the state.

The ride starts on the outskirts of Ayer and immediately heads through rolling orchards and farmlands to the classic New England town of Groton, one of the most elegant in the state. Just over the town line is the stately, meticulously landscaped campus of the Groton School, one of the most prestigious preparatory schools in the country. The most prominent landmark of the campus is the graceful Gothic-style stone chapel. A fine green, several graceful old churches, and the handsome brick buildings of Lawrence Academy, another prep school, dignify the center of town. Surrounding the town are broad acres of gentleman farms, estates, and orchards spreading over the rolling hills.

From Groton it's several miles along backroads to Pepperell, another classic town with a handsome old white church and town hall and an ornate, pillared red-brick library. Just outside of town you'll cross the Nashua River over the covered bridge, actually a replica of the original that was rebuilt in 1962. The return trip loops back through Groton across more inspiring rolling estate and orchard country to the center of Ayer, which is an old mill town trying to rebound. When the main line of the Boston and Maine Railroad between Boston, Fitchburg, and Albany declined, the town declined with it. Ayer became primarily an extension of Fort Devens, the large military base just outside of town that closed in 1994. The former base is now converting into a business and industrial park. Although a bit worn, the downtown area is still fascinating, with an ornate Victorian town hall and an old, arcaded commercial block.

The long ride heads north out of Pepperell along a broad, open ridge to Hollis, New Hampshire, just across the Massachusetts border. Hollis is a delightful old town with a classic New England church and green and a handsome white, pillared library. From Hollis you'll head back toward Pepperell through broad farms and orchards and pick up the route of the short ride just in time to go over the covered bridge.

Directions for the ride: 30 miles 🐛🐛🐛🐛🐛🐛🐛

1. Turn left (north) out of the parking lot onto Route 2A and go $^8/_{10}$ mile to Groton-Shirley Road (unmarked) on right, just before the bridge and the Shirley town line. You'll pass the Fort Devens airport on your left.

2. Turn right on Groton-Shirley Road and go $^9/_{10}$ mile to end (Route 111). You'll pass a state-run pheasant farm on your left; it is not open to the public.

3. Turn left on Route 111 and go 2 miles to where Route 225 West turns left and Route 111 goes straight. You'll pass the Groton School on your left after 1 mile. It's worth making a loop around the grounds to catch the flavor of this gracious and distinguished school.

4. Continue straight for $^2/_{10}$ mile to fork where Routes 111 and 225 bear right and a smaller road (Mill Street, unmarked) bears left.

5. Bear left on Mill Street and go $1^1/_{10}$ miles to end, at stop sign (merge left on Routes 111 and 119).

6. Bear left on Routes 111 and 119. Go $^8/_{10}$ mile to where Route 111 (River Road) turns right.

7. Turn right on Route 111 and go $^3/_{10}$ mile to Mount Lebanon Street on left. It's immediately after Yale Street, a dirt road on right.

8. Turn left on Mount Lebanon Street and go $^6/_{10}$ mile to a crossroads and stop sign (Shirley Street).

9. Continue straight for $1^3/_{10}$ miles to end (Townsend Street, Route 113). You'll climb a long hill and have a fine view from the top.

10. Turn right on Route 113 and go $1^4/_{10}$ miles to Route 111, at rotary.

You'll go through the center of Pepperell. Notice the handsome brick library on the right.

11. Bear left on Route 111 and go $^7/_{10}$ mile to where Route 111 turns right and Hollis Street (unmarked) goes straight. You'll cross the Nashua River, which flows over a low dam on your left, immediately before the intersection. The short ride turns right on Route 111, and the long ride goes straight.

12. Go straight ahead for $4^6/_{10}$ miles to a road that bears right at a large traffic island with a small white wooden building on it. You'll pass a great ice cream shop on your right near the beginning. The white building on the traffic island was originally a firehouse built in 1859. It is occasionally opened as a museum by the Hollis Historical Society.

13. Bear right on this road and then immediately bear right again (sign may say TO ROUTES 111, 111A). This is the center of Hollis, New Hampshire. Go 100 yards to stop sign (merge right). Notice the inviting domed library on your left.

14. Bear right at stop sign and go $^8/_{10}$ mile to fork where the main road curves left and Dow Road bears right.

15. Bear right on Dow Road and go $2^6/_{10}$ miles to end, at yield sign (merge right on Route 111).

16. Bear right on Route 111 and go $1^8/_{10}$ miles to crossroads and blinking light (Mill Street).

17. Turn left on Mill Street and go $^2/_{10}$ mile to crossroads and stop sign (Groton Street).

18. Turn left on Groton Street. Just ahead you'll cross the covered bridge over the Nashua River. Continue $^2/_{10}$ mile to stop sign where Route 113 West turns right. This is East Pepperell. Here the ride goes straight, but there are stores and restaurants if you turn right.

19. Continue straight at stop sign. Just ahead Route 113 East turns left, but go straight for $3^4/_{10}$ miles to end, at stop sign (merge right on Hollis Street).

20. Bear right on Hollis Street and go $^1/_2$ mile to School Street, which bears right.

21. Bear right on School Street and go $^1/_{10}$ mile to fork.

22. Bear left at fork and go $^1/_{10}$ mile to crossroads and blinking light (Routes 119 and 225).

23. Turn left on Routes 119 and 225. Go $^9/_{10}$ mile to Old Ayer Road (unmarked), which bears right at a small green. You'll go through the center of Groton.

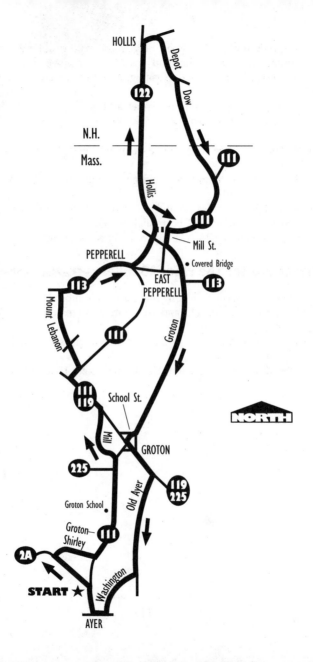

24. Bear right on Old Ayer Road. Stay on the main road for $2^4/10$ miles to fork immediately after the road passes under power lines (Groton-Harvard Road bears left and Washington Street, unmarked, bears right uphill).

25. Bear right on Washington Street and go $6/10$ mile to fork where Howard Street (unmarked) bears right and the main road bears slightly left.

26. Bear left on main road and go $\frac{1}{2}$ mile to end (Main Street), in the center of Ayer.

27. Turn right on Main Street and go $1/10$ mile to Routes 2A and 111 (Park Street) on right.

28. Turn right on routes 2A and 111. Go $6/10$ mile to fork where Route 2A bears left and Route 111 bears slightly right.

29. Bear left on Route 2A. The supermarket is just ahead on left.

Directions for the ride: 20 miles

1. Follow directions for the long ride through number 11.

2. Turn right on Route 111 and go $2/10$ mile to crossroads and blinking light (Mill Street)

3. Turn right on Mill Street and go $2/10$ mile to crossroads and stop sign (Groton Street).

4. Follow directions for the long ride from number 18 to the end.

34 Shirley–West Groton–Townsend–Lunenburg

Number of miles: 29 (16 without Townsend extension)
Terrain: Rolling, with one long hill.
Food: Groceries and restaurants in the towns.
Start: Center of Shirley. From Route 2 take the Shirley exit (exit 36). If you're heading west, turn right at end of ramp and just ahead turn left at end on Shirley Road. Go 2 miles to fork where Main Street bears right and Center Road bears left, just after police station on left. Bear right, and the center of town is just ahead. Main Street becomes Front Street. If you're heading east on Route 2, turn right at end of ramp on Shirley Road, go 2 miles to fork, and follow above directions.

Just east of Fitchburg is a prime area for biking. It has rolling hills and open ridges with fine views, crisscrossed by a network of lightly traveled secondary roads and winding rural lanes. The unspoiled classic New England towns of Shirley Center, Townsend, and Lunenburg are an attractive change of pace from the otherwise rural landscape.

The ride starts from Shirley, a small, somewhat tired-looking town that seems as though it's seen happier days. There's not much keeping the town going except the nearby business and inndustrial park on the grounds of the former Fort Devens military reservation. A couple of miles north is the town's better half, Shirley Center, one of the finest traditional villages in central Massachusetts. The small green is framed by an elegant old white church, pillared town hall, old cemetery, and gracious old wooden homes.

From Shirley Center you'll go through woods and farmland, with a run along Hickory Hills Lake, to the stately hilltop town of Lunenburg, another New England beauty with the traditional white church and old wooden town hall facing each other across the road and a handsome, pillared library. The return leg to Shirley leads through spectacular, rolling ridge country, with a run past unspoiled Massapoag Pond.

The long ride heads to West Groton, a tiny village with a lovely dam and an old brick mill. From here you'll head north to Townsend, yet another classic New England town. The handsome town green, highlighted by a bandstand in the center, is framed by the Victorian town hall and a magnificent church with a tall ornate steeple, dated 1770. You'll rejoin the short ride at Hickory Hills Lake.

Directions for the ride: 29 miles 〰〰〰〰〰

1. Head east on Front Street, paralleling the railroad tracks on your left, and go $^2/_{10}$ mile to crossroads (Phoenix Street on right), after house number 43.
2. Turn left at crossroads. Cross the tracks and go straight ahead onto Benjamin Road. Go $1^3/_{10}$ miles to end (Hazen Road, unmarked).
3. Turn right on Hazen Road and go $^2/_{10}$ mile to Brown Road (unmarked) on left.
4. Turn left on Brown Road. After $^1/_2$ mile you'll come to the graceful village of Shirley Center. Continue straight for $^9/_{10}$ mile to end (Route 2A).
5. Turn left on Route 2A and go $^1/_{10}$ mile to first right, Townsend Road.
6. Turn right on Townsend Road and go $^9/_{10}$ mile to crossroads and stop sign (Route 225). Just before the intersection is a fork; bear left on the main road here. The short ride turns left on Route 225, and the long ride turns right.
7. Turn right on Route 225 and go $1^4/_{10}$ miles to railroad tracks immediately after a dam and old brick mill on right. This is West Groton.
8. Turn 90 degrees left at the tracks onto Townsend Road, passing the country store on your right and following the tracks on your left. **CAUTION** crossing the tracks. Go $3^6/_{10}$ miles to diagonal crossroads and stop sign (Route 119). Notice the elegant stone church, set back off the road on a hill, after $^1/_4$ mile.
9. Cross Route 119 (**CAUTION:** busy intersection) and go $3^1/_2$ miles to end. **CAUTION:** You reach the end while you're going downhill.
10. Turn left at end and go $^1/_2$ mile to end (Route 13).
11. Turn left on Route 13 and go 2 miles to fork where Route 13 bears right, at the Townsend green.
12. Bear right on Route 13, passing the green on your left, and go $^2/_{10}$ mile to traffic light (Route 119), in the center of Townsend.
13. Cross Route 119 and go $1^3/_{10}$ miles to Emery Road on left.
14. Turn left on Emery Road and go $1^3/_{10}$ miles to end (South Row Road, unmarked).

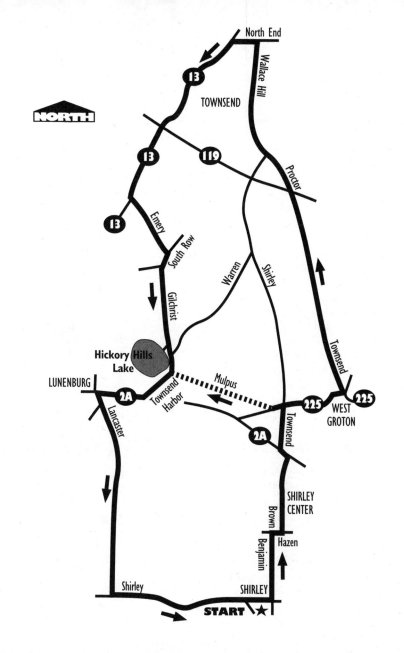

NORTH

North End

13

TOWNSEND

Wallace Hill

119

13

Proctor

13

Emery

South Row

Warren

Shirley

Gilchrist

Hickory Hills Lake

Townsend

LUNENBURG

2A

Townsend Harbor

Mulpus

225

225

WEST GROTON

Lancaster

2A

Townsend

SHIRLEY CENTER

Brown

Benjamin

Hazen

Shirley

SHIRLEY

START ★

15. Turn right on South Row Road and go $^3/_{10}$ mile to fork (Gilchrist Road bears left).

16. Bear left on Gilchrist Road and go $1^2/_{10}$ miles to where the main road bears left and Peninsula Drive goes straight.

17. Bear left on main road and go $^3/_{10}$ mile to stop sign (merge head-on into Townsend Harbor Road). You'll see Hickory Hills Lake on your right.

18. Continue straight for $^4/_{10}$ mile to fork, going along the shore of the lake. At the fork, Mulpus Road bears left, and Townsend Harbor Road (unmarked) bears right.

19. Bear right on Townsend Harbor Road and go $^8/_{10}$ mile to end (Route 2A, Massachusetts Avenue). You'll pass an attractive dam on your right.

20. Turn right on Route 2A and stay on it for $^9/_{10}$ mile to traffic light in the center of Lunenburg, at top of hill (Main Street on right, Lancaster Avenue on left).

21. Turn left at top of hill. You'll immediately come to a fork.

22. Go straight at fork on Lancaster Avenue (don't bear right on Leominster Road) and go $4^2/_{10}$ miles to end (Shirley Road, unmarked). This is a glorious run. You'll pass Massapoag Pond and a little dam on your right.

23. Turn left at end onto Shirley and go 1 mile to fork where Reservoir Road bears left downhill and the main road bears right.

24. Bear right on main road and go $1^7/_{10}$ miles to another fork immediately after an old wooden mill on your left. Shortly before the mill there's a delightful little millpond on your right.

25. Bear left at fork and go $^1/_{10}$ mile to another fork where Center Road bears left and Main Street bears slightly right.

26. Bear slightly right on Main Street. The center of town is just ahead.

Directions for the ride: 16 miles

1. Follow directions for the long ride through number 6.

2. Turn left on Route 225 and go $^4/_{10}$ mile to Mulpus Road (unmarked), a small road that bears right.

3. Bear right on Mulpus Road and go $2^1/_{10}$ miles to end, at traffic island. **CAUTION:** The first $^1/_2$ mile, to the Lunenburg town line, is bumpy. At the end Hickory Hills Lake is in front of you.

4. Turn left at end and go $^8/_{10}$ mile to end (Route 2, Massachusetts Avenue). You'll pass an attractive dam on your right.

5. Follow directions for the long ride from number 20 to end.

35 West Boylston– Sterling–Lancaster

Number of miles: 28 (14 without Lancaster extension)
Terrain: Rolling, with several hills, one a real monster.
Food: Grocery stores and snack bars in the towns.
Start: Picnic area at the fork of Routes 12 and 140 in West Boylston, just north of the bridge over the Wachusett Reservoir. Park at side of road.

Just north of the Wachusett Reservoir, midway between Worcester and Fitchburg, superb biking abounds on narrow roads winding through woods and along broad, open hilltops with impressive views. The area is very rural except for the two classic New England towns of Sterling and Lancaster.

You start from the western edge of the Wachusett Reservoir, second largest lake in the state, and head north along its slender western arm to the fine valley town of Sterling, best known as the locale of "Mary Had a Little Lamb." The fabled schoolhouse was reconstructed by Henry Ford 15 miles away, next to the Wayside Inn in Sudbury, instead of in its original location. A small statue of a lamb on the green commemorates the nursery rhyme. From Sterling you'll return to the start, traversing a broad, open hillside through farms and orchards with fine views of the surrounding countryside. You'll pass Davis's Farmland, a petting zoo with a full lineup of barnyard animals who'll eat out of your hand.

The long ride heads farther north along country lanes and over another open hilltop to the elegant town of Lancaster, oldest in Worcester County. The town is on the Nashua River, surrounded by broad expanses of farmland. The town green is uniquely impressive, flanked by the graceful brick First Unitarian Church; an ornate, domed Victorian library dated 1867; and two fine old schools. The church, designed by Charles Bulfinch, was built in 1816. Just past the green you'll pass the handsome campus of Atlantic Union College, run by the Seventh-Day Adventists. About 2 miles ahead, you'll see the entrance to the Maharishi

Ayurveda Health Center, a retreat for spiritual rejuventation, meditation, and self-discovery. Ayurveda is a system of holistic health and medicine from ancient India. Shortly beyond Lancaster you'll join the short ride, traversing the hillside near the end.

Directions for the ride: 28 miles

1. Head north on Route 140, paralleling the western arm of the reservoir on your left. As soon as you start, notice the Old Stone Church, built in 1890, on your left. Only the stone exterior remains. After $1^3/_{10}$ miles Route 140 curves sharply right at yield sign, in the village of Oakdale (part of West Boylston). Continue less than $^2/_{10}$ mile to Waushacum Street, which bears right (a sign may say TO STERLING).

2. Bear right on Waushacum Street and go $1^4/_{10}$ miles to crossroads and stop sign (Dana Hill Road on left).

3. Turn right at crossroads over a small metal-grate bridge and go $1^1/_{10}$ miles to fork (Jewett Road, a smaller road, bears left up a little hill). **CAUTION:** Walk across the metal-grate bridge if the road is wet. On your left you'll get a view of Mount Wachusett, 2,000 feet high. It's the tallest mountain in the state east of the Connecticut River.

4. Bear left on Jewett Road and go $^9/_{10}$ mile to end (Route 62).

5. Turn right on Route 62 and go $^4/_{10}$ mile to end, at stop sign (merge left on Route 12).

6. Bear left on Route 12. **CAUTION:** Busy intersection. Go $^3/_{10}$ mile, through the center of Sterling, to fork where Route 12 bears left and Route 62 goes straight. Notice the fine, brick Victorian library, built in 1885, on your left.

7. Go straight on Route 62 for $^1/_{10}$ mile to Redstone Hill Road, which bears right uphill.

8. Bear right on Redstone Hill Road and go $2^2/_{10}$ miles to end (Route 62). There's a tough climb to the top of the ridge, but you'll be rewarded with a long, lazy downhill through farms and orchards with views of distant hills. You'll pass Davis's Farmland on your right after $1^6/_{10}$ miles.

9. Turn right on Route 62 and go $^3/_{10}$ mile to crossroads (Chace Hill Road). There's an excellent farmstand on the right just before the intersection. At the crossroads the short ride turns right and the long ride turns left.

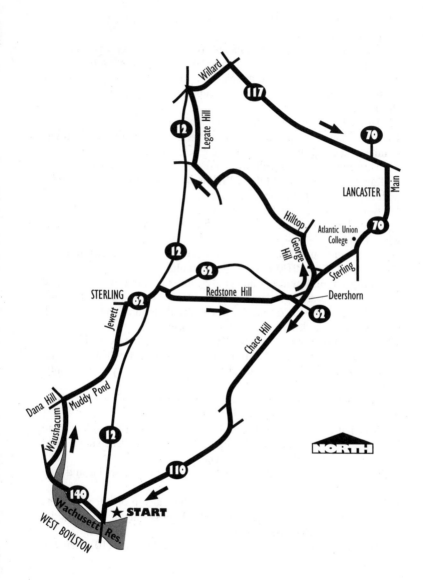

10. Turn left on Chace Hill Road. Go ⁶/10 mile to fork where the main road bears slightly right at a small green.

11. Bear left at fork and then immediately turn right on George Hill Road (unmarked). Go 1 mile to Hill Top Road on left, at bottom of hill (the main road bears right at the intersection). The large, wrought-iron gate on the far side of the intersection leads into the Maharishi Ayurveda Health Center.

12. Turn left on Hill Top Road and go 2⁴/10 miles to end.

13. Turn right at end (don't turn sharply right into a gravel pit) and go ½ mile to Legate Hill Road on right, just before Route 12.

14. Turn right on Legate Hill Road and go 1½ miles to end (merge right on Route 12 at bottom of hill). **CAUTION** here. You'll climb onto a ridge with fine views and then descend steeply.

15. Bear right on Route 12 and go 50 yards to crossroads and blinking light (Willard Street). It comes up while you're going downhill; don't whizz past it.

16. Turn right on Willard Street and go 1 mile to crossroads and stop sign (Route 117). **CAUTION:** Watch for potholes.

17. Turn right on Route 117 and go 3⁷/10 miles to Route 70 South (Main Street), which bears right (sign may say TO LANCASTER, 1 MILE). It comes up shortly after Route 70 North on left. You'll climb a long steady hill, but you'll be rewarded by an even longer descent.

18. Bear right on Route 70 South. After ⁹/10 mile you'll pass the Lancaster town green on your left. Continue 1²/10 miles to fork where the main road curves left and Sterling Road bears right. It's shortly after Atlantic Union College.

19. Bear right on Sterling Road and go ⁸/10 mile to another fork (Deershorn Road, unmarked, bears slightly left).

20. Bear left on Deershorn Road. After ⁴/10 mile, South Meadow Road bears left, but continue straight for ¹/10 mile to fork (Deershorn Road bears right, Chace Hill Road bears left).

21. Bear left on Chace Hill Road and go ¹/10 mile to crossroads and stop sign (Route 62).

22. Cross Route 62 and go 2¹/10 miles to fork at top of hill where the main road bears left and Squareshire Road goes straight. This is a delightful run through orchards and open fields.

23. Bear left on main road and go ⁷/10 mile to end (Route 110). Here the

Wachusett Reservoir, West Boylston

ride turns right, but if you turn left and go $2/10$ mile you'll get a sweeping view of the Wachusett Reservoir.

24. Turn right on Route 110 and go $2^7/10$ miles to traffic light (Route 12).
25. Bear left on Route 12. The picnic area is just ahead on right.

Directions for the ride: 14 miles

1. Follow directions for the long ride through number 9.
2. Turn right on Chace Hill Road and go $2^1/10$ miles to fork at top of hill where the main road bears left and Squareshire Road goes straight. This is a beautiful run through orchards and broad fields.
3. Follow directions for the long ride from number 23 to the end.

36 Apple Country Adventure:
Northboro–Berlin–Bolton

Number of miles: 23 (15 without Bolton extension)

Terrain: Rolling, with several good hills. Most of the hills come in the first half of the ride.

Food: Country store in Berlin. Grocery and snack bar in Bolton. Coffee shop at end.

Start: CVS Pharmacy, in a small shopping center at the junction of Routes 20 and 135 in the center of Northboro. It's on the north side of Route 20, at the corner of Church Street. From Interstate 290, take the Church Street exit if you're coming from the west, and the Solomon Pond Road exit if you're coming from the east. From either direction, turn right at the end of the exit ramp and go 2 miles into Northboro.

The rolling, refreshingly rural apple-orchard country along the western edge of Interstate 495 provides delightful bicycling on an elaborate network of winding country roads with no traffic. This is a region of classic New England scenery, with old barns, rambling wooden farmhouses, and stone walls crisscrossing the rolling pastureland. Berlin and Bolton are unspoiled towns with elegant village centers. The best time to take this ride is in mid-May, when the apple blossoms cover the orchards with a pink canopy, or in September and early October, when the foliage is peaking and you can stuff your saddlebag full of apples for pennies.

The ride starts in Northboro, an attractive town with a graceful old church and a couple of Victorian mills on the Assabet River, a small stream here. You'll head to Berlin (accented on the first syllable) on back roads winding through rolling hills crowned with orchards and open farmland. Berlin is a picture-postcard New England town with an exceptionally graceful church and green, a country store, and an old cemetery filled with weathered slate gravestones dating back to 1800. From Berlin you'll head north through the same type of countryside to Bolton, another gracious little town with a handsome stone library and a cluster of antiques shops. The return leg to Northboro brings you along ridgetops

223

with inspiring views and then down to the valley of the Assabet River through prosperous, well-landscaped farmland with grazing horses and cows. Just before the end you'll go underneath the graceful stone arches of the Wachusett Aqueduct, which carries water from the Wachusett Reservoir to metropolitan Boston.

The short ride bypasses Bolton by taking a more direct route from Berlin back to Northboro.

Directions for the ride: 23 miles

1. Turn right (west) out of parking lot onto Route 20 and immediately bear right on Church Street. (Don't get on Pierce Street.) Go $\frac{1}{10}$ mile to fork (Whitney Street, unmarked, bears right).

2. Bear left at fork, passing church on right. Immediately after the church turn right on Howard Street and go $\frac{9}{10}$ mile to fork (Green Street bears left).

3. Bear left at fork onto Green Street and go $\frac{1}{2}$ mile to crossroads just beyond the Interstate 290 overpass (Brewer Street on right).

4. Go straight at crossroads up steep hill (still Green Street) for $1\frac{7}{10}$ miles to fork (Smith Road bears right). There's a short steep hill at the beginning, and a long steep climb a half mile farther on.

5. Bear left at fork and go $\frac{8}{10}$ mile to Mile Hill Road (unmarked) on right, just past top of another hill. **CAUTION:** Bumps and potholes at the beginning. The rest of the ride is easier.

6. Turn right on Mile Hill Road. Don't worry about the name; it goes downhill. Go $1\frac{4}{10}$ miles to crossroads and stop sign (Linden Street). Here the ride turns right, but if you go straight for $\frac{1}{2}$ mile to the end, you'll have a good view of the Wachusett Reservoir. It's a steep descent and then a tough climb back up to Linden Street.

7. Turn right on Linden Street and go $2\frac{9}{10}$ miles to end (merge right at stop sign and blinking light on Route 62). This is Berlin. **CAUTION:** Bumpy railroad tracks at bottom of hill after about 2 miles.

8. Bear right at stop sign and then immediately bear left on Woodward Avenue (sign may say TO BOLTON). Go $\frac{1}{10}$ mile to stop sign, passing the church on your right. At the stop sign, the short ride bears slightly right on Walnut Street, and the long ride bears left.

9. Bear left at stop sign, passing the small brick library on right. Stay on the main road for $2\frac{8}{10}$ miles to a small, unmarked road that bears left.

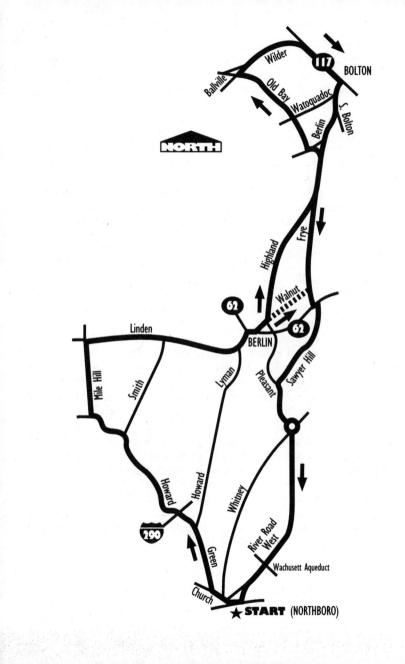

NORTH

Wilder

Ballville

Old Bay

Watoquadoc

BOLTON

117

S. Bolton

Berlin

Highland

Frye

62

Walnut

62

Linden

BERLIN

Sawyer Hill

Mile Hill

Smith

Lyman

Pleasant

Howard

Howard

Whitney

River Road West

290

Green

Wachusett Aqueduct

Church

★ START (NORTHBORO)

10. Bear left and go $1/10$ mile to end.

11. Turn left at end and go $1/10$ mile to Old Bay Road, which turns right up a steep hill.

12. Turn right on Old Bay Road and go $8/10$ mile to crossroads and stop sign. Most of this section is uphill.

13. Go straight for $9/10$ mile to traffic island immediately before stop sign. Here the road merges left, but you will turn sharply right.

14. Turn sharply right at traffic island and, just ahead, bear slightly right at yield sign. Continue $9/10$ mile to end, at stop sign (merge right on Route 117).

15. Bear right on Route 117 and go $7/10$ mile to Watoquadoc Road on right, at blinking light in the center of Bolton (sign may say to BERLIN, CLINTON). Notice the fine stone library on your right just before the intersection.

16. Turn right on Watoquadoc Road and go $1/4$ mile to Berlin Road, which bears left.

17. Bear left on Berlin Road and go $1/2$ mile to fork where South Bolton Road bears left.

18. Go straight ahead (don't bear left). Continue for $1\,1/10$ miles to fork where Frye Road bears left.

19. Bear left on Frye Road and go $1\,1/2$ miles to end (Route 62).

20. At end jog left and immediately right onto Sawyer Hill Road, up a steep hill. Go $1\,7/10$ miles to end (Pleasant Street), at grassy traffic island. There's a steep hill at the beginning, but at the top you'll be rewarded with a panoramic view of Mount Wachusett and a relaxing downhill run.

21. Turn left at end. After $4/10$ mile the main road curves sharply left. Stay on the main road for $1/4$ mile to rotary.

22. Bear slightly right onto the second road off the rotary, River Road West (don't turn 90 degrees right on Whitney Road). After 2 miles you'll go under the Wachusett Aqueduct. Just before the aqueduct you'll see a narrow sluiceway and a little dam on your left.

23. From the viaduct, continue $7/10$ mile to fork where Pierce Street (unmarked) bears right and the main road curves left.

24. Curve left on main road and go $2/10$ mile to end (Route 20). The shopping center is 100 yards to your right.

Wachusett Aqueduct, Northboro

Directions for the ride: 15 miles

1. Follow directions for the long ride through number 8.
2. Bear slightly right at stop sign onto Walnut Street, passing the small brick library on your left. Go 1 mile to end.
3. Turn right at end and go $\frac{2}{10}$ mile to end (Route 62).
4. Follow directions for the long ride from number 20 to the end.

Triboro Tour:
Westboro–Shrewsbury–
Northboro–Southboro

Number of miles: 29 (21 without Shrewsbury extension)
Terrain: Rolling. Several moderate hills, but nothing bad.
Food: Groceries and snack bars in the towns. Friendly's and McDonald's on Route 9, ½ mile east of starting point.
Start: Gold's Gym, on Lyman Street in Westboro, immediately north of Route 9. It's 2 miles west of Interstate 495 and ½ mile west of Route 30.

On this ride you'll explore the rolling, well-groomed farm country and graceful small towns east of Worcester. The region is just far enough from both the Boston and Worcester metropolitan areas to be rural rather than suburban. Smooth, well-maintained back roads weave among the hillsides and rolling pastures, providing relaxed and scenic biking.

You start from Westboro, an attractive town with a compact, Victorian brick business block, several fine churches, and gracious Colonial-style homes on the outskirts of town. From Westboro it's a smooth run to Northboro, with a spin along the Assabet Reservoir. The reservoir is one of the state's newest, formed in 1969 by damming the Assabet River. Northboro is another attractive community, with a graceful white church and a handsome stone Victorian library built in 1894. The stretch from Northboro to Southboro is a delight, heading across prosperous, open farmland with wooded hills rising in the background. You'll cross the Wachusett Aqueduct, which carries water from the Wachusett Reservoir to the Boston metropolitan area, and pass Saint Mark's School, one of the numerous prestigious preparatory schools scattered across the state. Its main building is an elegant, rambling hall with English Tudor architecture surrounded by extensive lawns.

Saint Mark's is just outside the center of Southboro, the most graceful New England classic of the three "boro" towns. The sloping, half-moon-shaped green is a beauty, framed by two fine old churches on a small rise. The return to Westboro heads along Route 30, a winner for biking among numbered routes, lightly traveled and passing through

229

sweeping expanses of open farmland. At the end of the ride, you'll detour past unspoiled Chauncy Lake. The grounds of Westboro State Hospital, dominated by a massive, ornate Victorian building, crown a hilltop overlooking the lake in a hauntingly beautiful setting that seems more like an old, distinguished college campus than a mental institution.

The long ride heads farther west to Shrewsbury through magnificent rolling countryside with some sharp ups and downs. You'll pass the new Veterinary School of Tufts University on the grounds of the former Grafton State Hospital, another mental institution. Massachusetts has dozens of state institutions for persons with mental and physical disabilities, most of them on large, gracious collegelike campuses in attractive rural surroundings. Adjacent to the Veterinary School, just off the route, is the Willard House and Clockshop, an eighteenth-century saltbox house with an impressive collection of antique clocks.

Shrewsbury is another handsome old town on a hilltop, with a classic white church and a fine brick library. The community is a well-to-do suburb of both Worcester and Boston, with the look and feel of a smaller, rural town. Most people know Shrewsbury only from the ugly commercial strip along Route 9; the rest of the town is pleasant. From Shrewsbury you'll head through wooded hills and past an orchard to Northboro, where you'll pick up the route of the shorter ride.

Directions for the ride: 29 miles

1. Turn right out of parking lot onto Lyman Street and immediately cross Route 9 at traffic light. Go 4/10 mile to end (Route 30, East Main Street).
2. Turn right on Route 30 and go 8/10 mile to center of Westboro, where you'll cross Route 135. **CAUTION** here—busy intersection.
3. Continue straight on Route 30 for 9/10 mile to Mill Road on right, just past top of hill. Here the short ride turns right and the long ride goes straight.
4. Continue straight on Route 30 for 3 3/10 miles to Pine Street on right, shortly after the Tufts Veterinary School. (Pine Street crosses a small railroad bridge at the beginning; you can see it from Route 30.) If you'd like to visit the clock museum, turn left after 2 9/10 miles on Willard Road, which leads into the grounds of the school, and go 6/10 mile to museum on right.

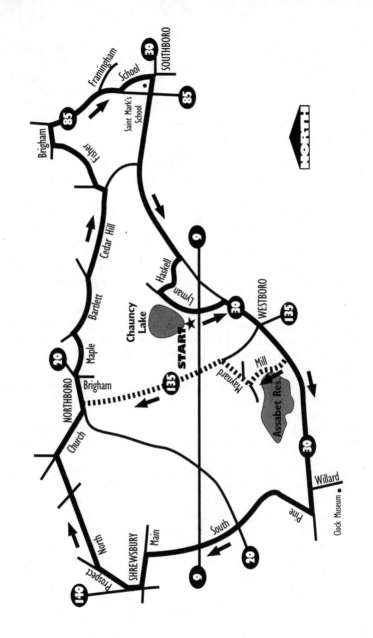

5. Turn right on Pine Street and go 2 miles to traffic light (Route 20). You'll pass a Job Corps center on the right near the beginning.

6. Cross Route 20 onto South Street. After $8/10$ mile you'll come to Route 9 at a traffic light. Continue straight for $1^3/10$ miles to another light.

7. Turn left at light onto Main and go $1/2$ mile to another light (Route 140) in the center of Shrewsbury. Notice the handsome brick library on your right, just before the intersection.

8. Turn right on Route 140 and go $1/10$ mile to fork where Route 140 bears left and Prospect Street bears right.

9. Bear right on Prospect Street and go $8/10$ mile to North Street, which bears right.

10. Bear right on North Street and go $1^8/10$ miles to crossroads and stop sign (Crawford Street, unmarked).

11. Go straight at crossroads onto West Street. Continue $7/10$ mile to another crossroads and stop sign (Church Street, unmarked).

12. Turn right on Church Street and go $1^2/10$ miles to end (Route 20), at traffic light. This is the center of Northboro. Shortly before the end there's a graceful church on your left.

13. Turn left on Route 20 and go $6/10$ mile to Maple Street on right, immediately after Brigham Street on right. You'll pass the Victorian library on your right and then a little dam at the bottom of the hill, also on the right. Just before Maple Street the White Cliffs Restaurant, an elegant, white Victorian mansion, is on the left.

14. Turn right on Maple Street. After $3/10$ mile Ridge Road turns right, but curve left on the main road for $4/10$ mile to end, opposite the entrance to the high school.

15. Turn right at end and go $1^2/10$ miles to Cedar Hill Street, which bears right at bottom of hill. You'll pass Bartlett Pond on your right near the beginning.

16. Bear right on Cedar Hill Street and go $1^9/10$ miles to Fisher Road (unmarked) on left, shortly after you go underneath Interstate 495. You'll pass office buildings for a mile as you nick a corner of Marlboro, a town that promotes commercial development.

17. Turn left on Fisher Road. Just ahead is a fork. Bear right at fork (still Fisher Road) and go $1^3/10$ miles to end (Brigham Street, unmarked).

18. Turn right on Brigham Street and go $4/10$ mile to traffic light (Route 85, Mill Street).

19. Turn right on Route 85 and go $9/10$ mile to fork where Route 85 bears right.

20. Bear right on Route 85 and go $4/10$ mile to School Street (unmarked), which bears left. There's a garage on your left at the intersection.

21. Bear left on School Street and go $7/10$ mile to crossroads and stop sign (Route 30, Main Street), in Southboro. You'll pass Saint Mark's School on right.

22. Turn right on Route 30 and go $2/10$ mile to traffic light (Route 85).

23. Go straight on Route 30 for $36/10$ miles to Haskell Street on right, just as you start to go downhill. It's just after the Windsor Ridge apartments on left.

24. Turn right on Haskell Street and go $9/10$ mile to end. **CAUTION:** Watch for potholes toward the end.

25. Turn left at end and go $8/10$ mile to parking lot on right, just before traffic light at Route 9. Just after you turn left you'll pass the entrance to Westboro State Hospital. Just beyond you'll pass Chauncy Lake on the right.

Directions for the ride: 21 miles

1. Follow directions for the long ride through number 3.

2. Turn right on Mill Road and go $9/10$ mile to end (Fisher Street). You'll pass the Assabet Reservoir on your left.

3. Turn right on Fisher Street. Just ahead is a fork where Maynard Street bears left.

4. Bear left on Maynard Street and go $6/10$ mile to crossroads, at traffic island (Route 135, Milk Street).

5. Turn left on Route 135 and go $33/10$ miles to end (Route 20) in the center of Northboro.

6. Turn right on Route 20 and go $6/10$ mile to Maple Street on right, immediately after Brigham Street on right. Notice the Victorian library and then the little dam at bottom of hill, both on your right. Just before Maple Street on the left is the White Cliffs, a restaurant in an elegant Victorian mansion.

7. Follow directions for the long ride from number 14 to the end.

38 Upper Blackstone Valley Tour:
Uxbridge–Whitinsville–Northbridge–Grafton

Number of miles: 29 (17 without Grafton extension)
Terrain: Rolling, with one tough hill. The long ride has an additional challenging climb.
Food: Groceries and snack bars in the towns. Pizza place at end.
Start: Uxbridge Shopping Center, Route 122, Uxbridge, ⁶⁄₁₀ mile north of Route 16.

Southeast of Worcester, between the city and the Rhode Island border, lies a fascinating and scenic area for bicycling dotted with ridges, wooded hills, and unspoiled little mill towns right out of the Industrial Revolution. Bisecting the region is the Blackstone River, among the first New England rivers to become industrialized. Traces of the old Blackstone Canal, which opened the valley to commerce during the 1830s, can still be seen in Uxbridge and Northbridge near Route 122. The river is currently being developed by both the state and the federal government into a linear historical park, called the Blackstone River and Canal Heritage State Park. Segments of the canal and its towpath have been restored; and in future years, the state plans to renovate some of the old mills into museums and visitors centers. Rhode Island has similar plans for its portion of the river. When the project is completed in both states, the Blackstone River will be a "heritage corridor" nearly 40 miles long.

The ride starts from Uxbridge, among the finest of the Blackstone Valley mill towns, with a compact old brick business block, a graceful brick library built in 1893, the Victorian Uxbridge Inn, and a distinctive Gothic-style church with a graceful turretlike steeple. Several of the mills have retail outlets where you can get bargains on clothing. Unlike many mill towns, Uxbridge has no congested tenements or even rows of identical mill housing, just old wooden homes that you'd expect to see in a more rural town.

From Uxbridge it's a short ride to Whitinsville, where you'll pass the unusually graceful Linwood Mill and ride along Linwood Pond about a mile before the center of town. Whitinsville is a fine example of a planned industrial community—a miniature Lowell. The formidable brick mill slants uphill for a quarter of a mile, and across the road are orderly rows of identical houses. As you climb the hill north of town you pass gracious old wooden homes and then enter inspiring, rolling farm country. You'll fly downhill into Farnumsville, another small mill town on the Blackstone River, and then climb onto a ridge through farms and orchards into the hilltop town of Grafton.

Grafton is among my favorite towns in the state. As you approach the center, you'll climb gradually past handsome Victorian homes. Suddenly the large oval green lies before you, complete with a bandstand in the middle and surrounded by several stately white churches, a handsome brick library, and the ornate brick Victorian town hall. From Grafton you'll return to Uxbridge along a succession of winding country lanes. Near the end you'll pass River Bend Farm, the main visitors center for the Massachusetts portion of the Blackstone corridor. Just ahead, ¼ mile off the route, is Stanley Woolen Mill, a handsome wooden building from the early 1850s on the Blackstone River and a good place to pick up bargains on woolen goods. It is the oldest operating textile mill in New England. Just ahead is the John Farnum House, built in 1715.

Directions for the ride: 29 miles

1. Turn left (north) out of parking lot. Follow Route 122 for ⁷⁄₁₀ mile to traffic light (Hartford Avenue).
2. Go straight at light for ⁴⁄₁₀ mile to Linwood Avenue on left, immediately before railroad bridge (it's unmarked; sign may say TO WHITINSVILLE).
3. Turn left on Linwood Avenue and go 1⁴⁄₁₀ miles to the second of two traffic lights 50 yards apart, in the center of Whitinsville (Douglas Road on left). As soon as you turn, notice the graceful Victorian mill on your left. Just past the mill, on your right, is a lovely Victorian mansion built in 1871. It is now a highly regarded country inn called, appropriately enough, The Victorian.
4. Turn right at second traffic light on Hill Street, which lives up to its name. Go 3²⁄₁₀ miles to crossroads and stop sign (Sutton Street) at blinking light. A turreted Victorian mansion, currently a funeral home, is on your right just after you turn onto Hill Street.

5. Continue straight for $1^2/_{10}$ miles to fork where Ferry Street (unmarked) bears left and Depot Street turns right across railroad bridge. The fork is just past the bottom of a long hill.

6. Turn right on Depot Street and go $^4/_{10}$ mile to end (Route 122). This is Farnumville, a mill village that is part of Grafton. There's a fine dam across the Blackstone River on your left. It's hidden by the bridge abutment; dismount to get a look. At Route 122, the short ride turns right and the long ride turns left.

7. Turn left on Route 122 and go $^2/_{10}$ mile to fork where Route 122A bears left and Route 122 bears slightly right.

8. Bear slightly right on Route 122 and then immediately turn right on Keith Hill Road. Go $1^7/_{10}$ miles to end (merge left at stop sign). The first mile is a steplike hill with some steep pitches.

9. Bear left at stop sign and go $^8/_{10}$ mile to fork where a smaller road bears left and the main road (South Street) bears right uphill.

10. Bear right on South Street and go $^4/_{10}$ mile to stop sign (Route 140) in the center of Grafton.

11. Go straight at stop sign and then immediately bear right, passing the tall monument on your left. Go $^8/_{10}$ mile to fork where the main road (Old Westboro Road, unmarked) bears right, and a smaller road (North Street) goes straight.

12. Bear right on main road and go $2^4/_{10}$ miles to Adams Road on right. You'll come within ½ mile of the Willard House and Clockshop, an eighteenth-century saltbox house with an impressive collection of antique clocks. To visit it, turn left after $1^6/_{10}$ miles on Wesson Street. Go $^4/_{10}$ mile to Willard Street on right. Turn right and go $^1/_{10}$ mile to museum on left.

13. Turn right on Adams Road and go $1^8/_{10}$ miles to traffic island where the main road bears right uphill and Merriam Road (unmarked) turns left.

14. Turn left at traffic island and go $^3/_{10}$ mile to George Hill Road on right. You'll pass an excellent farm stand on your left at the beginning.

15. Turn right on George Hill Road and go $1^9/_{10}$ miles to end (Leland Street). This is a pleasant narrow lane along a hillside. **CAUTION:** The end comes up suddenly at bottom of hill.

16. Turn right on Leland Street and go $^2/_{10}$ mile to end (Route 140).

17. Turn sharply left on Route 140 and go $1^7/_{10}$ miles to Glen Avenue on right. It comes up immediately after Williams Street, also on right. **CAUTION:** At the beginning you'll pass a weekend flea market; watch for traffic and pedestrians.

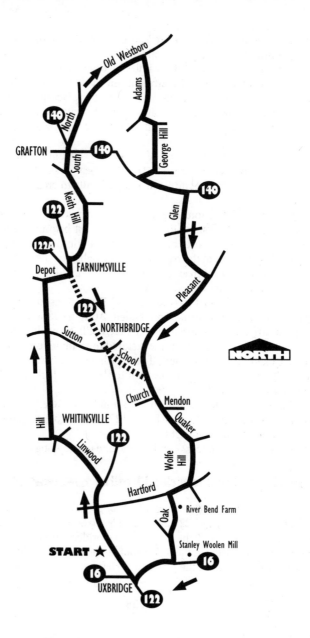

Old Westboro

Adams

140

North

George Hill

GRAFTON

140

South

140

Keith Hill

122

Glen

122A

Depot

FARNUMSVILLE

Pleasant

122

NORTHBRIDGE

Sutton

School

NORTH

Church

Mendon

Hill

WHITINSVILLE

Quaker

122

Linwood

Wolfe Hill

Hartford

River Bend Farm

Oak

Stanley Woolen Mill

START ★

16

16

UXBRIDGE

122

18. Turn right on Glen Avenue and go ½ mile to crossroads and stop sign. Continue straight for $\frac{9}{10}$ mile to end.

19. Turn right at end and go 2½ miles to fork where Mendon Road bears left and Quaker Street goes straight ahead downhill. After 1½ miles Riverdale Street on right leads $\frac{1}{10}$ mile to the Blackstone River and an old mill that is part of the Blackstone Heritage State Park system. Church Street, the next right after Riverdale Street, also leads $\frac{1}{10}$ mile to the river and the canal.

20. Continue straight on Quaker Street for $1\frac{3}{10}$ miles to fork where Quaker Road bears left and Wolfe Hill Road bears right.

21. Bear right on Wolfe Hill Road and go 1 mile to crossroads (Hartford Avenue).

22. Bear right on Hartford Avenue and go $\frac{4}{10}$ mile to Oak Street on left. You'll cross the Blackstone River and Canal just before the intersection; you can see the remains of a lock on your left. Rice City Pond, a dammed-up portion of the river, is on your right.

23. Turn left on Oak Street. Stay on the main road for $1\frac{3}{10}$ miles to end (Route 16), at T-intersection.

After $\frac{2}{10}$ mile you'll pass River Bend Farm, a visitors center for the Blackstone Heritage Corridor, on the left. At the end the ride turns right on Route 16, but to see the Stanley Woolen Mill, turn left and go ¼ mile.

Behind the visitors center, the restored towpath follows the east bank of the canal to the woolen mill. If you wish, you may walk your bike (or ride, with caution) along the towpath to the mill, which is on Route 16. Turn right on Route 16.

24. Turn right on Route 16 and go $\frac{3}{10}$ mile (½ mile if you're coming from the woolen mill) to end (Route 122). Just before the end, there's a picturesque dam on your right.

25. Turn right on Route 122 and go $\frac{6}{10}$ mile to shopping center on left.

Directions for the ride: 17 miles

1. Follow directions for the long ride through number 6.

2. Turn right on Route 122 and go 2 miles to School Street, which bears left uphill at blinking light. This is Northbridge, another mill town on the Blackstone River. Route 122 parallels the river on your right; there may be historic sites in the Blackstone Heritage State Park system in the future.

3. Bear left on School Street and go 1³/₁₀ miles to end (merge right at stop sign on Quaker Street). You'll pass a magnificent brick church on your right at the beginning.

4. Bear right on Quaker Street and go 1¹/₁₀ miles to fork where Mendon Road bears left and Quaker Street continues straight ahead downhill. At the beginning Riverdale Street on the right leads ¹/₁₀ mile to an old mill on the Blackstone River that is part of the Heritage State Park system. Church Street, the next right after Riverdale Street, also leads ¹/₁₀ mile to the river and the canal.

5. Follow directions for the long ride from number 20 to the end.

39

Purgatory Chasm Ride:
Uxbridge–Whitinsville–Sutton–Douglas

Number of miles: 27 (21 without Singletary Pond extension)
Terrain: Hilly.
Food: Refreshment stand at Purgatory Chasm, open during the summer in good weather. Grocery and snack bar in East Douglas. Pizza place at end.
Start: Uxbridge Shopping Center, Route 122, Uxbridge, 6/10 mile north of Route 16.

Southeast of Worcester, midway between the city and the Rhode Island border, is an area of ruggedly beautiful ridge-and-valley country dotted with picturesque small towns. Biking in this region is challenging but inspiring: There are several tough climbs, but each is balanced by a ridgetop run with sweeping views or a long, smooth downhill cruise. Highlighting this ride is a visit to Purgatory Chasm, a deep, boulder-strewn gorge between towering rocky cliffs.

The ride starts in Uxbridge, a beautiful old mill town on the upper Blackstone River, which slices diagonally from Worcester to Providence. In the center of town is a compact brick business block, the graceful brick library built in 1893, the Victorian Uxbridge Inn, and a distinctive Gothic-architectured church with a graceful turretlike steeple. From Uxbridge it's a short way to Whitinsville, one of the state's best examples of a planned, orderly mill village—a miniature Lowell or Holyoke. The original stone mill, a graceful bell-towered beauty, stands over a little dam in the center of town. Around the corner a more recent, massive brick mill extends along the road up a hillside for nearly a quarter of a mile. Across the road ordered rows of identical long, wooden mill houses with broad porches march along the side streets.

From Whitinsville it's not far to Purgatory Chasm, where a rocky trail leads half a mile along the bottom of the ravine to its far end. Beyond the Chasm there's a steady 2-mile climb, relieved by several flat spots, which more than one cyclist spontaneously named the Stairway to

Heaven. At the top you'll get a lift from the inspiring views and the screaming downhill plunge that awaits you around the corner. One more steep climb brings you to the classic New England village of Sutton, with a graceful church and green and an old wooden town hall.

Beyond Sutton the rest of the ride is easier, with only one more tough climb. Just ahead is a fine run along Singletary Pond and the three small Stockwell Ponds, followed by a long, lazy downhill through the little mill village of Manchaug. Then you'll head to East Douglas, another attractive town with a pair of old churches and a handsome little red-brick library. Beyond here you'll have one more climb onto an open ridge with superb views, followed by a long, well-earned descent back to Uxbridge.

Directions for the ride: 27 miles ~~~~~~~~~

1. Turn left (north) out of parking lot and go $^4/_{10}$ mile to fork where Rivulet Street bears left.

2. Bear left on Rivulet Street and immediately bear left at another fork, staying on the main road. Go $^3/_{10}$ mile to crossroads and stop sign.

3. Go straight (on Fletcher) at crossroads for $1^7/_{10}$ miles to end (Douglas Road), at yield sign. This is Whitinsville.

4. Bear right on Douglas Road across a little bridge. Go 100 yards to traffic light. From the left side of the bridge there's a fascinating view of the Mumford River flowing beside the massive mills and over a little dam.

5. Turn left at traffic light and go $^7/_{10}$ mile to fork (North Main Street bears right). It's shortly after Arcade Pond on right.

6. Bear right on North Main Street and go $^6/_{10}$ mile to another fork where the main road bears left downhill (becoming Purgatory Road) and a smaller road goes straight.

7. Bear left on main road. Just ahead you'll pass Whitins Pond on your left. Continue $1^1/_2$ miles to Purgatory Chasm on left. A long, tough hill leads up the Chasm.

8. Leaving the Chasm, continue uphill $1^8/_{10}$ miles to end. Just before the end there's a great view on your right.

9. Turn left at end and go $^2/_{10}$ mile to crossroads and blinking light (Uxbridge Road).

10. Turn right on Uxbridge Road and go $1^2/_{10}$ miles to crossroads and stop sign in the center of Sutton. You'll have a flying downhill run fol-

lowed by a hard climb. In Sutton the short ride turns left and the long ride goes straight.

11. Go straight at crossroads for $9/10$ mile to Winwood Road, a narrow lane that bears left. You'll follow Singletary Pond on your left.

12. Bear left on Winwood Road and go $8/10$ mile to crossroads and stop sign. You'll continue to follow the pond.

13. Turn left at crossroads and go $3/10$ mile to fork.

14. Bear left at fork, following the pond on your left, and go $3 \, 2/10$ miles to your fourth crossroads (Town Farm Road, unmarked). The first three come in quick succession, then it's $1 \, 2/10$ miles to the fourth where the right-hand road bears up a steep hill. You'll go along Singletary Pond and then the three small Stockwell Ponds on your left.

15. Turn left on Town Farm Road and go $8/10$ mile to end (merge left at stop sign).

16. Bear left at end and go $2/10$ mile to fork where the main road bears right.

17. Bear right, staying on main road, and go 1 mile to Putnam Hill Road (unmarked) on right, at stop sign, just past high school.

18. Turn right on Putnam Hill Road and go $1 \, 3/10$ miles to crossroads and stop sign (Central Turnpike).

19. Continue straight for $8/10$ mile to fork where the main road bears left, just beyond the top of the long hill. (Lackey Road, a smaller road, goes straight.)

20. Bear left, staying on main road, and go 2 miles to crossroads and blinking light (Whitins Road on left, Manchaug Road on right), in the small village of Manchaug. This stretch is nearly all downhill. You'll pass Tuckers Pond on the right.

21. Go straight at crossroads for 2 miles to fork where one road bears right and the other (Gilboa Street) goes straight. It's just after a red-brick church on left.

22. Bear right at fork, and after $1/10$ mile bear right again on the main road across a little bridge. Go $1/10$ mile to end (Route 16, Northeast Main Street). This is East Douglas.

23. Turn left on Route 16. Go $1/2$ mile to blinking light where Route 16 curves sharply right and Northeast Main Street bears left down a sharp hill.

24. Bear left downhill on Northeast Main Street. **CAUTION** here. Go $1 \, 4/10$ miles to Williams Street, which bears left shortly after the bridge over Route 146.

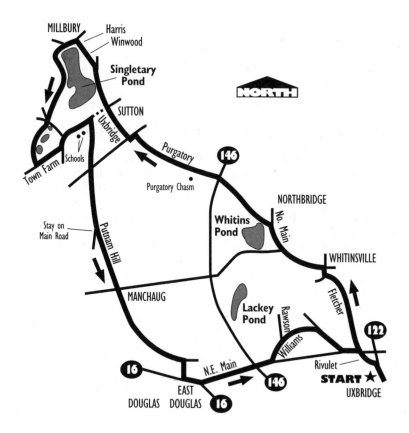

25. Bear left on Williams Street. After $8/10$ mile the main road curves right, and Rawson Street bears left. Continue on main road for $6/10$ mile to end.

26. Bear right at end and go $9/10$ mile to stop sign at bottom of hill (merge left). Enjoy the descent!

27. Bear left (almost straight) and go $1/10$ mile to crossroads and stop sign (Rivulet Street).

28. Turn right at crossroads and go $4/10$ mile to end, at stop sign (merge right on Route 122).

29. Bear right on Route 122 and go $4/10$ mile to parking lot on right.

Directions for the ride: 21 miles

1. Follow directions for the long ride through number 10.

2. Turn left at crossroads and go $1/2$ mile to Putnam Hill Road (unmarked) on left, just before school (sign may say TO MANCHAUG, EAST DOUGLAS).

3. Turn left on Putnam Hill Road and go $1 3/10$ miles to crossroads and stop sign (Central Turnpike).

4. Follow directions for the long ride from number 19 to the end.

Chapter 5:
The South Shore

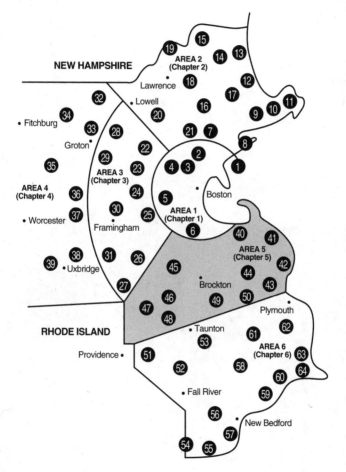

The numbers on this map refer to rides in this book.

Massachusetts Bay, Hingham

Hingham

Number of miles: 22 (17 without World's End extension)
Terrain: Gently rolling, with a few short, steep hills.
Food: Several grocery stores and restaurants. Burger King at end.
Start: Burger King on Route 228 at the Rockland-Norwell town line, immediately north of Route 3. Take exit 14.

This ride explores Hingham, the first town southeast of Boston that is spaciously and graciously suburban rather than congested. It is an affluent community graced with elegant wooden homes from the early 1800s, horse farms, country estates with gently rolling meadows, and a beautiful stretch of waterfront along Massachusetts Bay. Hingham is unique because it has two centers of town, Hingham and Hingham Center, a mile apart. Both are New England classics, with proud old churches and fine Colonial-style homes with peaked roofs and dormer windows.

Starting from the southern edge of the town, the ride heads north to the ocean at Crow Point, where you'll climb a short hill with a glorious view of Massachusetts Bay and the Boston skyline in the distance. You'll follow the waterfront and then head south for about 2 miles to the handsome center of town. Here you'll pass the Old Ship Church, built in 1681, the oldest church in America in continual use.

The route now heads to World's End, as idyllic a spot as any on the Massachusetts coast. It is a small peninsula originally designed by Frederick Law Olmsted and now maintained by the Trustees of Reservations. Its three drumlins are connected by a narrow neck between the first and second. Broad, grassy slopes lined with stately rows of trees slant gently down to the shore and give views of the Boston skyline. It's about a 3-mile loop on dirt roads to the far end of the peninsula; you may either ride or walk. The entrance fee is currently $3.50.

After leaving World's End you'll ride through Hingham Center, the older and less commercial of the two centers of town. The last part of the ride, south of Hingham Center, leads into a pastoral landscape of meticulous gentleman farms with broad fields and gracious old farmhouses.

Directions for the rides: 22 and 17 miles ~~~~~

1. Turn left on Route 228 and go less than $^2/_{10}$ mile to Gardner Street on right. Accord Pond is on your right at the beginning.

2. Turn right on Gardner Street and go $1^3/_{10}$ miles to traffic light (Route 53). You'll see Accord Pond again after $^6/_{10}$ mile.

3. Cross Route 53 (**CAUTION:** busy intersection). Go $1^1/_{10}$ miles to end (Route 228, Main Street).

4. Turn left at end. Go $2^7/_{10}$ miles to crossroads and stop sign where Route 228 (Main Street) turns right and Cedar Street (unmarked) turns left.

5. Turn left at crossroads onto Cedar Street and stay on main road for $1^1/_{10}$ miles to crossroads and stop sign at bottom of hill (South Street, unmarked). Cedar Street becomes Hersey Street.

6. Continue straight for $^7/_{10}$ mile to traffic light (Route 3A).

7. Continue straight for 1 mile to Marion Street, which turns sharply left up a steep hill at the Hingham Yacht Club. You'll follow Hingham Harbor on your right at the end. The yacht club is at the tip of Crow Point, a small peninsula.

8. Turn sharply left on Marion Street and go 50 yards to Merrill Street (unmarked) on right.

9. Turn right on Merrill Street, which continues steeply uphill. Go $^1/_{10}$ mile to end. Enjoy the view from the top of the hill!

10. Turn right at end down steep hill (**CAUTION** here). Go $^2/_{10}$ mile to crossroads (Jarvis Avenue). There's a small beach at the bottom of the hill.

11. Turn right on Jarvis Avenue. Go $^2/_{10}$ mile to fork where a dead-end road bears right and the main road (Bel Air Road) bears left. You'll climb another short, steep hill.

12. Bear left, and immediately curve right on the main road. Go $^6/_{10}$ mile to the intersection where Park Circle turns left and the main road curves sharply right.

13. Stay on main road for less than $^4/_{10}$ mile to end, at second stop sign. The road becomes a divided parkway at the end.

14. Turn right at end and go $^1/_{10}$ mile to fork.

15. Bear left at fork (don't go straight on Crow Point Lane). Go $^2/_{10}$ mile to traffic light (Route 3A).

16. Go straight for $^6/_{10}$ mile to crossroads and stop sign (North Street).

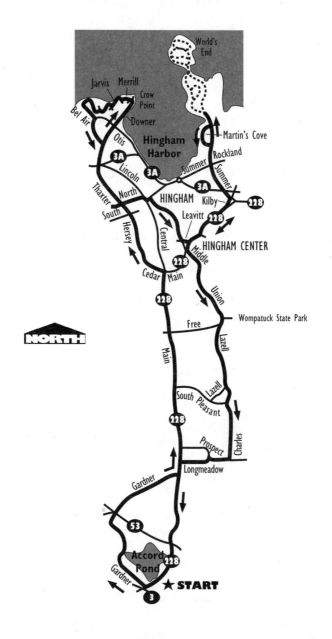

17. Turn left on North Street, and stay on main road for $^4/_{10}$ mile to fork in the center of Hingham. There's a handsome white church on the left just before the fork, and another one on the left just after it.

18. Bear left at fork, and immediately turn right on Main Street opposite Saint Paul's Church on left. Go $^8/_{10}$ mile to diagonal crossroads (Garrison Road on right, Leavitt Street on left). You'll pass the Old Ship Church on your left just past the business district.

19. Bear left on Leavitt Street and go 1 block to end (Route 228). Here the ride turns left, but if you wish to omit the World's End section of the ride ($4^2/_{10}$ miles round trip to the entrance and back), turn right. Go $^1/_{10}$ mile to Middle Street on left, at small traffic island. Resume with direction number 34.

20. Turn left on Route 228 and go less than $^2/_{10}$ mile to fork where Route 228 bears left.

21. Bear left at fork and go $^6/_{10}$ mile to Kilby Street (unmarked), which bears left.

22. Bear left on Kilby Street and go $^1/_{10}$ mile to crossroads (Summer Street, unmarked).

23. Turn left on Summer Street and go $^1/_{10}$ mile to diagonal crossroads and stop sign (Route 3A).

24. Cross Route 3A and go $^4/_{10}$ mile to traffic light (Summer Street on left, Rockland Street on right).

25. Go straight for $^7/_{10}$ mile to the entrance to World's End. **CAUTION:** If you bike onto the peninsula, some of the dirt roads have a soft or loose surface. Also, watch for pairs of wooden beams, with spaces wide enough to trap a bicycle tire between them, placed diagonally across the road to control erosion.

26. Leaving World's End, backtrack $^2/_{10}$ mile to the first right (Martins Cove Road, unmarked), just past top of little hill.

27. Turn right on Martins Cove Road and go less than $^1/_2$ mile to end (Martins Lane, unmarked).

28. Turn right at end and go $^2/_{10}$ mile to traffic light (Rockland Street on left, Summer Street on right).

29. Go straight for $^1/_{10}$ mile to diagonal crossroads (Route 3A).

30. Cross Route 3A and go $^1/_{10}$ mile to crossroads (Kilby Street, unmarked).

31. Turn right on Kilby Street and go $^1/_{10}$ mile to stop sign (merge right

on Route 228).

32. Bear right on Route 228 and go $^8/_{10}$ mile to fork where Leavitt Street bears right and Route 228 bears left.

33. Bear left on Route 228 and go $^1/_{10}$ mile to Middle Street on left, at small traffic island. This is Hingham Center.

34. Turn left on Middle Street, passing the town green on your left. Go $1^2/_{10}$ miles to fork where Free Street bears right and Lazell Street bears left up a little hill. Just before the fork, a road on your left leads to Wompatuck State Park, a massive, 3,000-acre expanse of woodland with campsites and 6 miles of bicycle paths.

35. Bear left on Lazell Street and go $^8/_{10}$ mile to another fork where Lazell Street (unmarked here) bears right and Charles Street bears slightly left.

36. Bear slightly left on Charles Street and go 1 mile to end (Prospect Street).

37. Turn right on Prospect Street and go $^3/_{10}$ mile to Longmeadow Road on left. The main road curves right at the intersection.

38. Turn left on Longmeadow Road and go $^4/_{10}$ mile to end (Route 228, Main Street).

39. Turn left on Route 228 and go $1^1/_{10}$ miles to Route 53, at traffic light.

40. Go straight for $^6/_{10}$ mile to Burger King on left. Accord Pond is on your right at the end. **CAUTION** turning left into Burger King.

Cohasset–Scituate

Number of miles: 26 (17 without Scituate extension)
Terrain: Gently rolling, with a couple of short hills.
Food: Grocery stores and restaurants in both Cohasset and Scituate.
Start: Cohasset High School on Pond Street, Cohasset, just north of Route 3A. There's a traffic light at the corner of Route 3A and Pond Street.

On this ride you explore the shoulder of land southeast of Boston where the coastline curves primarily from an east–west to a north–south direction. It is the first really nice stretch of coast heading southeast from the city, and the Cohasset section, just east of Hull, is among the most scenic in the state. A network of smooth secondary roads connecting these two affluent communities provides bicycling at its best.

The ride starts in Cohasset, an unspoiled community that is one of the finest of the Boston suburbs. Its splendid rocky coastline, rimmed by large, impressive homes hovering above the waves with the Boston skyline in the distance, rivals Cape Ann and Newport for elegance. The center of town is a New England jewel, with a long, stately green framed by a pair of graceful white churches, the town hall, and fine Colonial-style wooden homes. The church at the head of the green was built in 1747. Cohasset received a burst of publicity in 1986 when much of the movie *The Witches of Eastwick* was filmed here.

The long ride heads farther southeast into Scituate, another handsome community with a large green, a small, boat-filled harbor, and a compact row of shops along its shore. Just outside of town is the Lawson Tower, a handsome wooden-shingled landmark with a water tower inside. It was built in 1902 and given to the town by Thomas Lawson, a copper magnate. At the top is a set of bells that are played on special town occasions. The Scituate coast, not as elegant as the Cohasset section, is bordered by smaller homes and cottages. It is spectacular, however, especially on a windy day when the surf crashes against the seawalls, which are necessary to protect the shore from the brunt of northeasters. There's a graceful white lighthouse at the tip of Cedar Point, and the bridge over the tidal inlet that forms the border of the two towns is a great spot.

Directions for the ride: 26 miles 〰️〰️〰️

1. Turn right out of parking lot onto Pond Street and go $^2/_{10}$ mile to Route 3A, at traffic light.

2. Cross Route 3A and go $^2/_{10}$ mile to end (King Street, unmarked).

3. Turn left on King Street and go $^6/_{10}$ mile to end (Beechwood Street). You'll pass Lily Pond on your right.

4. Turn right on Beechwood Street and go 1 mile to crossroads (Doane Street).

5. Turn left on Doane Street and go less than $^2/_{10}$ mile to end (merge left at stop sign).

6. Bear left at end and go $^6/_{10}$ mile to crossroads (Clapp Road, unmarked).

7. Turn left on Clapp Road. **CAUTION** making this turn—there are no stop signs for any of the four roads. Go $1^7/_{10}$ miles to a wide fork where Grove Street (unmarked) bears right and Mann Lot Road bears left.

8. Bear left on Mann Lot Road and go $^4/_{10}$ mile to crossroads and stop sign (Route 3A).

9. Cross Route 3A and go $^6/_{10}$ mile to end (Country Way). A fine white church built in 1869 is at the intersection.

10. Turn right at end and go $^3/_{10}$ mile to Hollett Street, which turns left at a little traffic island. Here the short ride turns left and the long ride goes straight.

11. Continue straight for $^7/_{10}$ mile to fork where Country Way bears right and Branch Street goes straight.

12. Bear right on Country Way and go $^1/_2$ mile to traffic light (First Parish Road). A stately white church stands on the right just before the intersection.

13. Turn left at light and go $^3/_{10}$ mile to fork at the Scituate town green (Beaver Dam Road bears slightly left). There's a handsome Civil War monument on the green. Just before the green you'll pass the Lawson Tower on your left.

14. Bear slightly left on Beaver Dam Road and go $9/10$ mile to traffic light (Tilden Road).

15. Turn right on Tilden Road and go $8/10$ mile to crossroads and stop sign. Tilden Road becomes Brook Street.

16. Turn left at crossroads and go $4/10$ mile, through downtown Scituate, to Jericho Road on right, at traffic light. You'll see Scituate Harbor on your right just before the intersection.

17. Turn right on Jericho Road. Stay on the main road, following Scituate Harbor on your right, for $7/10$ mile to traffic island (Lighthouse Road bears right). To your right is Cedar Point, a small peninsula with a lighthouse at the tip. You will now loop counterclockwise around the peninsula.

18. Bear right at traffic island, following the water on your right. Go $8/10$ mile around Cedar Point back to this same traffic island.

19. Bear right at traffic island, following the ocean on your right, and go $1 2/10$ miles to end. The road turns 90 degrees left shortly before the end.

20. Turn right at end and go $1 8/10$ miles to traffic light (Gannett Road).

21. Turn right on Gannett Road and go $6/10$ mile to Bailey's Causeway on left. Here the ride turns left, but if you wish you can continue straight for $1/2$ mile until the road becomes a private driveway, and then backtrack to Bailey's Causeway.

22. Turn left on Bailey's Causeway and go $3/10$ mile to end (Hatherly Road). There's a golf course to the right.

23. Turn left on Hatherly Road and go $4/10$ mile to traffic light (Gannett Road).

24. Turn right on Gannett Road and go $4/10$ mile to where the main road curves left and a smaller road, Old Gannett Road, goes straight.

25. Go straight onto smaller road for $2/10$ mile to Border Street (unmarked), which turns right up a short, steep hill..

26. Turn right on Border Street and go $1 2/10$ miles to a little bridge over an inlet. This is a delightful spot, with Cohasset Cove on your right.

27. From the bridge continue $3/10$ mile to fork where Summer Street turns left and the main road bears right.

28. Bear right on the main road and immediately bear right again at large traffic island. Go 50 yards to end (Margin Street on right).

29. Turn right on Margin Street, following the water on your right, and go $3/10$ mile to fork where Atlantic Avenue bears left and Howard Gleason Road bears right.

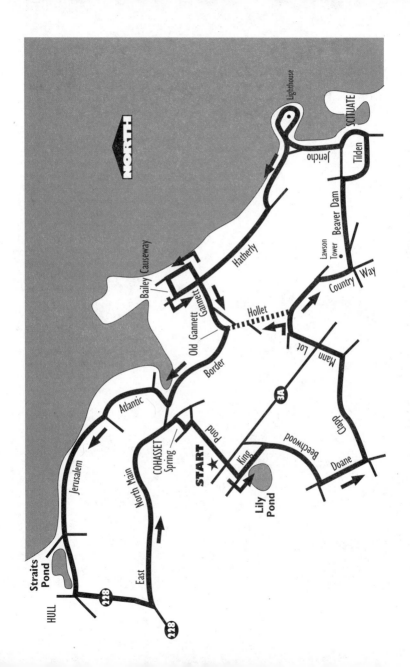

Atlantic surf, Scituate

30. Bear left on Atlantic Avenue and go $7/10$ mile to another fork with a large flower pot in the middle (Beach Street turns left, the main road bears right).

31. Bear right at fork (still Atlantic Avenue) and go $1^9/10$ miles to crossroads and stop sign. This is a magnificent run along the coast.

32. Go straight at crossroads onto Jerusalem Road (don't bear right along the ocean). Go 1 mile to another crossroads and stop sign (Hull Street, Route 228 on left). You'll ride along Straits Pond and pass a handsome stone Greek Orthodox church on your right just before the crossroads.

33. Turn 90 degrees left on Route 228 and go $1^1/10$ miles to East Street, which turns sharply left at several small traffic islands (a sign may say TO COHASSET). Just before the intersection, on your right, you'll pass Glastonbury Abbey, a Benedictine monastery open to visitors. It contains a bookstore, a chapel, a lovely stone bell tower, and an enclosure with barnyard animals.

34. Turn sharply left on East Street (**CAUTION** here). Go $2^7/10$ miles to fork where Elm Street (unmarked) bears left and the main road bears slightly right, in downtown Cohasset. You'll go past the lovely town green just before the fork.

35. Bear right on the main road and go less than $2/10$ mile to Spring Street, a small road that bears right opposite the library.

36. Bear right on Spring Street and go $1/10$ mile to end (Cushing Road).

37. Turn left at end and go 100 yards to your first right, Pond Street, which goes up a short, steep hill.

38. Turn right on Pond Street and go $1/2$ mile to school on right.

Directions for the ride: 17 miles

1. Follow directions for the long ride through number 10.

2. Turn left on Hollett Street and go $8/10$ mile to end, at stop sign (merge to your right at bottom of hill).

3. Bear right at end and go $1/10$ mile to fork.

4. Bear left at fork and immediately bear left again on Border Street (unmarked). Go $1^2/10$ miles to a little bridge over an inlet. This is a delightful spot, with Cohasset Cove on your right.

5. Follow directions for the long ride from number 27 to the end.

Scituate–Marshfield

Number of miles: 27 (16 without Marshfield extension)
Terrain: Gently rolling, with a couple of short hills and two long, gradual ones.
Food: Grocery store and restaurants in Scituate. Grocery store in Humarock.
Start: Scituate High School, Route 3A, just north of First Parish Road, next to the police station and town offices.

This ride takes you exploring the midsection of the South Shore, midway between Boston and Plymouth. This area, bisected by the marsh-lined North River, is more rural than suburban, with gentle wooded hills and some prosperous farms sloping down to the river. Paralleling the shore, you'll pass extensive salt marshes at the river's mouth and loop around three headlands standing guard above the ocean.

The ride starts from Scituate, an affluent community that boasts a large green with a Civil War monument in the middle, a graceful white church, and one of the state's more striking landmarks, the 150-foot-high Lawson Tower. This is a water tower covered on the outside by wooden shingles and donated to the town in 1902 by Thomas Lawson, a copper magnate. Atop the tower is a set of bells that are played on special town occasions.

From Scituate you'll head south to Marshfield, inland from the coast. Marshfield is primarily a gracious rural community that unfortunately is becoming suburban because of its proximity to Route 3. The ride sticks to the unspoiled sections, heading through wooded hills and then along the salt marshes bordering the South and North rivers. A small detour brings you through the beach community of Humarock, attractively located on a long, narrow peninsula with the open sea on one side and the South River, a tidal estuary, on the other. After crossing the North River back into Scituate, you'll pedal past broad salt marshes to the coast, where you'll go through two attractive oceanfront communities, Rivermoor and Second Cliff, both commanding headlands jutting into the ocean. From Second Cliff it's a short ride through the center of town back to your starting point.

Directions for the ride: 27 miles

1. Turn left from the school driveway onto Route 3A and just ahead turn right at traffic light onto First Parish Road. Go ⁶/₁₀ mile to crossroads (Grove Street).

2. Turn left on Grove Street and go 2⁴/₁₀ miles to end (Main Street, Route 123). You'll go straight at two crossroads and stop signs.

3. Turn left on Route 123 and go ³/₁₀ mile to Bridge Street on right.

4. Turn right on Bridge Street and go 1¹/₁₀ miles to fork where Highland Street bears left. You'll cross the North River and climb a long, gradual hill. **CAUTION:** The metal-grate bridge over the river is very slippery when wet. Walk across if the road is wet.

5. Bear left on Highland Street, and just ahead turn left at end (still Highland Street). Go ½ mile to Spring Street on left, just past bottom of big hill. Here the short ride turns left and the long ride goes straight.

6. Continue straight on Highland Street. After ⁹/₁₀ mile you'll merge head-on at a yield sign. Go straight for 2¹/₁₀ miles to the third crossroads and stop sign (Furnace Street), just after school on right.

7. Turn left on Furnace Street and go ⁴/₁₀ mile to traffic light (Route 3A, Main Street).

8. Turn right on Route 3A and go 1 mile to South River Street on left, immediately after the Marshfield Fairgrounds on left.

9. Turn left on South River Street. Just ahead on your right is the former Marshfield town hall, a handsome wooden Victorian building dated 1895. Continue 1½ miles to fork at traffic island (Grove Street bears left).

10. Bear right at fork (still South River Street) and go 1²/₁₀ miles to another fork where the main road bears slightly right. You'll climb a short, steep hill.

11. Bear slightly right at fork and go ¹/₁₀ mile to stop sign (merge to your right into Ferry Street, unmarked).

12. Bear right on Ferry Street and go ⁶/₁₀ mile to Bayberry Road on right. It's just after Blueberry Road, also on right.

13. Turn right on Bayberry Road. Stay on main road for ⁴/₁₀ mile to crossroads and stop sign after bridge. This is Humarock. The ocean is 100 yards in front of you.

14. Turn left at crossroads and go ¹/₂ mile to another crossroads and stop sign (Marshfield Avenue, unmarked). You'll follow the South River, a tidal inlet, on your left.

15. Turn left on Marshfield Avenue and go ²/₁₀ mile to crossroads immediately after bridge.

16. Turn right at crossroads, going along the harbor on your right. After ¹/₁₀ mile the main road turns 90 degrees left up a short, steep hill. Go 100 yards up the hill to Preston Terrace, which turns sharply right at the top of the hill.

17. Make a hairpin right turn on Preston Terrace and go ³/₁₀ mile to crossroads almost at top of hill (Pollard Street). There's a magnificent view of the South River and Humarock Beach to your right. You'll see another part of Pollard Street on your left before you come to the crossroads, but continue straight for ¹/₁₀ mile to the crossroads. **CAUTION:** Watch for bumps, potholes, and sandy spots along this street.

18. Turn right on Pollard Street and go 1 short block to another crossroads.

19. Turn right at crossroads and go ⁴/₁₀ mile to end (merge head-on into a larger road). **CAUTION:** There is no stop sign here.

20. Go straight at end for ³/₁₀ mile to Summer Street, which bears right at traffic island.

21. Bear right on Summer Street and go 1⁶/₁₀ miles to a large, grassy traffic island where Summer Street bears right and Prospect Street goes straight. A little pond is on your right at the intersection.

22. Bear right on Summer Street and go ⁷/₁₀ mile to Route 3A, at another large, grassy traffic island. You'll climb a long, gradual hill.

23. Bear right at traffic island onto Route 3A. Go 1⁴/₁₀ miles to a road that bears right just before traffic light (sign may say SCITUATE, 2 MILES).

24. Bear right just before light, and immediately turn right on Driftway. Go 1³/₁₀ miles to where Driftway bears right onto a smaller road (a sign may say THIRD CLIFF, SCITUATE COUNTRY CLUB).

25. Bear right on Driftway. After ⁶/₁₀ mile the road turns 90 degrees right along the ocean onto Collier Road. Continue ⁸/₁₀ mile to end. You'll loop around the headland of Rivermoor.

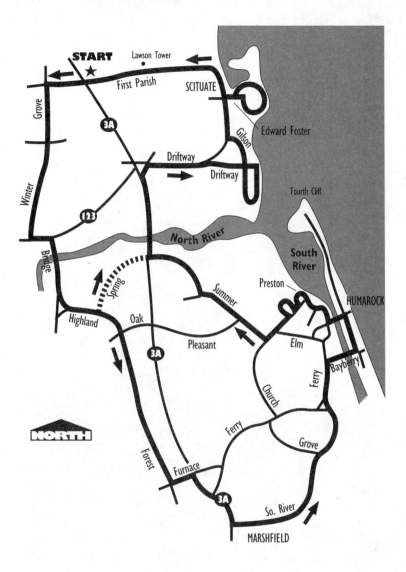

Lawson Tower, Scituate

26. At end turn left and then immediately right on Gilson Road. Go $^7/_{10}$ mile to end.

27. Turn right at end and go $^6/_{10}$ mile to crossroads and stop sign (Edward Foster Road).

28. Turn right on Edward Foster Road and go $^3/_{10}$ mile to crossroads immediately after little bridge (Peggotty Beach Road on right). You will now loop around the Second Cliff headland.

29. Turn right at crossroads, following a tidal marsh and then the ocean on your right. After $^7/_{10}$ mile, bear right across the same bridge and go $^3/_{10}$ mile to crossroads and stop sign (Front Street on right).

30. Turn right at crossroads and go $1^8/_{10}$ miles to a five-way intersection where Branch Street bears right and Beaver Dam Road bears slightly left (almost straight). You'll go through downtown Scituate and then straight at two traffic lights.

31. Bear slightly left on Beaver Dam Road, passing the Scituate town green on your left, and go $^4/_{10}$ mile to traffic light (Country Way). You'll see the Lawson Tower on your right just beyond the green.

32. Go straight at light for $^1/_2$ mile to Route 3A, at traffic light.

33. Turn right on Route 3A. The high school is just ahead on right.

Directions for the ride: 16 miles 〰️〰️〰️

1. Follow directions for the long ride through number 5.

2. Turn left on Spring Street and go $1^3/_{10}$ miles to wide crossroads and stop sign (Route 3A).

3. Turn left on Route 3A and go $1^4/_{10}$ miles to a road that bears right just before traffic light (sign may say SCITUATE, 2 MILES).

4. Follow directions for the long ride from number 24 to the end.

Duxbury–Marshfield

Number of miles: 27 (20 without Marshfield extension)
Terrain: Gently rolling.
Food: Grocery stores in Marshfield. McDonald's at end.
Start: McDonald's, in the Kingsbury Square shopping center, at the junction of Routes 3A and 53 in Kingston. It's just west of Route 3; take exit 10. If you're heading south on Route 3, turn right at the end of the exit ramp. If you're heading north on Route 3, turn left at end of ramp.

The South Shore coast just north of Plymouth provides superb bicycling. The protected waters of Kingston and Duxbury bays are lined with graceful old homes from the 1800s and even earlier. The coast itself, consisting mainly of slender peninsulas with the sea on one side and salt marshes on the other, is beautiful; inland lies a serene, rural landscape of cranberry bogs, small ponds, and snug, cedar-shingled homes.

The ride starts from Duxbury, one of the most affluent and thoroughly unspoiled of the Boston suburbs. The town green, graced by the handsome, pillared town hall and a classic white church, is one of the most dignified in the state. First you'll parallel the shore of Kingston Bay to the Myles Standish monument, a graceful stone tower 100 feet high on top of a hill that rises 200 feet from the shore. The view from the top is as dramatic as any in the state. Unfortunately, like so many of the most interesting places in Massachusetts, it's open only during the summer. From here you'll follow Duxbury Bay to the picturesque Currier-and-Ives village of Snug Harbor, with a rambling wooden block of stores and gracious old homes just inland from the harbor full of boats. Just ahead is Powder Point, a peninsula lined with mansions and estates. One of them, the King Caesar House, is a Federal-era beauty open to the public on summer afternoons. It was built in 1807 by Ezra Weston, nicknamed King Caesar, one of the many post-Revolutionary merchant princes who made millions in shipbuilding and the China trade and then flaunted their success by constructing mansions on the Massachusetts coast.

From Powder Point you'll cross the bay over the Powder Point Bridge, a narrow wooden span nearly half a mile long. On the far side is Duxbury Beach, the South Shore's finest. Completely undeveloped, it extends southward 4 miles along a fragile sandy spit of land only a tenth of a mile wide. You'll head north along the ocean to Brant Rock, another peninsula with a road hugging the rocky coastline. Beyond Brant Rock you'll enter an area of beach cottages across the town line in Marshfield, which is more built-up and not as well-to-do as Duxbury. You'll now head a short distance inland and then return south into Duxbury along Route 3A, a smooth, quiet road lined with handsome houses and small farms. At the end of the ride you can visit the Duxbury Art Complex Museum, a striking modern building opened in 1971. From here it's a short trip back to the start past the town green.

The short ride takes a more direct route back to the start after crossing the Powder Point Bridge. You'll pass the Governor Winslow House, built in 1699 and one of the finer historic houses on the South Shore, with a full complement of period furnishings. On the grounds are Daniel Webster's law office and a blacksmith shop. Across the street is a schoolhouse built in 1857, now headquarters of the Marshfield Historical Society.

Directions for the ride: 27 miles

1. When you leave the shopping center, go straight at traffic light onto Route 3A for $8/10$ mile to crossroads (Oak Street on left, Park Street on right).
2. Turn right on Park Street and go $4/10$ mile to fork (Loring Street bears left).
3. Bear left at fork and go $2/10$ mile to stop sign (Bay Road).
4. Turn left on Bay Road and go $2^1/10$ miles to crossroads and stop sign in the village of South Duxbury. Some fine views of Kingston Bay lie to your right.
5. Turn right at stop sign on Standish Street. Go $4/10$ mile to Crescent Street, a smaller road that bears right.
6. Bear right on Crescent Street. After $4/10$ mile, the road to the Myles Standish Monument bears left uphill. It's a steady grade, $3/10$ mile to the top.

7. Continue 1 mile to stop sign (Marshall Street on right). **CAUTION:** Midway along this stretch the road curves sharply left at bottom of steep hill.

8. Continue straight at stop sign for $\frac{1}{2}$ mile to crossroads and stop sign (Washington Street on right). You're back in South Duxbury.

9. Turn right at crossroads and go $1\frac{9}{10}$ miles to an intersection with a flagpole in the middle. (There's a fork immediately after the intersection.) Half a mile before the intersection you'll go through Snug Harbor. It's worth taking one of the little lanes on the right to the bay.

10. Immediately after the flagpole, bear right on main road (Powder Point Avenue), following the harbor on your right. Go $\frac{2}{10}$ mile to King Caesar Road, which bears right.

11. Bear right on King Caesar Road and go $\frac{1}{2}$ mile to fork (Weston Road bears left). You'll pass the King Caesar House.

12. Bear right at fork (still King Caesar Road) and go $\frac{7}{10}$ mile to the beginning of the Powder Point Bridge.

13. Cross the bridge. During the summer a police officer may be stationed at either end of the bridge to make sure that only Duxbury residents drive across, but you're perfectly okay on a bike. At the far end of the bridge, the ocean is 100 yards in front of you. Turn left into the Duxbury Beach parking lot.

14. At the far end of the parking lot, continue $\frac{1}{4}$ mile along a dirt road. Walk your bike; most of this stretch is soft sand. At the end of the dirt section, you'll enter another beach parking lot.

15. Continue straight for $1\frac{2}{10}$ miles to Bay Street on right, immediately after the Marshfield town line. Here the short ride goes straight and the long ride turns right.

16. Turn right on Bay Street and go $\frac{7}{10}$ mile to dead end, where you have a fine view of Green Harbor. Backtrack $\frac{1}{10}$ mile to your first right, at stop sign.

17. Turn right, crossing little bridge, and go less than $\frac{2}{10}$ mile to Marginal Street on right.

18. Turn right on Marginal Street and go $\frac{3}{10}$ mile to end (Route 139). You'll pass an old-fashioned country store on your right after $\frac{1}{10}$ mile.

19. Turn right on Route 139 and go $\frac{6}{10}$ mile to end, at a wide intersection. This is the village of Brant Rock. At the end, notice the fine stone church on the left. You will now head out to the Brant Rock peninsula.

20. Turn right at end onto a wide divided road and go $\frac{2}{10}$ mile to fork

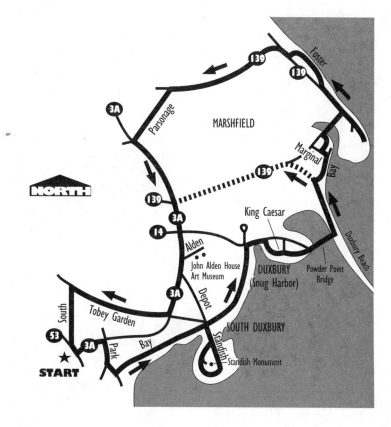

Myles Standish Monument

(Island Street, unmarked, bears right).

21. Bear left at fork, following the ocean on your left, and go ½ mile to the dead end.

22. Make a U-turn at the end and backtrack ⁷/₁₀ mile until you come back to Route 139. You'll see Brant Rock jutting into the ocean.

23. Go straight onto Route 139, still following the ocean on your right, for ⁶/₁₀ mile to Foster Avenue (unmarked), which bears right.

24. Bear right on Foster Avenue. After ⁷/₁₀ mile, the road turns 90 degrees left. Continue ¹/₁₀ mile to end (Route 139 again).

25. Turn right on Route 139. Just ahead Route 139 bears left at a fork. Stay on Route 139 for 1⁸/₁₀ miles to Parsonage Street on left, immediately after police station on left.

26. Turn left on Parsonage Street. After ½ mile you'll come to a crossroads and stop sign (Webster Street). Continue straight for ⁷/₁₀ mile to traffic island.

27. Bear left at traffic island and immediately turn left on Route 3A. Go 2⁴/₁₀ miles to traffic light (Saint George Street on left, Route 14 on right).

28. Continue straight on Route 3A for 1⁸/₁₀ miles to crossroads and blinking light (Tobey Garden Street on right). You'll go by the Duxbury town green on your right. To visit the Duxbury Art Complex Museum, turn left after ⁴/₁₀ mile on Alden Street. The Museum is just ahead on your right. The John Alden House, built in 1653, is ²/₁₀ mile beyond the museum, set back from the road on your right.

29. Turn right on Tobey Garden Street and go 1⁹/₁₀ miles to South Street (unmarked), which turns left at a little green. It's ³/₁₀ mile after bridge over Route 3. This is the Tree of Knowledge Corner. A tablet on the green explains the origin of the name.

30. Turn left on South Street and go 1²/₁₀ miles to end (Route 53).

31. Turn left on Route 53. Shopping center is just ahead on right.

Directions for the ride: 20 miles

1. Follow directions for the long ride through number 15.

2. Continue straight for ⁷/₁₀ mile to wide crossroads (Route 139).

3. Turn left on Route 139 and go 2 miles to Route 3A (Enterprise Street), at stop sign. You'll pass the Governor Winslow House on your right after ⁶/₁₀ mile.

4. Turn left on Route 3A and go $8/10$ mile to traffic light (Route 14 on right).

5. Continue straight on Route 3A for $1\,8/10$ miles to crossroads and blinking light (Tobey Garden Street on right). To visit the Duxbury Art Complex Museum, turn left after $4/10$ mile to Alden Street. The Museum is just ahead on your right. The John Alden House, built in 1653, is $2/10$ mile beyond the museum, set back from the road on your right. Beyond Alden Street you'll go by the Duxbury town green on your right.

6. Follow directions for the long ride from number 29 to the end.

South Shore Scenic Circuit:
Norwell–Pembroke–Hanson–Hanover

Number of miles: 27 (17 without Pembroke–Hanson extension)
Terrain: Gently rolling, with several gradual hills.
Food: Groceries and restaurants in the towns. McDonald's at end.
Start: McDonald's, Route 53 in Hanover, ⁴⁄₁₀ mile south of Route 3. It's opposite Hanover Mall. Take exit 13 from Route 3.

If the parking lot is designated "Customers Only" or limited to a short period of time, start from Circuit City at the southern end of Hanover Mall. Park in the lot at the side of the building, near the customer pick-up area.

The pond-studded, largely rural landscape just inland from the shoulder of land jutting east between Boston and Plymouth offers delightful bicycling. The region is fairly affluent, with large, spacious homes nestled among pine groves; impeccable gentleman farms with rustic barns and rambling Colonial-style farmhouses; and trim, cedar-shingled houses with peaked roofs. The area is far enough from Boston to be more rural than suburban, although new homes and businesses keep springing up near Route 3 in Pembroke. The North River, a tidal stream meandering through salt marshes, flows through the area.

The ride starts through the gracious town of Norwell, an affluent but unpretentious community filled with homes dating back to the early 1800s and even the 1700s. From Norwell you'll proceed to Hanover, another fine old town with a beautiful town hall topped by a cupola, built in 1863, and a handsome brick library next to it. Most people know Hanover by its congested commercial strip on Route 53, where the ride starts, but when you get away from this road, the rest of the town is delightful.

The long ride heads farther south across the North River into a more rural area of pines and ponds. In Pembroke you'll skirt the edge of the cranberry-growing region farther south and ride along the Pembroke Herring Run, a small cascading stream and picnic area that makes a great rest stop. Every spring, millions of herring swim upstream to spawn. The migration, which lasts about a week, occurs around April 19, although the actual dates vary each year depending on the temperature of the water. Just past the Herring Run is the center of Pembroke, with an attractive library, old school building, and white church.

From Pembroke you'll weave past a pleasing cluster of ponds into Hanson. Hanson is another attractive town—with a marvelous Victorian town hall, built in 1872—which commands the head of Wampatuck Pond. From Hanson you'll head over to Hanover, where you'll pick up the route of the short ride.

Directions for the ride: 27 miles

1. Turn right out of parking lot onto Route 53 and go $\frac{2}{10}$ mile to Mill Street on left, at traffic light.

If you start from Hanover Mall, turn left from the southern end of the shopping center onto Mill Street, a narrow two-lane road (don't get on Route 53). Go $\frac{2}{10}$ mile to a wide fork where South Street bears left. Resume with direction number 3.)

2. Turn left on Mill Street. **CAUTION** making this turn. Go less than $\frac{4}{10}$ mile to a wide fork (South Street bears left).

3. Bear left on South Street and go $\frac{3}{10}$ mile to fork just beyond the bridge over Route 3 (Pleasant Street bears right).

4. Bear left (still South Street) and go $\frac{8}{10}$ mile to end (Route 123, Main Street).

5. Turn left on Route 123 and go 100 yards to Prospect Street on right.

6. Turn right on Prospect Street and go $1\frac{6}{10}$ miles to crossroads and stop sign (Grove Street).

7. Turn right on Grove Street and go $1\frac{1}{10}$ miles to fork (School Street bears left).

8. Bear left on School Street and go $\frac{1}{2}$ mile to end (Mount Blue Street).

9. Turn right on Mount Blue Street and go $\frac{6}{10}$ mile to fork (Lincoln Street bears right).

10. Bear left at fork (still Mount Blue Street) and go $1\frac{2}{10}$ miles to end (Old Oaken Bucket Road, unmarked).

11. Turn right at end and go $\frac{3}{10}$ mile to end (Central Street on left, Norwell Avenue on right).

12. Turn left on Central Street and go $\frac{9}{10}$ mile to crossroads and stop sign (Route 123, Main Street). On the far side of the intersection is a little

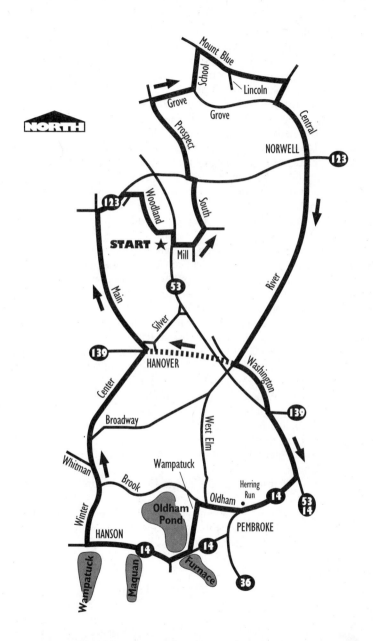

green and a fine, traditional white church. This is the center of Norwell.

13. Continue straight for 3^6/10 miles to crossroads and stop sign (Washington Street). Here the short ride turns right and the long ride turns left.

14. Turn left on Washington Street and go ^{8}/10 mile to end (Routes 53 and 139). You'll cross the North River.

15. Turn left on Routes 53 and 139. **CAUTION:** Busy intersection. Just ahead, continue straight at traffic light onto Route 53. Go 1^3/10 miles to Route 14 West (Barker Street), which bears right.

16. Bear right on Route 14 and go 1^1/2 miles to where Route 14 curves left and Oldham Street goes straight, as you come into the center of Pembroke. You'll pass the Pembroke Herring Run on your right after a mile.

17. Go straight on Oldham Street for ^{7}/10 mile to fork where West Elm Street bears right.

18. Bear left (still Oldham Street) and go ^{2}/10 mile to Wampatuck Street on left.

19. Turn left on Wampatuck Street and go ^{9}/10 mile to end (Route 14, Mattakeesett Street). You'll follow Oldham Pond on the right and pass a beach near the end. At the end, Furnace Pond is in front of you.

20. Turn right on Route 14 and go ^{2}/10 mile to fork where Route 14 bears right onto Maquan Street.

21. Bear right on Route 14 and go 1^4/10 miles to stop sign (merge right on Route 58). You'll pass Maquan Pond on your left.

22. Bear right on Route 58 and go ^{3}/10 mile to Winter Street on right, at traffic light. The striking Hanson town hall is on your left immediately after the intersection, overlooking Wampatuck Pond.

23. Turn right on Winter Street. Stay on main road for 1^1/2 miles to crossroads and stop sign (East Washington Street).

24. Continue straight for ^{6}/10 mile to fork where Center Street bears left and Broadway bears right.

25. Bear left on Center Street and go ^{7}/10 mile to crossroads and stop sign (Myrtle Street).

26. Continue straight for 1^1/10 miles to end (Route 139) in the center of Hanover.

27. Turn right on Route 139 and immediately left before the church onto Center Street. Go 50 yards to stop sign (Main Street). Notice the town hall and library across from the church.

28. Bear left at stop sign and go 2^4/10 miles to traffic light (Webster Street, Route 123).

29. Turn right on Route 123 and go ⁶⁄₁₀ mile to Woodland Drive on right.

30. Turn right on Woodland Drive. Just ahead the main road bears left. Bear left and go ¹⁄₁₀ mile to where the main road turns right; it's a dead end if you go straight.

31. Turn right and stay on the main road for ⁹⁄₁₀ mile to end (Route 53, Washington Street).

32. Turn right on Route 53. McDonald's is just ahead on right. If you started from the mall, jog right on Route 53 and immediately left into mall (**CAUTION** here).

Directions for the ride: 17 miles

1. Follow directions for the long ride through number 13.

2. Turn right on Washington Street and go ¹⁄₁₀ mile to fork (Rockland Street bears left).

3. Bear left on Rockland Street (don't turn sharply left on Church Street). Go ¹⁄₄ mile to traffic light (Route 53).

4. Cross Route 53 onto Route 139. **CAUTION:** Busy intersection. Go 1³⁄₁₀ miles to Center Street on right, immediately after old white church on right. This is the center of Hanover. Notice the town hall opposite the church and the brick library next to the town hall.

5. Turn right on Center Street and go 50 yards to stop sign (Main Street).

6. Follow directions for the long ride from number 28 to the end.

45

Canton–Stoughton–
North Easton–Sharon

Number of miles: 26 (16 without North Easton extension)
Terrain: Gently rolling.
Food: Grocery stores and snack bars in the towns. Ground Round Restaurant at end.
Start: Ground Round, junction of Routes 1 and 27 in Walpole, just north of the Sharon line. The restaurant is on the southeast corner of the intersection.

This ride takes you exploring a cluster of four pleasant suburban communities about 20 miles south of Boston and just northwest of Brockton. The landscape is semirural and semisuburban. The long ride goes through North Easton, a classic nineteenth-century planned industrial community with a collection of magnificent stone buildings.

The ride heads first through a rural stretch of Sharon into Canton, where you'll see the Canton Viaduct, a graceful stone-arched railroad abutment crossing a small valley. It was built in 1834 and is a landmark of early railroad engineering. Built to accommodate the small, slow-moving early trains, it now supports the continuous traffic of the Boston to New York main line. Beyond the viaduct you'll bike past Reservoir Pond and head into Stoughton, a middle-class residential community, and then into Easton.

Shortly after you cross the town line, you'll come to North Easton, a village of impressive elegance bearing the stamp of one man, Oliver Ames. Ames was a nineteenth-century industrialist who amassed his fortune making shovels, of all things, including most of the shovels used to build the railroads and mine the earth of the developing West. After making his millions, he decided to donate money to construct a village that his workers could be proud of, and so he hired the foremost architect of the day, H. H. Richardson, and the foremost landscape designer, Frederick Law Olmsted, to do the job. Coming into town, you'll pass the handsome stone railroad station with its graceful arched entryway. Then you'll see the Ames Memorial Hall, an imposing Victorian building. Next to this is the Ames Free Library, one of the most beautiful in the state, a fine stone edifice with a clock tower and an ornate, wood-paneled interior. It was built in 1883. Just past the library is an ornate stone church with a tall, slender spire. In the middle of the town's main intersection is a small, rocky terraced park, complete with a stone archway, called the Rockery. It was designed by Olmsted in 1879.

Leaving North Easton, you can go about a mile off the route to visit the largest solar-heated community in New England. The route goes along lovely Ames Long Pond (it seems everything in town is named Ames) and proceeds into the center of Sharon, a pleasant upper-middle-class community with lots of rural land. Just outside town is the Kendall Whaling Museum, a one-man collection of whaling objects and art. The homestretch brings you past an Audubon sanctuary at the base of 530-foot Moose Hill, the highest point in southeastern Massachusetts outside of the Blue Hills.

Directions for the ride: 26 miles

1. Turn right (east) out of parking lot onto Route 27 and go 1 mile to crossroads and stop sign where Route 27 turns right.
2. Go straight at crossroads for 2^7/10 miles to end. The first half mile is downhill. At the end, the Canton Viaduct is on your right.
3. Turn left at end and go ¼ mile to fork where Chapman Street bears right. As soon as you turn, there's a little dam on the right, with the stream flowing from beneath the viaduct.
4. Bear right on Chapman Street and go 1^2/10 miles to end (Washington Street). If you make a hairpin right turn just after the railroad bridge and go ^{2}/10 mile, you'll come to an old stone railroad station.
5. Turn left on Washington Street and go ^{3}/10 mile to Pleasant Street on right. Here the ride turns right, but if you go straight for 200 yards you'll come to a beautiful old church and school on the left.
6. Turn right on Pleasant Street and go 3^3/10 miles to Central Street, at the second of two traffic lights about ^{2}/10 mile apart. Here the short ride turns right and the long ride goes straight. Just after you turn onto Pleasant Street, you'll see Pequitside Farm, a small recreation area owned by the town of Canton, on your right. A short distance ahead you'll see Reservoir Pond on your left.

7. Go straight at traffic light for $^7/_{10}$ mile to second stop sign (Route 138), in the center of Stoughton.

8. Go straight at stop sign onto Route 138 for $^1/_{10}$ mile to fork where Route 138 bears right and Route 27 bears left.

9. Bear left on Route 27 and go $^3/_{10}$ mile to Sumner Street, which bears right.

10. Bear right on Sumner Street and go 2$^6/_{10}$ miles to end.

11. Turn right at end onto Union and go $^8/_{10}$ mile to end (Route 138). You'll pass French Pond on your right.

12. Turn left on Route 138 and go $^7/_{10}$ mile to Elm Street. It's a cross-roads with a cemetery on the far right-hand corner.

13. Turn right on Elm Street and go $^8/_{10}$ mile to Oliver Street on left. You'll pass on your left an arched stone gatehouse designed by H. H. Richardson.

14. Turn left on Oliver Street and go $^1/_{10}$ mile to Mechanic Street on left. The road turns 90 degrees right immediately before the intersection.

15. Turn left on Mechanic Street and go $^3/_{10}$ mile to end. You'll pass the railroad station, built in 1881, on your right, now maintained by the Easton Historical Society. Behind the station are the long stone buildings of the Ames shovel factory, recently recycled into offices. A children's museum, formerly an old fire station, is on the left just before the end.

16. Turn right at end. Just ahead is a fork. The little terraced park in the middle of the fork is the Rockery. Here the ride bears right, but if you bear slightly left on Lincoln Street for $^8/_{10}$ mile and turn left on Mahoney Road (sign may say TO MILITIA PARK) and go 200 yards, you'll come to the solar condominiums.

17. Bear right at fork and go $^4/_{10}$ mile to Canton Street, which bears left. You'll pass the Memorial Hall, the library, and the stone church on the left. The library is worth going to if it's open.

18. Bear left on Canton Street and go 1$^3/_{10}$ miles to West Street, which bears right at stop sign. You'll go along Ames Long Pond.

19. Bear right on West Street, crossing the lake over a causeway, and go 1$^7/_{10}$ miles to crossroads and stop sign (Plain Street).

20. Go straight at crossroads. After $^7/_{10}$ mile School Street bears right, but go straight on West Street for $^8/_{10}$ mile to Chemung Street, which bears left uphill at a wooded traffic island.

21. Bear left on Chemung Street and go $^6/_{10}$ mile to crossroads and stop sign (Bay Road).

22. Turn right at crossroads onto Bay Road and go $^4/_{10}$ mile to East Street

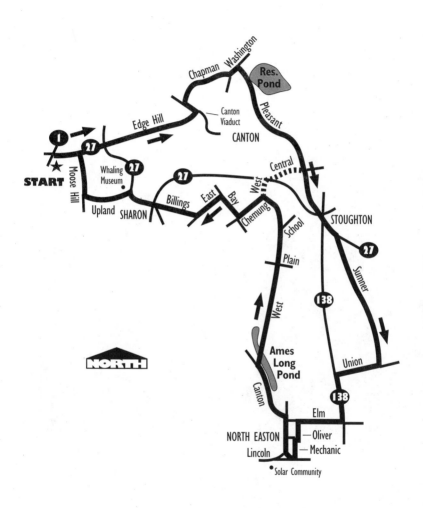

Stoughton Water Works

on left. There's a fantastic ice cream place at the intersection.

23. Turn left on East Street and go $7/10$ mile to Billings Street, which bears right at bottom of hill.

24. Bear right on Billings Street and go 1 mile to traffic light in the center of Sharon (Route 27 goes straight and right). After $2/10$ mile you'll pass a small dam on your left and Manns Pond. When you get to Route 27, notice the fine white church on the far side of the intersection.

25. Go straight at traffic light onto Route 27. After $1/2$ mile the road curves sharply right at large traffic island with a house on it.

26. At the far end of the traffic island, make a U-turn to the left, then immediately bear right downhill on Upland Road, a narrow lane (sign may say KENDALL WHALING MUSEUM). Go $2/10$ mile to where Upland Road curves sharply left and Everett Street turns right. Here the ride bears left, but if you turn right and continue 200 yards you'll come to the Whaling Museum.

27. Bear left, staying on Upland Road, and go $1/2$ mile to stop sign (merge head-on onto Moose Hill Parkway).

28. Continue straight for $1/2$ mile to end (Moose Hill Street). Here the ride turns right, but the entrance to the Moose Hill Audubon Sanctuary is 50 feet to your left.

29. Turn right at end and go $14/10$ miles to end (Route 27).

30. Turn left on Route 27 and go $4/10$ mile to Ground Round on left. **CAUTION** turning left into parking lot.

Directions for the ride: 16 miles

1. Follow directions for the long ride through number 6.

2. Turn right on Central Street and go $8/10$ mile to end, at stop sign (merge right on Route 27).

3. Bear right on Route 27 and go $2/10$ mile to West Street on left. It's immediately after the Stoughton Water Works, an ornate building dated 1892, on your left.

4. Turn left on West Street and go $3/10$ mile to fork (Chemung Street bears right uphill).

5. Bear right on Chemung Street and go $6/10$ mile to crossroads and stop sign (Bay Road).

6. Follow directions for the long ride from number 22 to the end.

46

Sharon–Easton–Norton–Mansfield–Foxboro

Number of miles: 32 (15 without Easton–Norton–Foxboro extension)
Terrain: Flat.
Food: None on the short ride. Grocery and snack bar in Mansfield. Snack bar at end.
Start: Shaw's Plaza, South Main Street, Sharon, just east of Interstate 95 at the South Main Street–Mechanic Street exit (exit 8).

On this ride you'll explore a delightfully rural, lake-dotted area 10 miles west of Brockton. Flat terrain, smooth secondary roads, and a spin along the shore of Massapoag Lake in Sharon make for relaxed pedaling. The longer ride passes the gracious old campus of Wheaton College in Norton.

The ride starts from Sharon, an attractive, upper-middle-class community. It has a few housing developments, but most of the town is still rural. The focal point of the community is refreshingly unspoiled Massapoag Lake, most of its shoreline graced by handsome older homes. You'll follow the lakeshore for half its perimeter and then head through woods and farmlands into Easton. At the town line you'll pass Borderlands State Park, an idyllic expanse of meadows and woodland surrounding Leach Pond, with paths looping around its shore. The park headquarters is a magnificent stone mansion that formerly belonged to the Ames family, whose legacy is concentrated in nearby North Easton.

The long ride heads farther south through prosperous farmlands into Norton, one of the most pleasantly rural towns within commuting distance of Boston. In the center of town is Wheaton College, a small, high-quality school with a traditional, tree-shaded campus of stately ivy-covered buildings. At the center of the campus is a perfect little pond. Just north of the campus is the Norton Reservoir, another good-sized lake that you'll skirt briefly. The return to Sharon passes through the rural eastern edges of Mansfield and Foxboro.

Directions for the ride: 32 miles ～～～～～～～～

1. Turn right (northeast) out of parking lot and go $^6/_{10}$ mile to Wolomolopoag Street on your right.

2. Turn right on Wolomolopoag Street and go $1\frac{1}{2}$ miles to end (East Foxboro Street).

3. Turn left at end and go $1\frac{1}{2}$ miles to fork where one road bears left and Beach Street goes straight.

4. Continue straight at fork. You'll immediately see Massapoag Lake on your right. Go $^9/_{10}$ mile to end (Pond Street).

5. Turn right at end. Just ahead is a little rotary. Continue straight, following the lake, for $4\frac{1}{2}$ miles to crossroads and stop sign (Rockland Street). Here the short ride turns right and the long ride goes straight. The entrance to Borderlands State Park is 1 mile before the crossroads and the Ames mansion is just beyond the entrance. **CAUTION:** Watch for bumps and potholes for the last mile.

6. Go straight at crossroads for $1^3/_{10}$ miles to end, at stop sign. **CAUTION:** Watch for potholes on this direction and the next one.

7. Turn right at end and go $1^2/_{10}$ miles to South Street on left. The main road curves sharply right at the intersection.

8. Turn left on South Street and go $^2/_{10}$ mile to crossroads and stop sign (Foundry Street, Route 106).

9. Cross Route 106 and go $^3/_{10}$ mile to end.

10. Turn left at end and go $^3/_{10}$ mile to end (Bay Road, unmarked).

11. Turn right on Bay Road and go $4^4/_{10}$ miles to Myles Standish Industrial Park Road on right at traffic light, just after the Interstate 495 overpass. You'll pass Winnecunnet Pond on your right about a mile before the intersection.

12. Turn right on Myles Standish Industrial Park Road and go $^3/_{10}$ mile to first right, North Boundary Road.

13. Turn right on North Boundary Road and go $2^1/_{10}$ miles to crossroads, and stop sign (Plain Street).

14. Turn left at crossroads and go $^8/_{10}$ mile to end (Pine Street).

15. Turn right at end and go $^1/_{2}$ mile to crossroads and stop sign (Route 123). Just before Route 123, Wheaton College is on your left. The campus is worth visiting.

16. Cross Route 123 onto Elm Street and go $^8/_{10}$ mile to end (Reservoir Street).

17. Turn right on Reservoir Street. You'll immediately see the Norton Reservoir on your left. Go ½ mile to Cobb Street (unmarked), which bears right just after a little bridge.

18. Bear right on Cobb Street and go ½ mile to end (North Washington Street).

19. Turn left at end and go ³⁄₁₀ mile to fork shortly after the bridge over Interstate 495 (Essex Street, unmarked, bears slightly right).

20. Bear right at fork and go 1⁴⁄₁₀ miles to end (Mill Street).

21. Turn left on Mill Street. After ½ mile, at a little green, Cherry Street (unmarked) turns right, but bear left, staying on the main road. Just ahead is a stop sign.

22. Bear slightly left at stop sign and go ½ mile to end (Route 106, Eastman Street).

23. Turn left on Route 106 and go ⁴⁄₁₀ mile to Franklin Street on right, at traffic light. There's a grocery on the right just before the corner.

24. Turn right on Franklin Street and go 2¹⁄₁₀ miles to fork where East Foxboro Street bears right and Cocasset Street (unmarked) bears left.

25. Bear left on Cocasset Street and go 1 mile to Oak Street on right, at blinking light.

26. Turn right on Oak Street and go 2¹⁄₁₀ miles to end (Mechanic Street).

27. Turn right at end and go ½ mile to shopping center on right. **CAUTION:** Watch for potholes and cracks on the bridge over Interstate 95.

Directions for the ride: 15 miles 〰️〰️〰️

1. Follow the directions for the long ride through number 5.

2. Turn right at crossroads and go 1⁶⁄₁₀ miles to crossroads and stop sign (Franklin Street).

3. Turn right on Franklin Street and go ⁹⁄₁₀ mile to fork where East Street bears right and Cocasset Street (unmarked) bears left.

4. Follow directions for the long ride from number 25 to the end.

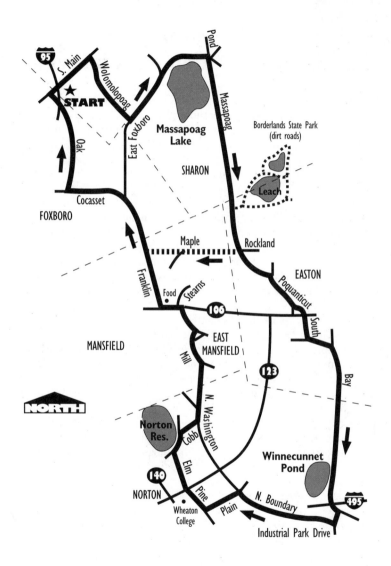

47 Foxboro–Mansfield–North Attleboro–Plainville

Number of miles: 23 (14 without Mansfield–North Attleboro extension)
Terrain: Gently rolling, with a few short hills.
Food: McDonald's and Burger King in Plainville. Country store in Mansfield. Snack bar in North Attleboro. Friendly's at end, $\frac{1}{10}$ mile south of starting point on Route 140.
Start: Foxboro town green, Route 140. Park on the southbound side of Route 140, facing the green on the left side of the road. There are no time restrictions here.
How to get there: If you're heading south on Interstate 95, take the South Main Street–Mechanic Street exit (exit 8). Turn right at end of ramp and go about $2\frac{1}{2}$ miles to the Foxboro green. Park on the far side of the green. If you're heading north on Interstate 95, exit north onto Route 140 and go about $1\frac{1}{2}$ miles to the Foxboro green. Park on the opposite side of the green.

On this ride we explore the pleasantly rural, lake-dotted countryside just south of the midpoint between Boston and Providence. The ride starts from Foxboro, an attractive town with two fine churches and a well-kept green forming a central square. A landmark in the town is a small, ornate, churchlike building that was constructed as a Civil War memorial and for many years served as the town library. From Foxboro you'll head through tidy residential areas to Plainville, a pleasant rural town consisting mainly of woods, farmland, and orchards. You'll bicycle along the shores of two unspoiled ponds, Turnpike Lake and Lake Mirimichi, in quick succession. The return to Foxboro brings you along winding, narrow lanes bobbing up and down little rises through dense forests.

The long ride proceeds further south past small farms into Mansfield, a compact mill town surrounded by rural countryside. The route stays in the sparsely settled western part of Mansfield and does not go into the center of town. As you cross into North Attleboro, you'll ride along Greenwood Lake. Just ahead you'll pass the North Attleboro National

Fish Hatchery, a fascinating spot to visit if open (its hours change frequently). You'll descend steeply into Plainville and rejoin the short ride just before Turnpike Lake.

Directions for the ride: 23 miles

1. Head south on Route 140 and just ahead turn right on South Street at end of green. As you approach South Street, notice the small, stone, churchlike Civil War memorial in front of you. Follow South Street $2^3/10$ miles to crossroads where West Street turns right and North Grove Street turns left uphill.
2. Turn left on North Grove Street and go $^6/10$ mile to end (Route 106). There's a steep hill at the beginning.
3. Turn right at end and go $^1/10$ mile to South Grove Street on left, immediately after the bridge over Interstate 495. Here the short ride goes straight and the long ride turns left.
4. Turn left on South Grove Street and go $^6/10$ mile to crossroads and stop sign (West Street).
5. Go straight at crossroads for $^9/10$ mile to end. **CAUTION:** Bumps and potholes.
6. Turn left at end and go $^4/10$ mile to stop sign where the main road bears right. **CAUTION:** Bumps and potholes.
7. Bear right at end and go $^3/10$ mile to end.
8. Turn right at end. Go $^1/10$ mile to crossroads just before a railroad overpass (White Tail Lane on left, Otis Street on right).
9. Turn right on Otis Street and go $1^2/10$ miles to end. There's a country store on your left at the beginning. You'll pass Sweets Pond on your right at the end.
10. Turn right at end and go $^9/10$ mile to fork where Bungay Road bears left and the main road goes straight. **CAUTION:** Watch for potholes.
11. Go straight at fork for $^3/10$ mile to end.
12. Turn left at end and go $^7/10$ mile to Bungay Road on right. (There are two Bungay Roads, one in Mansfield and one in North Attleboro.) You'll see Greenwood Lake on the right.
13. Turn right on Bungay Road and go $^1/2$ mile to end (Route 152). You'll pass the North Attleboro National Fish Hatchery on your right, worth visiting if it's open. Just ahead there's a little red schoolhouse built in 1810, currently used as an office, also on the right.

14. Turn left on Route 152 and go 1³/₁₀ miles to Robert F. Toner Boulevard (unmarked) on right, at traffic light (sign may say TO ROUTE 95).

15. Turn right on Robert F. Toner Boulevard and go ⁴/₁₀ mile to John Dietsch Boulevard on right, immediately before shopping center on right. **CAUTION:** Watch for traffic entering and exiting Interstate 95.

16. Turn right on John Dietsch Boulevard and go 6/10 mile to small crossroads (Towne Street, unmarked). Bliss Ice Cream, on your left in the shopping center, is a good halfway stop (the back of the snack bar is next to the road).

17. Turn left on Towne Street and go 8/10 mile to crossroads and stop sign (Commonwealth Avenue, unmarked).

18. Turn right at crossroads and go less than 4/10 mile to traffic light (Mount Hope Street, unmarked). The round brick building on the far right corner was built as a gasworks in 1855. This area is Attleboro Falls, a section of North Attleboro.

19. Turn right on Mount Hope Street and go ⁷/₁₀ mile to stop sign and blinking light (Landry Avenue).

20. Continue straight for ⁹/₁₀ mile to end (Elmwood Street, unmarked). Shift into low gear at end.

21. Turn right at end onto Elmwood Street and go 1²/₁₀ miles to end (Route 106), shortly after bottom of steep hill. After ½ mile you'll pass World War I Memorial Park on the right; there's a small zoo here and a good view from the base of a fire tower.

22. Turn left on Route 106 and go less than ²/₁₀ mile to crossroads (George Street).

23. Turn right on George Street and go ½ mile to Route 1, at stop sign.

24. Turn right on Route 1 and go ⁴/₁₀ mile to Shepard Street, which bears right. You'll pass Turnpike Lake on your right.

25. Bear right on Shepard Street, following the shore of Turnpike Lake, and go ⁴/₁₀ mile to end (Route 152).

26. Turn left on Route 152 and go ⁴/₁₀ mile to Mirimichi Street on right.

27. Turn right on Mirimichi Street. After ⁴/₁₀ mile the main road bears right and a dead-end road goes straight. Stay on main road for 1⁹/₁₀ miles to end, at traffic island. You'll go across Lake Mirimichi.

28. Turn left at end onto West and go ³/₁₀ mile to Mill Street on right (sign may say TO STATE FOREST).

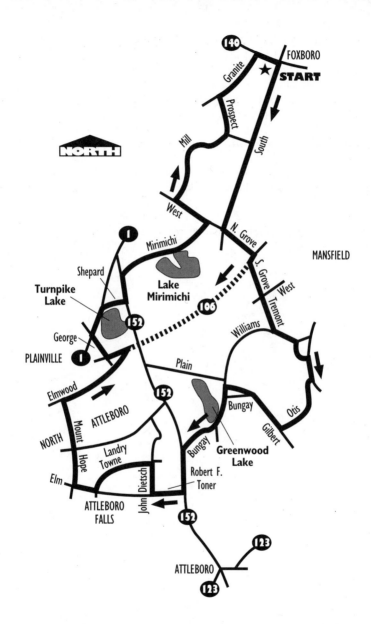

29. Turn right on Mill Street and go $1^3/_{10}$ miles to fork where Prospect Street (unmarked) bears left.

30. Bear left on Prospect Street and go $^8/_{10}$ mile to end.

31. Turn right at end onto Granite and go $^9/_{10}$ mile to end (Route 140). You'll pass Sunset Lake on your left at the beginning.

32. Turn right on Route 140. The Foxboro green is just ahead.

Directions for the ride: 14 miles

1. Follow directions for the long ride through number 3.

2. Continue straight on Route 106 for $2^1/_2$ miles to Route 152, at traffic light.

3. Cross Route 152 and go $^4/_{10}$ mile to crossroads (George Street).

4. Follow directions for the long ride from number 23 to the end.

Norton–Taunton

Number of miles: 28 (13 without Taunton extension)
Terrain: Flat to gently rolling.
Food: None on the route. McDonald's at end.
Start: McDonald's, Great Woods Marketplace, on Route 140 in Norton. Park in the shopping center; McDonald's has parking "for customers only." It's about a mile south of Interstate 495 and 1⁶/10 miles north of Route 123.
How to get there: From the north, head south on Interstate 95 to the Interstate 495 South exit. Go about 3 miles to the Route 140 South exit (exit 11). Turn right at end of ramp and go 1²/10 miles to McDonald's on left.

If you're coming from the southeast on Interstate 495, there is no exit onto Route 140 South. Instead, take the Route 123 exit (exit 10). Turn left (west) on Route 123 and go 2 miles to Route 140, in the center of Norton. Turn right (north) on Route 140 and go 1⁶/10 miles to McDonald's on right.

Midway between Taunton and Attleboro, about 30 miles south of Boston, is a very enjoyable area for biking. The terrain is nearly level, with an extensive network of little-traveled country roads looping past ponds and prosperous farmland. The region is far enough from Boston to be fairly rural, without much infiltration of suburban development.

The ride starts from Norton, one of the most pleasantly rural towns within commuting distance of Boston and a graceful New England classic. The centerpiece of the community is Wheaton College, a high-quality school with a lovely campus graced by elegant, ivy-covered wood and brick buildings. A small pond with a footbridge across it adds to the beauty of the setting. Adjacent to the campus are a stately white church and a handsome brick turn-of-the-century former library. You'll go through the center of town near the end of the ride.

At the beginning of the ride, you'll pass the Great Woods Performing

Arts Center, which is the summer home of the Pittsburgh Symphony Orchestra and the scene of many popular concerts. Just ahead you'll follow the north shore of the Norton Reservoir and go through the small lakeside community of Norton Grove. After a few miles of woods and farmland, you pass Winnecunnet Pond, Watson Pond, and Lake Sabbatia in quick succession. Across from the latter pond is the Paul A. Dever School, a state institution for children who have mental disabilities and a port of embarkation for troops during World War II. Watson Pond and Lake Sabbatia are just over the town line in Taunton, a city of 40,000 covering a wide area in the southeastern part of the state. The city, best known for the manufacture of fine silver products, is rural around its outer edges. You'll bike through a pleasant, tree-shaded residential area and then quickly get back into the undeveloped western edge of the city. The return run to Norton brings you through a fine mixture of woods, farmland, and old wooden houses. You'll pedal through the center of town and finish with a spin along the western shore of the Norton Reservoir.

Directions for the ride: 28 miles

1. Turn right (north) on Route 140 and go 1 mile to Reservoir Street (unmarked) on right, just before the bridge over Interstate 495. Just before the intersection you'll pass the Great Woods Performing Arts Center on your left.
2. Turn right on Reservoir Street and go 1$\frac{9}{10}$ miles to Elm Street on left. It's $\frac{1}{2}$ mile after a laundromat and Cobb Street on left. You'll follow the Norton Reservoir on your right.
3. Turn left on Elm Street and go $\frac{4}{10}$ mile to Cross Street (unmarked) on your left, immediately after a factory on left.
4. Turn left on Cross Street and go $\frac{7}{10}$ mile to end. A little dam is on the left just past the factory.
5. Turn left at end and go $\frac{4}{10}$ mile to Newcomb Street on right.
6. Turn right on Newcomb Street and go 1$\frac{1}{10}$ miles to crossroads and stop sign (dirt road if you go straight).
7. Turn right at crossroads and go $\frac{6}{10}$ mile to end (Route 123).
8. Turn right on Route 123 and go $\frac{6}{10}$ mile to Leonard Street on left, just before the bridge over Interstate 495.
9. Turn left on Leonard Street and go 1 mile to end. At the end the short ride turns right and the long ride turns left.

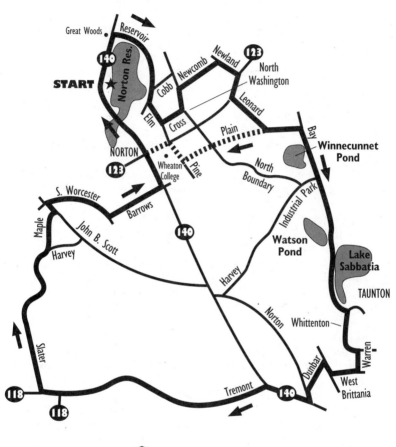

Great Woods

Reservoir

START

Norton Res.

140

Cobb

Newcomb

Newland

123

North
Washington

Leonard

Elm

Cross

Plain

Bay

**Winnecunnet
Pond**

NORTON

123

Wheaton
College

Pine

North
Boundary

S. Worcester

Barrows

Industrial Park

Maple

John B. Scott

140

Harvey

Harvey

**Watson
Pond**

**Lake
Sabbatia**

TAUNTON

Norton

Whittenton

Slater

Warren

118

118

Tremont

140

Dunbar

West
Brittania

10. Turn left at end. Just ahead, Burt Street is on your left, but curve right on the main road. Continue ⁶⁄₁₀ mile to end (Bay Road).

11. Turn right on Bay Road and go 1⁴⁄₁₀ miles to traffic light (Myles Standish Industrial Park on right).

12. Continue straight for 2¹⁄₁₀ miles to Whittenton Street, which bears right at the end of a pond on your left. The main road curves sharply left at the intersection over a small bridge. On this stretch you'll pass Winnecunnet Pond, Watson Pond, and finally Sabbatia Lake. There's a small state park with a beach at Watson Pond. The Dever State School is on your right across from Sabbatia Lake.

13. Bear right on Whittenton Street and go ⁸⁄₁₀ mile to fork at a traffic island (Warren Street bears right).

14. Bear right at fork and go ³⁄₁₀ mile to end (West Britannia Street, unmarked).

15. Turn right on West Britannia Street and go ⁶⁄₁₀ mile to end (Fremont Street). You'll pass an attractive brick school built in 1888 on your left at the beginning.

16. Turn right at end and go ¹⁄₁₀ mile to Dunbar Street on left.

17. Turn left on Dunbar Street and go ¹⁄₂ mile to end, at stop sign (merge left on Norton Avenue).

18. Bear left at end and go ¹⁄₁₀ mile to end (Route 140).

19. Turn right on Route 140 and go ⁷⁄₁₀ mile to Tremont Street, which bears left (sign may say LASALLETTE). It's several streets after Glebe Street, which also bears left.

20. Bear left on Tremont Street and go ³⁄₁₀ mile to fork (Worcester Street bears right).

21. Bear left at fork (still Tremont Street). Go 4³⁄₁₀ miles until you come to Route 118, which turns left and also goes straight ahead at the intersection.

22. Continue straight on Route 118 for ¹⁄₄ mile to Slater Street on right.

23. Turn right on Slater Street. Stay on the main road for 2³⁄₁₀ miles to fork where Harvey Street bears right and Maple Street bears left.

24. Bear left on Maple Street and go ⁷⁄₁₀ mile to where the main road bears right and a dead-end road goes straight.

25. Bear right on main road and go 100 yards to end (John B. Scott Boulevard).

26. Turn left at end and go ¹⁄₁₀ mile to crossroads and stop sign just after the diagonal railroad tracks (**CAUTION** here).

27. Turn right at crossroads onto South Worcester Street. Go $^9/_{10}$ mile to Barrows Street on left, just before railroad tracks.

28. Turn left on Barrows Street and go $1^2/_{10}$ miles to wide crossroads and stop sign (Route 140).

29. Turn left on Route 140 and go $^7/_{10}$ mile to end (Route 123, East Main Street), in the center of Norton. The town green is in front of you at the intersection. Here the ride jogs left and then right (still Route 140), but if you turn right on Route 123 you'll come to Wheaton College on your right after $^2/_{10}$ mile.

30. Jog left and immediately right, staying on Route 140 North. Go $1^6/_{10}$ miles to McDonald's on right. You'll follow the Norton Reservoir on your right just before the end.

Directions for the ride: 13 miles 🐛🐛🐛🐛🐛🐛

1. Follow directions for the long ride through number 9.

2. Turn right at end of Leonard Street and go $1^2/_{10}$ miles to crossroads and stop sign (South Washington Street).

3. Continue straight for $^8/_{10}$ mile to end (Pine Street).

4. Turn right on Pine Street and go $^1/_2$ mile to crossroads and stop sign (Route 123).

5. Turn left on Route 123. As soon as you turn left, Wheaton College is on your left. Go $^1/_4$ mile to fork just before Route 140, at blinking light in the center of Norton.

6. Go straight at fork (don't bear left), passing the green on your left. Go 100 yards to end (Route 140). Notice the handsome brick former library on the far side of the intersection.

7. Turn right on Route 140 and go $1^6/_{10}$ miles to McDonald's on right. You'll follow the Norton Reservoir on your right just before the end.

The Bridgewater Ride:
West Bridgewater–East Bridgewater–
North Middleboro–Bridgewater

Number of miles: 28 (20 without North Middleboro extension)
Terrain: Gently rolling, with one hill.
Food: Grocery stores and restaurants in the towns.
Start: Center Shopping Plaza, junction of Routes 28 and 106, West Bridgewater, 2 miles east of Route 24.

The three Bridgewaters, just south of Brockton and about 30 miles south of Boston, mark the transition between suburbia to the north and an extensive rural area to the southeast, encompassing nearly all the land down to the Cape Cod Canal and New Bedford. As you head south and southeast from Brockton, the landscape acquires characteristics unique to the southeastern portion of the state—sandy soil, scrub pine, cranberry bogs, generally flat and often swampy terrain, and cedar-shingled houses with peaked roofs. This landscape provides some of the most scenic and easiest bicycling in the state on a superb network of well-maintained country lanes and secondary roads. Most of southeastern Massachusetts has a tidy, prosperous look that is subtly pleasing. This ride is the closest to Boston that offers some of the ambience of this section of the state.

The ride starts from West Bridgewater, a pleasant community with some tract housing (which you won't go through) toward the Brockton line and lots of undeveloped land. You'll quickly cross into East Bridgewater, which is somewhat more rural. The center of town is beautiful, if you can somehow ignore the broad slash of Route 18 that bisects it. The large green is framed by an unusually graceful white church and a handsome old schoolhouse. Heading east of town you'll go through broad farms and past unspoiled Robbins Pond. You'll now start seeing cranberry bogs as you pass through the eastern edge of Halifax, one of the most thoroughly rural towns within commuting distance of Boston, and then into Bridgewater itself, which lies south of its East and West companions. The town center is a New England classic, with a small green smack in the middle of Route 18, framed by a compact row of old business buildings, a fine church, and an ornate brick former library built in 1881. Adjoining the center of town is the campus of Bridgewater State College, the earliest state college in Massachusetts, with attractive redbrick buildings. From Bridgewater it's not far back to West Bridgewater on back roads. Just before the end you'll pass a beautiful park along the Town River, originally the site of a factory during the 1800s.

The long ride heads farther south through broad sweeps of farmland bordered by stately rows of shade trees. Looming in the distance on a hilltop is the Bridgewater Correctional Institution, a grim, turreted monstrosity resembling a medieval fortress, strangely out of place in this pastoral setting. You'll go right by the prison and then follow the Taunton River into North Middleboro, a charming, unspoiled village. Its small green is framed by a graceful yellow wooden church with a clock tower; a white, pillared mansion; and a classic old schoolhouse. From here you'll have a fine run past farms and meadows to Bridgewater, where you'll pick up the route of the short ride.

Directions for the ride: 28 miles ᕦᕤᕦᕤᕦᕤᕦᕤᕦᕤ

1. Turn right out of parking lot onto Route 106, heading east, and go ⁹/₁₀ mile to crossroads and blinking light (East Street).

2. Turn left on East Street (**CAUTION** here) and go ⁴/₁₀ mile to fork (Union Street bears right).

3. Bear right on Union Street. After ½ mile, North Central Street bears left, but continue straight for 1 mile to crossroads and stop sign (North Central Street again), in East Bridgewater.

4. Turn right at crossroads. Just ahead is a traffic light (Route 18). Cross Route 18 and go ³/₁₀ mile to fork at the East Bridgewater town green (Plymouth Street bears right).

5. Bear left at fork (still Central Street) and stay on the main road for 1⁸/₁₀ miles to traffic light (Washington Street).

6. Turn right on Washington Street and go 1⁹/₁₀ miles to second crossroads (Pond Street). There's a convenience store on the left at the intersection.

7. Turn left on Pond Street (it's a fairly sharp left) and go 1⁸/₁₀ miles to fork, staying on the main road. It's after Hudson Street on left. You'll pass Robbins Pond on your right.

8. Bear right at fork and go ½ mile to another fork where the main road bears left and Furnace Street bears right.

9. Bear left on main road and go ³⁄₁₀ mile to end (merge left at yield sign).

10. Bear left at end and go ¹⁄₁₀ mile to Pine Street, which bears right.

11. Bear right on Pine Street. After 100 yards you'll cross Route 106. Continue straight for ½ mile to end (merge to right into Route 105). You'll pass a cranberry bog on the right.

12. Bear right on Route 105 and go 1²⁄₁₀ miles to fork (Summit Street bears right).

13. Bear right on Summit Street and just ahead curve right on the main road. Continue ⁴⁄₁₀ mile to end (merge right on Walnut Street).

14. Bear right at end and go ²⁄₁₀ mile to Cherry Street (unmarked) on left.

15. Turn left on Cherry Street and go ⁹⁄₁₀ mile to fork where Cherry Street bears right and Short Street bears left.

16. Bear left on Short Street and go ³⁄₁₀ mile to end (Auburn Street), at large traffic island.

17. Bear right on Auburn Street and stay on the main road for 1⁷⁄₁₀ miles to crossroads and stop sign (Summer Street, unmarked). Here the short ride turns right and the long ride turns left.

. **18.** Turn left at crossroads and go 1⁸⁄₁₀ miles to Titicut Street on right. You'll see the prison on your right in the distance.

19. Turn right on Titicut Street and go ⁶⁄₁₀ mile to crossroads and stop sign immediately before the prison.

20. Bear left at crossroads (still Titicut Street) and go 1 mile to end. **CAUTION:** Watch for bumps and potholes while going down the hill. You'll cross the Taunton River shortly before the end.

21. Turn right at end onto Plymouth and go ³⁄₁₀ mile to traffic light (Routes 28 and 18, Bedford Street).

22. Go straight at light for ⁸⁄₁₀ mile to fork at the North Middleboro green, where the main road bears right. Notice the fine old buildings in the graceful village.

23. Bear right at fork and go ⁶⁄₁₀ mile to another fork just after you cross the Taunton River (South Street bears right).

24. Bear right on South Street and go 2³⁄₁₀ miles to another fork where South Street bears left and Winter Street bears right.

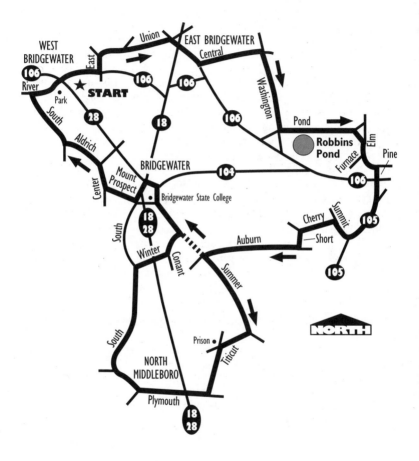

25. Bear right on Winter Street and go $^4/_{10}$ mile to crossroads and stop sign (Route 18).

26. Cross Route 18 and go $^4/_{10}$ mile to end.

27. Turn left at end and go $^1/_2$ mile to end, at stop sign (merge left at bottom of hill).

28. Bear left at end and go $^9/_{10}$ mile to fork (Grove Street, unmarked, bears left). Bridgewater State College is in front of you.

29. Bear right at fork and go $^2/_{10}$ mile to end (Route 104).

30. Turn left on Route 104 and go $^2/_{10}$ mile to traffic light (Routes 18 and 28).

31. Turn left at light. This is the center of Bridgewater. Just ahead Routes 28 and 18 bear left, but continue straight on Route 104 for $^1/_{10}$ mile to crossroads (Grove Street on left, Mount Prospect Street on right). Notice the old library on your right, immediately after the new one.

32. Turn right on Mount Prospect Street and go $^1/_2$ mile to end.

33. Turn right at end and go $^4/_{10}$ mile to Aldrich Road on left, just before a large brick church on left.

34. Turn left on Aldrich Road. After $^7/_{10}$ mile the main road bears left and Bedford Street turns right. Bear left and go 100 yards to end.

35. Turn right at end onto South and go 1 mile to end, immediately after a little bridge.

36. Turn right at end onto River. After $^2/_{10}$ mile, the road curves sharply left and there's a delightful riverfront park on your right. Continue $^2/_{10}$ mile to Route 28 (South Main Street). The shopping center is on the far side of Route 28.

Directions for the ride: 20 miles

1. Follow directions for the long ride through number 17.

2. Turn right at crossroads and stop sign. Go $1^1/_2$ miles to fork where Grove Street (unmarked) bears left. In front of you is Bridgewater State College.

3. Follow directions for the long ride from number 29 to the end.

Middleboro–Halifax

Number of miles: 25 (16 without Halifax loop)
Terrain: Flat.
Food: Grocery store and restaurant in Halifax.
Start: Oliver Mill Park, corner of Route 44 and Nemasket Street in Middleboro, 3 miles east of Interstate 495. Entrance is on Nemasket Street.

On this ride you explore the lakes and broad expanses of farmland midway between Boston and the Cape Cod Canal and about 10 miles inland from the coast. The area is far enough from Boston, about 35 miles, to be completely rural. Very flat terrain, good secondary roads without much traffic, and fine rural scenery make bicycling in this region a pleasure. A section of the ride parallels Great Cedar Swamp, an extensive wetland bordered by large, prosperous farms.

The ride starts from the outskirts of Middleboro at Oliver Mill Park, site of an industrial enterprise dating back to the 1700s. It included a gristmill, a sawmill, a forge, and other operations. The area has recently been landscaped and the old stone channel for the Nemasket River restored. In the early spring, this is a prime spot to watch the annual herring run, when millions of the fish swim up the rivers to their spawning grounds. Shortly after you leave the park, you'll pass a magnificent white church on a splendid green in the middle of nowhere. You'll now head toward Halifax, passing a couple of cranberry bogs and skirting Great Cedar Swamp on narrow lanes. Halifax is one of the most rural communities within commuting distance of Boston, consisting primarily of woods, cranberry bogs, swampland, and Monponsett Pond. The town center is beautiful, with a fine, white-pillared town hall and old schoolhouse. Just north of town you'll thread across Monponsett Pond along a causeway splitting the lake in half. From here you'll make a loop, passing unspoiled Stetson Pond, going along the far side of Monponsett Pond, and arriving back in Halifax. The return trip to Middleboro goes along Route 105, one of the best numbered routes in the state for biking. This section is narrow, well surfaced, almost traffic-free, and passes through magnificent open farmland.

Directions for the ride: 25 miles ~~~~~~~~~~

1. From the parking lot, go straight ahead opposite the entrance onto Plymouth Street, which parallels Route 44 on your left. Go 1^4/10 miles to stop sign at a five-way intersection (Route 105, East Main Street). Notice the one-room schoolhouse on the far side of the intersection.

2. Turn left on Route 105 and go ^{2}/10 mile to traffic light (Route 44), passing a classic white church on left.

3. Cross Route 44 and go ^{7}/10 mile to where Route 105 turns left onto Thompson Street.

4. Turn left, staying on Route 105, and go ^{2}/10 mile to Fuller Street, which bears right.

5. Bear right on Fuller Street and go 1^1/2 miles to fork where Winter Street bears right.

6. Bear left at fork (still Fuller Street). Go 1^8/10 miles to another fork (East Street bears right, South Street bears left).

7. Bear left on South Street and go ^{3}/10 mile to where Hayward Street bears right and the main road curves left.

8. Curve left and stay on main road for 1^6/10 miles to fork where Carver Street (unmarked) bears left and South Street (unmarked) bears right. Here the short ride bears left and the long ride bears right.

9. Bear right on South Street and go ^{3}/10 mile to end (Route 106), opposite a graceful white church. The pillared town hall is to the right of the church.

10. Turn right on Route 106 and go 1 mile to traffic light (Route 58, Monponsett Street).

11. Turn left on Route 58 and go 2^7/10 miles to South Street on right, immediately before the modern Calvary Baptist Church on right. You'll cross Monponsett Pond at the beginning.

12. Turn right on South Street and go ^{3}/10 mile to stop sign, where the main road curves right and another road turns left.

13. Curve right on main road (Plymouth) and go 1^4/10 miles to crossroads and stop sign (Route 36). You'll pass Stetson Pond on your left.

14. Turn right on Route 36 and go 1^7/10 miles to end (Route 106, Plymouth Street). You'll pass the other side of Monponsett Pond near the end.

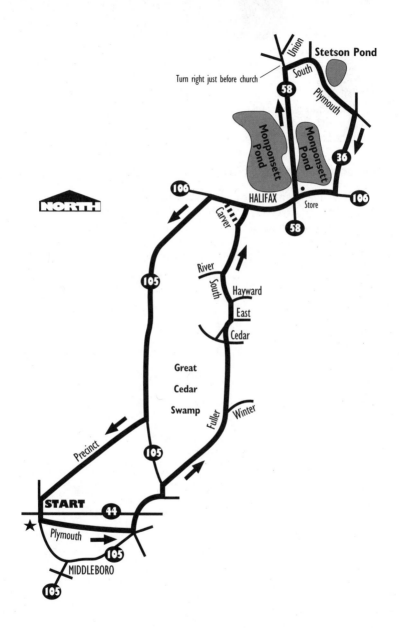

15. Turn right on Route 106 and go $^7/_{10}$ mile to traffic light (Route 58, Monponsett Street).

16. Cross Route 58 and go $1^6/_{10}$ miles to Route 105 (Thompson Street) on left.

17. Turn left on Route 105 and go 5 miles to Precinct Street on right.

18. Turn right on Precinct Street and go 2 miles to end.

19. Turn left at end and go $^2/_{10}$ mile to traffic light (Route 44). The park is on the far side of the intersection.

Directions for the ride: 16 miles

1. Follow directions for the long ride through number 8.

2. Bear left on Carver Street and go $^4/_{10}$ mile to end (Route 106).

3. Turn left on Route 106 and go $^2/_{10}$ mile to Route 105 (Thompson Street) on left.

4. Follow directions for the long ride from number 17 to the end.

Chapter 6:
Southeastern Massachusetts

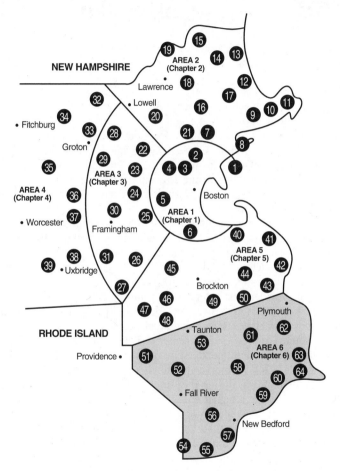

The numbers on this map refer to rides in this book.

Seekonk–Rehoboth

Number of miles: 28 (15 without southern extension)
Terrain: Gently rolling, with one hill. The long ride has an additional hill.
Food: Country store in Rehoboth.
Start: Seekonk High School, corner of Arcade Avenue and Ledge Road in Seekonk, 7/10 mile north of Route 44.
How to get there: From the north, exit south from Interstate 95 onto Route 1A, Newport Avenue (exit 2A). Go 1 mile to the third traffic light (Central Avenue). Turn left on Central Avenue and go 1 mile to end (Route 152). Turn right on Route 152 and go 3⁴/10 miles to Arcade Avenue on left, at a blinking light. Turn left on Arcade Avenue and go 6/10 mile to school on right.

If you're coming from Interstate 195, exit north onto Route 114A (exit 1). After 1 mile, Route 114A bears left, but go straight onto Arcade Avenue for 8/10 mile to traffic light (Route 44). Cross Route 44 and go 7/10 mile to school on left.

Just east of Providence is a very rural, gently rolling area that provides superb bicycling. An extensive network of well-paved, narrow country lanes winds past large farms, a couple of ponds, and rustic, weathered old barns and farmhouses. The center of Rehoboth is a beauty, with a perfect little dam and millpond, a fine small church, and a graceful brick building called Goff Memorial that holds the town library and hosts a classical music festival during the summer. The only problem with Rehoboth is that it has a higher concentration of dogs than average; it's a good idea to carry dog repellent.

The ride starts off from Seekonk, a residential suburb of Providence that quickly becomes rural toward its eastern edge. You'll bike past gentleman farms and large, gracious homes and then cross into Rehoboth, where you'll head to Rehoboth Village, the center of town, through a pastoral landscape of gently rolling farmland. The return run to Seekonk leads through more of this landscape. The long ride heads farther east and south through an even more rural area. You'll go along the Warren Upper Reservoir and follow the beautiful valley of the Palmer River, lined with large farms. Just ahead you'll pass Shad Factory Pond, a small millpond with a nice dam. From here you've a short ride back to the start.

Directions for the ride: 28 miles ~~~~~~~~~

1. Turn left out of south end of parking lot onto Ledge Road (don't get onto Arcade Avenue). **CAUTION:** Speed bump as you leave the parking lot. Go ^{1}/10 mile to crossroads and stop sign (Arcade Avenue).
2. Cross Arcade Avenue and stay on the main road for 1^2/10 miles to end, at stop sign. (After ^{1}/2 mile Hope Street bears right, but go straight here).
3. Turn sharply left at end, up a gradual hill, and go ^{4}/10 mile to Prospect Street (unmarked) on left.
4. Turn left on Prospect Street and go 1^4/10 miles to fork where Walker Street (unmarked) bears left. It's shortly after Woodward Avenue on left.
5. Bear right at fork, and stay on main road for 1^1/2 miles to end (Pine Street, unmarked).
6. Turn right on Pine Street and go 2^2/10 miles to end (Broad Street, unmarked).
7. Turn left on Broad Street and go ^{3}/10 mile to fork where the main road bears slightly left.
8. Bear left at fork and go ^{3}/10 mile to crossroads and stop sign (River Street).
9. Bear left at crossroads and go ^{7}/10 mile to end (Danforth Street).
10. Turn right on Danforth Street and go ^{3}/10 mile to wide crossroads and stop sign (Route 44).
11. Cross Route 44 onto Bay State Road. Go ^{8}/10 mile to fork where Bay State Road bears left and County Street bears right. You'll go through Rehoboth Village just before the fork.
12. Bear right at fork and go ^{3}/10 mile to crossroads and blinking light (Route 118). Here the short ride turns right and the long ride goes straight.
13. Cross Route 118 and go 2^2/10 miles to crossroads and stop sign at top of hill. There's a country store on the far right corner.
14. Turn right at crossroads and go 2 miles to end (Gorham Street, un-

marked). You'll enjoy a nice downhill run to the Warren Upper Reservoir on your right.

15. Turn left on Gorham Street and go $^2/_{10}$ mile to end, at stop sign (Cedar Street on left, Plain Street on right).

16. Turn right at end and go $^6/_{10}$ mile to stop sign (Route 118). At the intersection, Route 118 turns right and also goes straight.

17. Turn right on Route 118. Just ahead Route 118 turns right, but continue straight. Go $^7/_{10}$ mile to fork where Brook Street bears right and the main road, Pleasant Street, bears left.

18. Bear left on the main road and go 1 mile to Providence Street on right, immediately beyond fire station on right.

19. Turn right on Providence Street and go $1^3/_{10}$ miles to Mason Street, which turns sharply left at traffic island.

20. Make a sharp left on Mason Street and go $1^9/_{10}$ miles to Route 6, at stop sign.

21. Cross Route 6 (**CAUTION** here). Go $^1/_{10}$ mile to end (Old Providence Road).

22. Turn right at end and go 1 mile to Route 6 again, at stop sign. The bridge over the Palmer River is a delightful spot. It's currently blocked off to cars, but you can bike across. **CAUTION:** Bumps and potholes at end.

23. Cross Route 6 diagonally (**CAUTION** again). Go $1^9/_{10}$ miles to end.

24. Turn left at end and go $^1/_{10}$ mile to your first right, Reed Street (unmarked).

25. Turn right on Reed Street and go $^6/_{10}$ mile to crossroads and stop sign (Water Street, unmarked). You'll pass Shad Factory Pond and the dam on your left.

26. Turn left on Water Street and go $^3/_{10}$ mile to traffic island at bottom of hill (Wheeler Street bears right).

27. Bear right at traffic island and go $1^1/_{10}$ miles to fork where French Street bears right and Wheeler Street (unmarked) bears left.

28. Bear left at fork and go $^3/_{10}$ mile to end, at stop sign.

29. Turn left at end onto Lake. Stay on main road for 2 miles to end, at stop sign (merge left onto Route 44).

30. Bear left on Route 44 (**CAUTION** here) and go 50 yards to Jacob Street on right.

31. Turn right on Jacob Street and immediately bear left on Ledge Road. Go $1^2/_{10}$ miles to crossroads and stop sign (Arcade Avenue, unmarked).

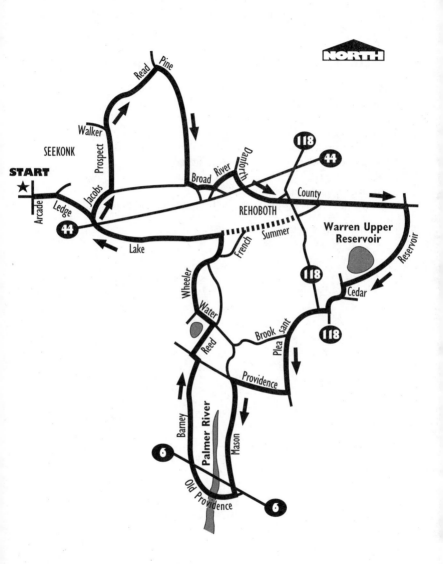

32. Go straight for $1/10$ mile to school entrance on right. **CAUTION:** Speed bump at entrance.

Directions for the ride: 15 miles

1. Follow directions for the long ride through number 12.
2. Turn right on Route 118 and go $3/10$ mile to crossroads (Elm Street on left, Summer Street on right).
3. Turn right on Summer Street. Stay on the main road for $1\frac{1}{2}$ miles to fork where French Street bears left and the main road bears slightly right. It's shortly after you climb a steep little hill.
4. Bear slightly right at fork. Stay on the main road for $2\frac{4}{10}$ miles to end, at stop sign (merge left on Route 44).
5. Follow directions for the long ride from number 30 to the end.

52 Swansea–Somerset– Dighton–Rehoboth

Number of miles: 30 (17 without Rehoboth extension)
Terrain: Gently rolling, with one moderate hill and one steep one.
Food: Grocery in Dighton. McDonald's at end.
Start: McDonald's, Route 6, Swansea, 3 miles west of Route 138 and ½ mile east of Interstate 195 (exit 3). The McDonald's is in a shopping center.

This ride takes you exploring the gently rolling countryside along the west bank of the lower Taunton River, the major river in the southeastern part of the state. The route parallels the river for several miles and then returns along the ridge rising just inland from the west bank. The long ride heads farther west into farm country and then finishes with a relaxing run along Mount Hope Bay, the broad estuary at the mouth of the river.

You'll start from Swansea, a pleasant rural community midway between Fall River and Providence, and just far enough from either to have so far avoided suburban development. The center of town boasts a handsome stone town hall with a clock tower, built in 1890, and a fine stone library next door.

From Swansea you'll traverse a low ridge into Somerset, which lies along the Taunton River across from Fall River. Most of Somerset is suburban, but you'll bike through the older and less-developed northern portion of town. You'll follow the river on a narrow street lined with fascinating old wooden buildings in a wide variety of architectural styles and then continue along the water into an increasingly rural landscape to the center of Dighton, another attractive riverfront town extending westward into gently rolling farm country.

In Dighton you'll head back toward Swansea along a ridge a short distance inland from the riverbank, with impressive views of the river and the surrounding landscape. The long ride heads farther inland to Rehoboth, a beautiful rural town of broad farms and winding, wooded

311

roads. You'll cross briefly into a little strip of Rhode Island to the shore of Mount Hope Bay, just back over the Massachusetts line. After a scenic, curving run along the shore, you've a short ride back to the start.

Directions for the ride: 30 miles 〰〰〰〰〰

1. Turn right out of *back* of parking lot onto Milford Road, which parallels Route 6 one block north of it, and go $^6/_{10}$ mile to end (Hortonville Road). **CAUTION:** There are speed bumps when you leave the parking lot. Ride around the sides.

2. Turn right on Hortonville Road and go $^2/_{10}$ mile to Main Street on left, at traffic light. An attractive brick school, now an administration building, is on the right at the intersection.

3. Turn left on Main Street and go $2^8/_{10}$ miles to traffic light at bottom of hill (County Street, Route 138). Just after you turn left, there's a little dam on your left. Then, just ahead, you'll pass the handsome stone Swansea town hall and library.

4. Cross Route 138 and go $^3/_{10}$ mile to end (Riverside Avenue). The Taunton River is in front of you.

5. Turn left at end onto Riverside Avenue and go $^4/_{10}$ mile to fork where the main road bears right along the river.

6. Bear right at fork, following the river. Go $1^1/_{10}$ miles to diagonal crossroads where South Street bears right up a little hill.

7. Bear right on South Street and go $^4/_{10}$ mile to end (Main Street, unmarked).

8. Turn left on Main Street and go $^1/_2$ mile to Avon Street on left. As soon as you turn left, notice the pillared mansion on the left. Farther on you'll pass a varied mixture of fascinating old buildings on both sides of the street.

9. Turn left on Avon Street and go 100 yards to a traffic island immediately before end (Pleasant Street).

10. Turn right at traffic island and go $2^6/_{10}$ miles to Water Street on your right. It's a little lane that comes up just after a small bridge with concrete abutments. You'll pass Broad Cove, an inlet of the river, on your left.

11. Turn right on Water Street, still following the river on your right. Go $^6/_{10}$ mile to Route 138 (County Street), at stop sign and blinking light. This is the center of Dighton.

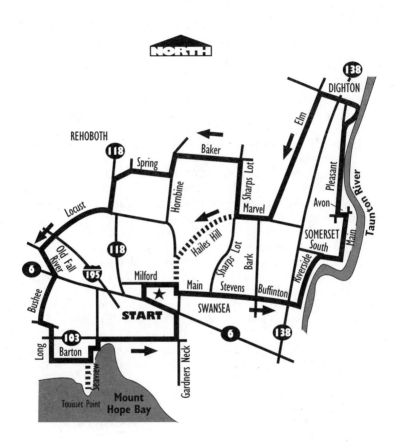

12. Cross Route 138 and go $^4/_{10}$ mile to crossroads (Elm Street). You'll pass a grocery on the right. Notice the graceful church a little to the right at the crossroads.

13. Turn left on Elm Street and go 3 miles to end (Whetstone Hill Road on left, Marvel Road on right). As soon as you turn left, a lovely dam is on your right. Then you'll climb a steep hill. As you're going down the far side, there's a crossroads—continue straight ahead. Farther on you'll go along a ridge with fine views of the river to your left.

14. Turn right at end and go 1 mile to crossroads and blinking light (Sharps Lot Road, unmarked). Here the short ride goes straight and the long ride turns right.

15. Turn right on Sharps Lot Road and go $1^7/_{10}$ miles to crossroads (Williams Street on right, Baker Road on left).

16. Turn left at crossroads and go $1^6/_{10}$ miles to end (Hornbine Road). Opposite the intersection is the Hornbine School, a one-room wooden schoolhouse. It was built during the 1830s and used until 1934.

17. Turn left at end and go $^1/_2$ mile to Spring Street on right.

18. Turn right on Spring Street and go 1 mile to fork where the main road bears left and Martin Street (unmarked) turns right.

19. Bear left on main road and go $^2/_{10}$ mile to end (Route 118).

20. Turn left on Route 118 and go $^8/_{10}$ mile to end (Locust Street), where a big water tower stands on the right. Route 118 turns left here.

21. Turn right at end and go $1^8/_{10}$ miles to end (Old Fall River Road).

22. Turn left at end and go $^8/_{10}$ mile to end, at stop sign (merge left on Route 6).

23. Bear left on Route 6 and immediately turn right on a small road (Bushee Road). **CAUTION** here. Go $1^4/_{10}$ miles to end (Schoolhouse Road, unmarked).

24. Turn left on Schoolhouse Road and go $^2/_{10}$ mile to Long Lane (unmarked) on right, at traffic island.

25. Turn right on Long Lane and go $^2/_{10}$ mile to crossroads and stop sign (Route 103).

26. Cross Route 103. After $^8/_{10}$ mile, the road turns 90 degrees left onto Barton Avenue. Continue $1^8/_{10}$ miles to traffic light (Route 103 again, Wilbur Avenue). When you come to Mount Hope Bay the road twists and turns, but stay on the main road until you come to Route 103.

If you wish you can turn right immediately before the bay onto Seaview Avenue, which parallels the water 1 mile to a dead end, and then backtrack to Barton Avenue. The massive building across the bay is the coal-fueled Brayton Point power plant.

27. Turn right on Route 103 and go 1³/₁₀ miles to blinking light at top of hill (Gardners Neck Road, unmarked).

28. Turn left on Gardners Neck Road (**CAUTION** here) and go ⁹/₁₀ mile to Route 6, at traffic light.

29. Turn left on Route 6 (**CAUTION** here) and go ⁹/₁₀ mile to McDonald's on right.

Directions for the ride: 17 miles

1. Follow directions for the long ride through number 14.

2. Continue straight at blinking light and go 1⁸/₁₀ miles to end (merge left at stop sign).

3. Bear left at stop sign (don't go through the intersection onto Wood Street) and go ½ mile to Milford Road on right.

4. Turn right on Milford Road and go ⁶/₁₀ mile to shopping center on left. You enter the shopping center from the back, just as you left it. **CAUTION:** Watch out for speed bumps as you enter parking lot.

53 Profile Rock and Dighton Rock:
Taunton–Berkley–Assonet–North Dighton

Number of miles: 24 (13 without Profile Rock–Dighton Rock extension)
Terrain: Gently rolling, with one moderate hill.
Food: Country store in Berkley. The delightful Assonet Inn, Assonet. Burger King and Papa Gino's at end.
Start: Burger King or Papa Gino's at the corner of Route 44 and Joseph E. Warner Boulevard, in Taunton, about 1½ miles west of the center of town.

The region just south of Taunton, along the east bank of the Taunton River, is ideal for bicycling. Country lanes wind through a fairly flat landscape of farms and woodland, with some stretches along the river. You'll go through the pleasingly rural town centers of Berkley and Assonet and then through North Dighton, an unusually attractive mill village in the middle of nowhere. On the ride you investigate two unique landmarks—Profile Rock, a large boulder with a striking resemblance to an Indian's profile, and Dighton Rock, on which are inscriptions of disputed origin.

The ride starts from Taunton, a city of 40,000 best known for the manufacture of fine silver products. In the downtown area (not on the route) is the majestic, domed Bristol County courthouse standing proudly over a grassy square. At the beginning of the ride, you'll pass the massive nineteenth-century plant of the F. B. Rogers Silver Company stretching along the riverbank. As soon as you cross the river, you get into gently rolling countryside with broad farms. It's not far to Berkley, a pretty village with an unusually large green. From here you'll proceed to Profile Rock, where a short path leads to a spot from which the profile is best seen. Just downhill from the rock is the attractive mill village of Assonet, which is part of Freetown. The Assonet River is dammed here into a tiny millpond. You'll follow the river, where you'll pass the Assonet Inn, a rambling Victorian building with broad porches. It looks elegant, but inside is an informal, old-fashioned restaurant serving good food at reasonable prices.

Leaving Assonet you'll traverse a hillside with fine views of the Taunton River, which widens into an estuary as it flows between Taunton and Fall River. A short pedal across broad meadows brings you to Dighton Rock State Park, a lush, grassy area along the riverbank. The rock itself is enclosed in a small museum open during the summer. Its strange pictographs are clearly visible; their origins have been attributed to a Portuguese explorer (the most generally accepted theory), Vikings, Phoenicians, and Indians.

After you leave Dighton Rock, another carefree run follows the river on a narrow lane; then you'll cross it over the narrow, steel-trussed Berkley Bridge, one of the more picturesque spots in southeastern Massachusetts. From here you make a brief run to North Dighton, where an unusual sight greets you. Completely surrounded by farmland, a massively grim brick mill on one side of the road contrasts with a large, well-kept green and fine old homes on the other. From here, it's a couple of miles back to Taunton through broad farms.

Directions for the ride: 24 miles ~~~~~~~~~~

1. Turn right out of east side of parking lot onto Warner Boulevard. Go $^2/_{10}$ mile to crossroads and blinking light (Cohannet Street).

2. Turn left on Cohannet Street. Just ahead Dighton Avenue bears right, but continue straight for $^1/_2$ mile to crossroads and stop sign.

3. Turn right at crossroads (Highland) and go $^9/_{10}$ mile to end (Route 138, Somerset Avenue). **CAUTION:** Bumps and potholes.

4. Turn left on Route 138 and go $^3/_{10}$ mile to Fifth Street, which bears right under railroad bridge.

5. Bear right on Fifth Street and go $^2/_{10}$ mile to end (West Water Street).

6. Turn left at end, passing the Rogers Silver Company, and go $^3/_{10}$ mile to your first right (Plain Street), which crosses the Taunton River. **CAUTION:** Bumps and potholes.

7. Turn right. Immediately after the bridge, turn right again and then immediately bear left, staying on the main road (Berkley Street). Go $1^7/_{10}$ miles to North Main Street on your left.

8. Turn left on North Main Street and go $1^2/_{10}$ miles to fork at the Berkley

town green. Here the short ride bears slightly right and the long ride bears left. Notice the small brick library in the middle of the fork.

9. Bear left at fork and go less than $^2/_{10}$ mile to crossroads and stop sign (Porter Street).

10. Go straight onto Locust Street for $1^8/_{10}$ miles to fork shortly beyond the overpass over Route 24. At the fork Algerine Street bears right and Bryant Street bears left.

11. Bear right on Algerine Street and stay on the main road for $1^9/_{10}$ miles to end (Mill Street, Route 79). There's a nice dam and an old mill on your left just before the end.

12. Turn left at end onto Route 79 and go 100 yards to Walnut Street on right.

13. Turn 90 degrees right on Walnut Street and go $^3/_{10}$ mile to end (Elm Street, unmarked).

14. Turn left at end and go $^3/_{10}$ mile to the entrance to Profile Rock on left, at a long, grassy traffic island.

15. Turn left onto entrance road and go $^2/_{10}$ mile to end. From here a gravel path leads about 100 yards to the viewpoint for the rock.

16. Leaving the rock, turn right at end of entrance road. Go $^6/_{10}$ mile to stop sign (merge left onto Route 79, Mill Street).

17. Bear left at stop sign. As you turn, notice the dam on your right. Go $^1/_{10}$ mile to crossroads and yield sign. This is Assonet.

18. Go straight at crossroads for $^9/_{10}$ mile to end, just past top of hill. The Assonet Inn is on your right shortly after the crossroads.

19. Bear left at end and go $^9/_{10}$ mile to Friend Street on left (sign may say STATE PARK).

20. Turn left on Friend Street and go $^8/_{10}$ mile to end (Bay View Avenue).

21. Turn left at end and go $^3/_{10}$ mile to the entrance to Dighton Rock on your right. It's about $^6/_{10}$ mile to the museum and picnic area on the bank of the river.

22. Leaving Dighton Rock, turn left at end of entrance road. Go 1 mile to the second left, Point Street.

23. Turn left on Point Street and go $^7/_{10}$ mile to Berkley Street on right (dead end if you go straight).

24. Turn right on Berkley Street and go $^9/_{10}$ mile to crossroads and stop sign (Elm Street).

25. Turn left at crossroads, crossing the river, and go $^7/_{10}$ mile to traffic light (Route 138, Somerset Avenue).

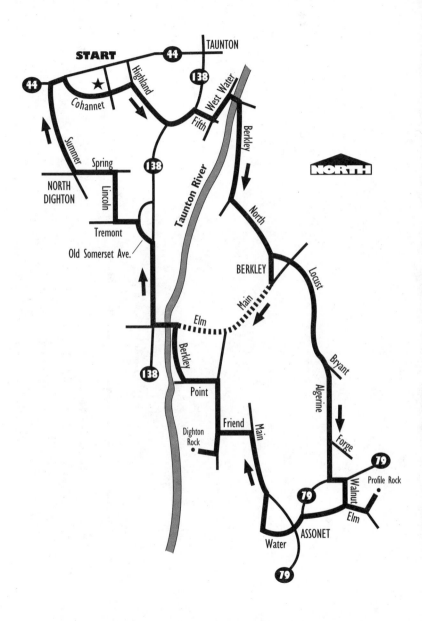

Profile Rock, Assonet

26. Turn right on Route 138 and go 1 mile to Old Somerset Avenue, which bears left.

27. Bear left on Old Somerset Avenue and go $^2/_{10}$ mile to Tremont Street on left.

28. Turn left on Tremont Street and go $^3/_{10}$ mile to Lincoln Avenue on right.

29. Turn right on Lincoln Avenue and go $^7/_{10}$ mile to end (Spring Street). A picturesque little dam is on the right just before the end.

30. Turn left on Spring Street. After $^4/_{10}$ mile, go straight ahead, passing a long brick mill on your right and a green on your left. Continue $^2/_{10}$ mile to crossroads and stop sign at end of mill (Summer Street). This is North Dighton.

31. Turn right on Summer Street and go $1^4/_{10}$ miles to end (Route 44). **CAUTION:** Bumps and potholes.

32. Turn right on Route 44 and go $^2/_{10}$ mile to Cohannet Street (unmarked) on right. A bridge at the beginning of this street is blocked off to cars but is passable by bike.

33. Turn right on Cohannet Street and go $^8/_{10}$ mile to crossroads and stop sign (Joseph E. Warner Boulevard). **CAUTION:** Bumpy spots. (If the bridge at the beginning becomes impassable or is torn down, simply stay on Route 44 for $^8/_{10}$ mile to starting point on right.) You'll pass an attractive park and bird sanctuary on the right.

34. Turn left at stop sign and go $^2/_{10}$ mile to parking lot on left, just before traffic light.

Directions for the ride: 13 miles 〰️〰️〰️

1. Follow the directions for the long ride through number 8.

2. Bear slightly right at fork and go $1^2/_{10}$ miles to another fork where Bay View Avenue bears left and the main road bears right.

3. Bear right on main road and go $1^4/_{10}$ miles to traffic light (Route 138, Somerset Avenue). You'll cross the Taunton River.

4. Follow directions for the long ride from number 26 to the end.

54 Westport–Tiverton, Rhode Island–Little Compton, Rhode Island

Number of miles: 34 (20 without Tiverton–Little Compton extension)
Terrain: Gently rolling, with one tough hill.
Food: Country store and restaurant in Adamsville. Country store in Little Compton.
Start: Lees Supermarket on Main Road, Westport, just north of the town hall.
How to get there: From Interstate 195, exit south onto Route 88 and go about 5 miles to Charlotte White Road, at third traffic light. Turn right and go $3/10$ mile to crossroads and stop sign (Main Road). Turn left on Main Road and go 1½ miles to supermarket on left. It's just past Village Commons, a small shopping center on left.

The southwestern corner of coastline directly south of Fall River, extending into Rhode Island along the broad Sakonnet River, has some of the most ideal and idyllic bicycling in the state. The region is a pedaler's paradise of untraveled country lanes winding past salt marshes and snug, cedar-shingled homes with immaculately tended lawns, trim picket fences, and broad meadows sloping down to the bay.

The ride starts from Westport, a slender town stretching from east of Fall River all the way down to the coast. The Westport River, a broad tidal estuary, bisects the town, and you'll be exploring the thin strip of land between the river and the Rhode Island border. You'll ride across sweeping expanses of farmland to the tiny village of Adamsville, which lies in Little Compton, Rhode Island, 100 yards over the state line. In the town are a country store in a rambling old wooden building, a little millpond, and a monument to the Rhode Island Red breed of poultry. From Adamsville you'll head south to the most southwesterly bit of coast in Massachusetts, an unspoiled strand framed by salt ponds and stately homes. At its eastern tip, guarding the mouth of the Westport River, is the exclusive summer colony of Acoaxet. From here you have a beautiful ride back to Adamsville along the West Branch of the Westport River and a short spin through farms to the starting point.

The long ride heads west into the little strip of Rhode Island south of Fall River lying along the mile-wide Sakonnet River, which is the easternmost section of Narragansett Bay. The landscape is beautiful as you hug the river on narrow country lanes and then climb onto a ridge with dramatic views of broad meadows sloping down to the shore. You'll pass Sakonnet Vineyards, which is open for wine-tastings. Just ahead is the center of Little Compton, the finest traditional New England village in Rhode Island. The long green is framed by a classic white church, a delightful country store, and an old cemetery where Elizabeth Pabodie, daughter of John and Priscilla Alden and the first white girl born in New England, is buried. From here you'll wind through gently rolling, open farmland to Adamsville, where you'll pick up the short ride heading toward Acoaxet.

Directions for the ride: 34 miles ༽ᗡᑫᗠᑫᗠᑫᗠᑫᗠᑫᗠ

1. Turn left (south) out of the parking lot and go ½ mile to Adamsville Road on right.

2. Turn right on Adamsville Road and go ⁸⁄₁₀ mile to Sodom Road on right (sign visible from opposite direction).

3. Turn right on Sodom Road and go 2¹⁄₁₀ miles to traffic island where the main road curves sharply right.

4. Go straight at traffic island (don't curve right) and immediately turn left at end on Narrow Avenue (unmarked). Go 1⁶⁄₁₀ miles to end (Route 81). Shortly before the end you'll cross the state line into Tiverton, Rhode Island. The short ride turns left on Route 81 and the long ride turns right.

5. Turn right on Route 81 and go ⁴⁄₁₀ mile to crossroads where a dirt road is on the right and King Road (unmarked) is on the left.

6. Turn left on King Road and go 1 mile to your second right, Brayton Road (unmarked).

7. Turn right on Brayton Road and go 1⁸⁄₁₀ miles to crossroads and blinking light (Bulgarmarsh Road, Route 177).

8. Turn left on Route 177 and go 1⁸⁄₁₀ miles to end (Route 77). There's a great downhill run at the end. **CAUTION** at end, at bottom of hill.

9. Turn right on Route 77 and go ½ mile to Nannaquaket Road on left. It crosses a little bridge.

10. Turn left on Nannaquaket Road and go 1⁶/10 miles to end, at yield sign (merge right on Route 77).

11. Bear right on Route 77 and go ½ mile to small crossroads at top of hill (Seapowet Avenue on right).

12. Turn right on Seapowet Avenue and go 2²/10 miles to the intersection where the main road bears right and another road turns left. You'll cross a rustic bridge over an inlet of the Sakonnet River.

13. Bear right on the main road (Neck Road; the sign is visible after the intersection). Go 1³/10 miles to your first left (Pond Bridge Road, unmarked), just past top of hill.

14. Turn left on Pond Bridge Road and go ½ mile to end (Route 77). You'll pass a curved wooden dam and a fish ladder on your left.

15. Turn right on Route 77 and go 3⁶/10 miles to a road that turns left at traffic island (a sign may say TO THE COMMONS). After about 1½ miles you'll pass the Sakonnet Vineyards on your left.

16. Turn left at traffic island and go ⁶/10 mile to fork, at the Little Compton green.

17. Bear right at fork and go ²/10 mile to end, in the center of Little Compton.

18. Turn left at end and go ¹/10 mile to your first right (Simmons Road).

19. Turn right on Simmons Road and go ⁶/10 mile to a traffic island where the main road curves sharply left and a smaller road turns right.

20. Turn right at traffic island and go ³/10 mile to William Sisson Road on left.

21. Turn left on William Sisson Road and go ⁶/10 mile to end.

22. Turn left at end and go ⁶/10 mile to fork where one branch bears slightly left and the other bears right. The fork is immediately after a stop sign.

23. Bear right at fork onto Pottersville and go ⁹/10 mile to another fork, where the main road bears right at a traffic island.

24. Bear right on the main road and go ⁸/10 mile to end. You cross back into Massachusetts just before the end.

25. Turn right at end and go ½ mile to Howland Road on right.

26. Turn right on Howland Road and go 1¹/10 miles to Atlantic Avenue on left, just before the ocean.

27. Turn left on Atlantic Avenue and go ⁷/10 mile to end, in the village of Acoaxet. Here the ride turns left, but if you turn right a dirt road leads ½ mile through the dunes to a high boulder at the tip of the point between

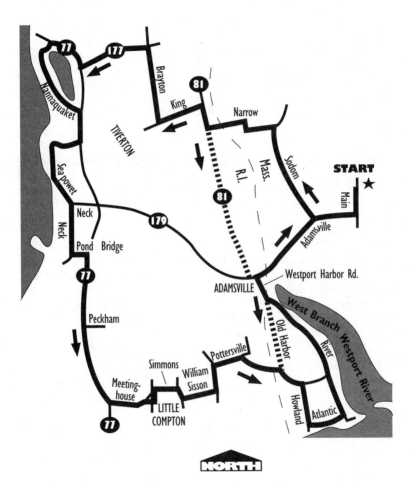

NORTH

the Westport River and the ocean. There's a great view from the boulder.

28. Turn left at end of Atlantic Avenue onto River and go $3^3/_{10}$ miles to end (merge right at stop sign).

29. Bear right at stop sign and go $^1/_2$ mile to end, in the village of Adamsville. At the end, notice the unique, three-story white tower on the right. It covers a well. On the left-hand corner is a plaque commemorating the Rhode Island Red breed of poultry. Abraham Manchester's, opposite you, is a good lunch spot.

30. Turn right at end and go $2^1/_2$ miles to end (Main Road, unmarked).

31. Turn left on Main Road and go $^1/_2$ mile to supermarket on right, just beyond the town hall.

Directions for the ride: 20 miles

1. Follow directions for the long ride through number 4.

2. Turn left on Route 81 and go $3^3/_{10}$ miles to end, in the village of Adamsville.

3. Turn left at end and go 100 yards to Westport Harbor Road on right. A plaque commemorating the Rhode Island Red breed of poultry is on the near corner, and an unusual three-story wooden tower, covering a well, is on the far corner. Abraham Manchester's, on your left, is a good lunch spot.

4. Turn right on Westport Harbor Road and go $^1/_2$ mile to fork where River Road bears left and Old Harbor Road goes straight up a steep hill.

5. Go straight up the hill for $2^2/_{10}$ miles to Howland Road on right. It's $^1/_2$ mile after Mullen Hill Road, also on right.

6. Follow directions for the long ride from number 26 to the end.

Westport–
Horseneck Beach

Number of miles: 21 (9 without Horseneck Beach extension)
Terrain: Gently rolling, with one tough hill.
Food: Snack bar just before Horseneck Beach. Grocery just before end.
Start: Tennis courts behind Westport Middle School, Old County Road. From Route 24, head east on Interstate 195 for 2 miles to Route 88. Go south on Route 88 for 3½ miles to Old County Road, at second traffic light. Turn left at light and go ⁶/₁₀ mile to school on left.

If you draw a line from Fall River to New Bedford and chip away the urban areas, everything south of that line is an absolute paradise for biking. This is a gently rolling landscape of little-traveled country roads winding past snug, cedar-shingled homes with trim picket fences, flawless lawns, and broad meadows sloping gently down to wide tidal rivers and salt marshes. This ride takes you exploring the heart of this area, heading along the east bank of the East Branch of the Westport River, a broad tidal estuary, and returning along the west bank. You'll stay within the borders of Westport, a slender town stretching from Route 195 to the ocean at Horseneck Beach, among the most unspoiled in the state. With its splendid harbor and the broad reaches of both the east and west branches of the river, Westport is an active boating center.

The ride starts from the broad, gradual hillside stretching along the river and heads down to its narrow northern end. You'll go by the Westport Vineyard and Winery, open most afternoons for tours and tastings. The ride down to Horseneck is delightful, and when you reach the ocean, the road hugs the shoreline for nearly a mile. Just before the public portion of the beach, you can bike onto a narrow pendant of land that extends a mile into Buzzards Bay. At the end of the beach, you'll enjoy superb views of the harbor from the bridge across the mouth of the river. Near the end you'll go along the top of the ridge that runs along the west bank of the river, enjoying splendid views of the river below and the neighboring ridge on the other side.

Directions for the ride: 21 miles

1. Turn left out of parking lot and go ⁷⁄₁₀ mile to Pine Hill Road on right, just past steep part of hill. You'll go through the small village of Head of Westport at the bottom of the hill.

2. Turn right on Pine Hill Road. Go 2¹⁄₁₀ miles to where Pine Hill Road bears right shortly after Riverview Drive on right.

3. Bear right (still Pine Hill Road) and go 1⁴⁄₁₀ miles to crossroads and stop sign (Hix Bridge Road, unmarked). Here the short ride turns right and the long ride goes straight. If you turn right, you'll come to the Westport Vineyard and Winery after ²⁄₁₀ mile.

4. Go straight at crossroads for 5 miles to the ocean, where the road turns 90 degrees right. (Just before this point is the Bayside Restaurant on the right, a great lunch spot.)

5. Continue ⁸⁄₁₀ mile to Route 88 (unmarked) on right, at grassy traffic island. (A sign for Horseneck Beach State Reservation is visible after you turn right.) The ride turns right on Route 88, but if you continue straight for ½ mile you'll cross a dramatic causeway with open ocean on both sides. On the far side of the causeway is Gooseberry Neck, a narrow pendant protruding into the bay.

6. Turn right on Route 88 and go 3²⁄₁₀ miles to traffic light (Drift Road). You'll pass the main part of Horseneck Beach, set back from the road on your left. **CAUTION:** The metal-grate bridge shortly before the light is very slippery when wet. If the road is wet, walk across. For a side trip, you can turn left immediately before the bridge and go ½ mile along the harbor to the Westport Yacht Club.

7. Turn right on Drift Road and go 3³⁄₁₀ miles to crossroads and stop sign (Hix Bridge Road).

8. Go straight for 3⁷⁄₁₀ miles to fork with a small green in the middle. The little square building on the green is a powder house built in 1812.

9. Bear right at fork and go 100 yards to end (Old County Road). You're back in Head of Westport. At the end, there's a grocery on your right.

10. Turn left at end and go ¼ mile to school on right. It's uphill—the same hill that you went down at the beginning.

Directions for the ride: 9 miles

1. Follow directions for the long ride through number 3.

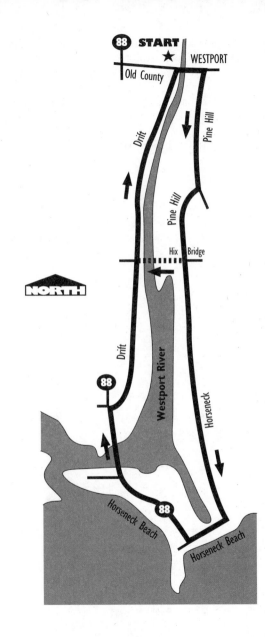

2. Turn right on Hix Bridge Road and go 1 mile to crossroads and stop sign (Drift Road). You'll pass the Westport Vineyard and Winery on the left after $^2/_{10}$ mile. The bridge over the river is a pretty spot. There's a short, steep hill after the bridge.

3. Turn right on Drift Road and go $3^7/_{10}$ miles to a fork with a small green in the middle. The little square building on the green is a powder house built in 1812.

4. Follow directions 9 and 10 for the long ride.

56 North Dartmouth–
Westport–Freetown

Number of miles: 29 (13 without Freetown extension)
Terrain: Gently rolling, with two long, gradual hills and one short, steep one.
Food: Grocery in Westport. Fast-food places on Route 6 near end.
Start: North Dartmouth Mall, at the junction of Faunce Corner Road and Route 6 in North Dartmouth. From Interstate 195 take the Faunce Corner– North Dartmouth exit (exit 12) and turn south at end of exit ramp. Go almost 1 mile to mall on right. Park near Faunce Corner Road.

This ride takes you exploring the surprisingly rural area midway between Fall River and New Bedford. The region is an attractive mixture of forest and farmland crisscrossed by smooth secondary roads. The architectural highlight of the ride is the bold, strikingly modern campus of University of Massachusetts at Dartmouth, the major educational facility for this part of the state.

The ride starts from North Dartmouth, the section of town near the university and along the Route 6 commercial strip (which you won't ride along). Within a mile and a half you'll pass the university campus, which crowns a broad hill. The main road looping around the perimeter of the campus is worth following. The route descends into the lovely small village of Head of Westport, where a stream flows between grassy banks and some graceful old Colonial-style homes. From here you'll head north, passing the back of Lincoln Park, a former amusement park (now sometimes used for flea markets) with a big roller-coaster. Just ahead you'll enjoy riding along Noquochoke Lake. As you continue north, the landscape becomes more rural and wooded. After turning south back toward the starting point, you'll climb gradually to a small hilltop reservoir within an embankment and then be rewarded with a fast downhill run toward the tiny village of Hixville. A quiet secondary road brings you past small farms back to the starting point.

Directions for the ride: 29 miles

1. Turn right onto Faunce Corner Road and go $^2/_{10}$ miles to Route 6, at traffic light.

2. Cross Route 6 (**CAUTION:** busy intersection) and go $^4/_{10}$ mile to fork where Chase Road bears left and Old Westport Road bears right.

3. Bear right on Old Westport Road. After $^8/_{10}$ mile you'll pass the entrance to University of Massachusetts at Dartmouth on your left. Continue 3 miles to Reed Road on right, at bottom of hill. Here the route turns right, but immediately after the intersection is the attractive village of Head of Westport and a country store.

4. Turn right on Reed Road and go $1^9/_{10}$ miles to traffic light (Route 6). You'll see the Lincoln Park roller-coaster on your left shortly before Route 6.

5. Cross Route 6 (**CAUTION** here) and go 3 miles to Hixville Road on right. You'll pass Noquochoke Lake on your left. At Hixville Road the short ride turns right and the long ride goes straight.

6. Continue straight for $^2/_{10}$ mile to Old Fall River Road on right. This is the tiny village of Hixville. Notice the fine church on your left just past the intersection.

7. Turn right on Old Fall River Road and go $^3/_{10}$ mile to Collins Corner Road on left.

8. Turn left on Collins Corner Road and go $2^2/_{10}$ miles to crossroads and stop sign (Flagg Swamp Road).

9. Turn left at crossroads. After $1^1/_{10}$ miles the road turns 90 degrees right onto Quanapoag Road. Continue $^7/_{10}$ mile to crossroads and stop sign (Bullock Road; sign visible from opposite direction).

10. Turn left on Bullock Road and go $1^3/_{10}$ miles to Chipaway Road, which turns sharply right while you're going uphill.

11. Turn sharply right on Chipaway Road and go $1^9/_{10}$ miles to crossroads and stop sign (Braley Road on left, Quanapoag Road on right).

12. Turn right on Quanapoag Road and go 2 miles to another crossroads and stop sign (Bullock Road again).

13. Turn left on Bullock Road and go $2^1/_{10}$ miles to fork where High Hill Road bears slightly left and Faunce Corner Road bears right.

14. Bear right on Faunce Corner Road and go $1^1/_2$ miles to crossroads and stop sign (Old Fall River Road). You'll pass the High Hill Reservoir on your left, hidden behind a tall embankment.

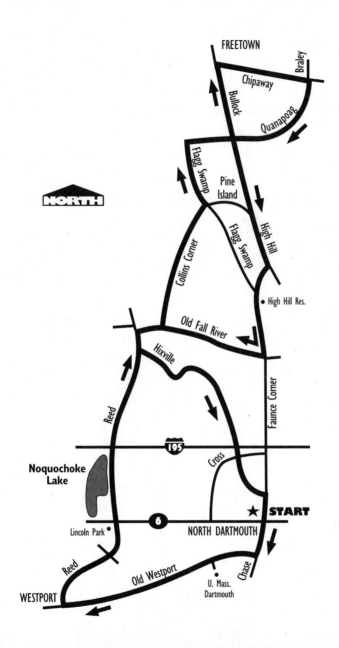

15. Turn right at crossroads onto Old Fall River Road and go 2³/₁₀ miles to end, back in Hixville. There's a great downhill run halfway along this stretch.

16. Turn left at end and go ²/₁₀ mile to where Hixville Road turns left.

17. Turn left (still Hixville Road) and go 2⁹/₁₀ miles to crossroads and stop sign (Cross Road). **CAUTION:** Diagonal railroad tracks after 2¹/₂ miles.

18. Continue straight for ⁸/₁₀ mile to end (Faunce Corner Road, unmarked).

19. Turn right at end and go ¹/₁₀ mile to mall on right, at traffic light.

Directions for the ride: 13 miles

1. Follow directions for the long ride through number 5.

2. Turn right on Hixville Road and go 2⁹/₁₀ miles to crossroads and stop sign (Cross Road). **CAUTION:** Diagonal railroad tracks after 2¹/₂ miles.

3. Follow directions 18 and 19 for the long ride.

Dartmouth

Number of miles: 27 (29 if you visit Demarest Lloyd Memorial State Park; 18 without southwestern loop; 13 with shortcut)
Terrain: Flat, with a couple of gradual, easy hills.
Food: Grocery and restaurant in Padanaram. Ponderosa and Burger King at end.
Start: Ponderosa Steak House, corner of Route 6 and Tucker Road, in North Dartmouth. From Interstate 195 take exit 12 (the Faunce Corner–North Dartmouth exit), and turn south at the end of the ramp. Go 1 mile to Route 6. Turn left on Route 6; Ponderosa is just ahead on the right.

Dartmouth, an extensive oceanfront town south and west of New Bedford, offers ideal biking on numerous back roads. The landscape is flat, with broad stretches of farmland and salt marshes. The ride starts in North Dartmouth, commercial center of the town and home of University of Massachusetts at Dartmouth. The bold, modern campus is about 1 mile off the route. You'll head down to the picturesque village of Padanaram on Apponagansett Bay, with antiques shops and fine old homes. From here you'll cross the bridge over the bay and enjoy a run along its shore. The marvelous Children's Museum, one of the best in New England, is on the 13-mile ride. From Padanaram you'll work your way to the southern coast and the tiny village of Russells Mills on winding, wooded roads. The focal point of Russells Mills is Davoll's General Store, a wonderful country store built in 1793. You'll pass the Lloyd Center for Environmental Studies, dramatically located on Buzzards Bay at the mouth of the Slocum River. Nature trails wind through the grounds, and there's a spectacular view from the top of the main building.

The long ride heads farther into Dartmouth to the Westport line, passing broad, well-tended farms. Demarest Lloyd Memorial State Park is about 1 mile from the route and worth visiting. It's a lovely expanse of woods and shoreline, with a good beach that doesn't get as crowded as nearby Horseneck Beach.

Directions for the ride: 27 miles 🍂🍂🍂🍂🍂🍂🍂🍂

1. Turn right onto Route 6 and immediately turn right at traffic light on Tucker Road. Go 3 miles to Russells Mills Road on left, at the bottom of a long, very gradual hill. A snack bar is on the far left corner.

2. Turn left on Russells Mills Road and go 1²/10 miles to Elm Street on right, immediately before the brick police station on left.

3. Turn right on Elm Street and go 1³/10 miles to the second crossroads and stop sign (Bridge Street) at bottom of hill. This is the center of Padanaram. Notice the handsome stone former library, built in 1889, on your right at the first crossroads.

4. Turn right on Bridge Street, which crosses the bay, and go ⁴/10 mile to Smith Neck Road on left. Here the 13-mile ride goes straight and the longer rides turn left.

5. Turn left on Smith Neck Road, following the bay. Go 1⁸/10 miles to where Rock o'Dundee Road turns right and the main road bears slightly left.

6. Stay on the main road for 1⁴/10 miles to Little River Road (unmarked) on right (it's a dead end if you go straight). You'll pass an ice cream stand shaped like a milk bottle on your right. Shortly before the intersection you'll see a grand mansion in the distance on your left. This is Round Hill, a former estate divided into multimillion-dollar condominiums.

7. Turn right on Little River Road and go 3³/10 miles to stop sign at bottom of hill, at traffic island (Rock o'Dundee Road on right). **CAUTION:** Watch for sand at the intersection. After 1⁶/10 miles, you'll pass the Lloyd Center for Environmental Studies on your left. The main building is ¹/10 mile down the dirt entrance road.

8. Bear left at the traffic island and then immediately bear right on main road. Go ⁸/10 mile to Tannery Lane, which bears left. Here the 18-mile ride goes straight and the 27-mile ride bears left. There's a small dam on your right immediately before the intersection.

9. Bear left on Tannery Lane and immediately turn left at end onto Horseneck. Go 1⁹/10 miles to fork where the main road curves left (becoming Barney's Joy Road) and Horseneck Road bears right. This is a nice run past broad farms with views of the river to your left.

10. Curve left on main road and go ⁸/10 mile to end (Allens Neck Road). Here the ride turns right, but if you turn left you'll come to Demarest Lloyd Memorial State Park after 1¹/10 miles.

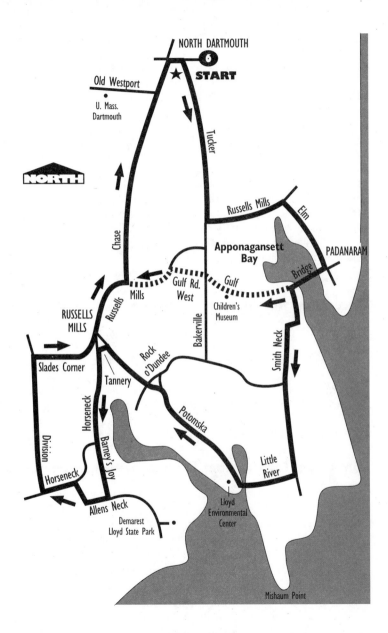

11. Turn right on Allens Neck Road and go $^7/_{10}$ mile to end (Horseneck Road, unmarked).

12. Turn left on Horseneck Road and go $^7/_{10}$ mile to Division Road on right.

13. Turn right on Division Road and go $2^7/_{10}$ miles to Slades Corner Road on right. Division Road runs along the border of Dartmouth on your right and Westport on your left.

14. Turn right on Slades Corner Road and go $1^1/_2$ miles to end, at stop sign. This is the tiny village of Russells Mills. Davoll's General Store is in front of you at the intersection.

15. Turn left at end and go 1 mile to Chase Road (unmarked) on left, immediately after the public works building on right.

16. Turn left on Chase Road and go 4 miles to traffic light (Route 6). If you'd like to visit University of Massachusetts at Dartmouth, turn left after $3^1/_2$ miles on Old Westport Road and go $^8/_{10}$ mile to the strikingly modern campus on your left.

17. Turn right on Route 6. Ponderosa is just ahead on right.

Directions for the ride: 18 miles

1. Follow the directions for the 27-mile ride through number 8.

2. Bear right at fork, up short hill, and go 100 yards to end (Russells Mills Road). This is the tiny village of Russells Mills. Davoll's General Store is on your left at the intersection.

3. Turn right on Russells Mills Road and go $^9/_{10}$ mile to Chase Road (unmarked) on left, immediately after the public works building on the right.

4. Follow directions 16 and 17 for the 27-mile ride.

Directions for the ride: 13 miles

1. Follow the directions for the 27-mile ride through number 4.

2. Continue straight for $1^1/_2$ miles to crossroads and stop sign (Bakerville Road). You'll pass the Children's Museum on your left after 1 mile.

3. Continue straight for $^6/_{10}$ mile to end (Russells Mills Road, unmarked).

4. Turn left at end and go $^7/_{10}$ mile to Chase Road on right.

4. Follow directions 16 and 17 for the 27-mile ride, turning right on Chase Road instead of left.

58

Land o' Lakes:
Lakeville–Freetown–Acushnet–Rochester

Number of miles: 27 (16 without Freetown–Acushnet–Rochester extension).

Terrain: Gently rolling, with two short hills.

Food: Snack bar in Acushnet. Grocery in Rochester.

Start: Savas Plaza, a small shopping center on Routes 18 and 105 in Lakeville, 4 miles south of Route 44. From Interstate 495, exit south on Routes 18 and go 4 miles to shopping center on right. It's just south of where Route 105 North turns left at traffic light.

Ten miles north of New Bedford is a cluster of large, unspoiled lakes surrounded by woods, prosperous farms, and a few cranberry bogs. Lightly traveled roads threading between the lakes make this one of the nicest regions for biking in southeastern Massachusetts.

The ride starts from the rural town of Lakeville, which is accurately named. Most of Assawompset Pond and adjacent Long Pond, two of the largest lakes in the state, lie within its borders. Lakeville is unusual in that it has no distinct town center; the closest approximation is where the ride starts. The combination town hall and fire station, housed in a handsome brick building with a bell tower, is close to the starting point. A little beyond is a fine church overlooking the water. You start off by going along the shore of Assawompset Pond, which, along with most of the other lakes in the area, supplies Taunton and New Bedford with water. Shortly you'll weave between Great Quittacas and Little Quittacas Ponds, both surrounded by pine groves. On the south shore of Little Quittacas Pond is the graceful stone New Bedford Waterworks building; just ahead the lane carves through a perfectly groomed, symmetrical row of trees.

For a few miles you'll ride past small farms and a couple of cranberry bogs on narrow lanes. Then you'll cross the New Bedford Reservoir to the little village of Long Plain (part of the town of Acushnet), which is surrounded by broad farms. It contains a museum of local history housed in a fine Victorian building dated 1875. A little farther along you'll pass Snipatuit Pond and bike across the gracefully curving causeway between Great Quittacas Pond and Assawompset Pond. At the end you'll go along the latter pond back to the start.

Directions for the ride: 27 miles

1. Turn right (south) out of parking lot and go $2^6/_{10}$ miles to where Route 18 turns right and Route 105 goes straight. You'll ride along Assawompset Pond on your left. Notice the brick town hall and fire station on the right shortly after you leave the lot.

2. Go straight on Route 105 for $2^1/_{10}$ miles to Negus Way, which bears right at the bottom of a little hill. **CAUTION:** Watch for bumps and potholes. You'll pass Little Quittacas Pond on your right.

3. Bear right on Negus Way, following the water on your right, and go $1^1/_{10}$ miles to end (Route 18). **CAUTION:** Several speed bumps. You'll pass the New Bedford Water Works.

4. Turn left on Route 18 and go $^1/_2$ mile to where Route 18 curves sharply right and a smaller road goes straight. You'll see Long Pond on the right.

5. Go straight on smaller road and then immediately turn left at end on Morton Road (unmarked). Go $1^1/_{10}$ miles to crossroads and stop sign (Route 105, Braley Hill Road). Here the short ride goes straight and the long ride turns right.

6. Turn right on Route 105 and go $^1/_2$ mile to your first right, Doctor Braley Road (unmarked).

7. Turn right on Doctor Braley Road and go 1 mile to fork where Rounsevell Drive bears right and the main road curves sharply left.

8. Curve left on main road. After $1^6/_{10}$ miles the paved road turns 90 degrees left and a dirt road goes straight. Stay on paved road for $1^8/_{10}$ miles to end (Peckham Road, unmarked).

9. Turn left on Peckham Road and go $^1/_4$ mile to Lake Street on left.

10. Turn left on Lake Street and go 1 mile to end (Route 105). You'll cross the New Bedford Reservoir.

11. Turn right on Route 105 and go $^2/_{10}$ mile to where Robinson Road (still Route 105) turns left. You'll pass the Long Plain Museum on your right. A snack bar is on the right immediately after the intersection.

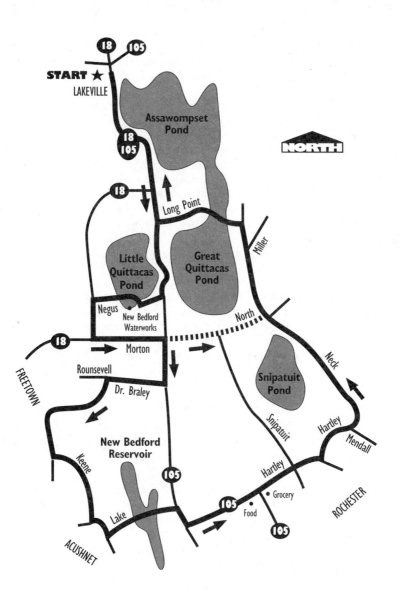

12. Turn left on Route 105 and go 1½ miles to where Route 105 turns right onto Cushman Road and Hartley Road goes straight.

13. Go straight on Hartley Road. After ⁷/10 mile you'll come to a crossroads (Snipatuit Road). Continue straight for ²/10 mile to fork (Vaughn Hill Road bears right).

14. Bear left at fork (still Hartley Road) and go ⁶/10 mile to another fork where Neck Road bears left. A sign may point left TO MIDDLEBORO.

15. Bear left at fork and go 3¹/10 miles on Neck to crossroads and stop sign (North Avenue). You'll go along Snipatuit Pond on your left.

16. Go straight at crossroads. After 1½ miles Miller Street bears right, but go straight for ³/10 mile to Long Point Road on left.

17. Turn left on Long Point Road and go 2 miles to end (Route 105).

18. Turn right on Route 105 and go 3¹/10 miles to shopping center on left, just before Route 105 bears right at traffic light.

Directions for the ride: 16 miles

1. Follow directions for the long ride through number 5.

2. Cross Route 105. After ⁸/10 mile Snipatuit Road bears right, but continue straight downhill for 1³/10 miles to crossroads (Neck Road).

3. Turn left at crossroads. After 1½ miles Miller Street bears right, but continue straight for ³/10 mile to Long Point Road on left.

4. Follow directions 17 and 18 for the long ride.

Mattapoisett–Rochester

Number of miles: 30 (18 without northern loop)
Terrain: Flat or gently rolling.
Food: Great country store in Rochester.
Start: Commuter parking lot on North Street, Mattapoisett, just south of Interstate 195 (exit 19A).

The cranberry bog country of southeastern Massachusetts provides some of the finest biking in the state. On this ride you explore a sample of that country just inland from Buzzards Bay, midway between New Bedford and the Cape Cod Canal. The area is very rural but there's a tidiness about it—in the cozy, cedar-shingled homes behind picket fences and stone walls; the broad fields bordered by rustic wooden fences; and the close-cropped, reddish-hued cranberry bogs surrounded by pine groves. Smooth, lightly traveled, narrow lanes and back roads spin their web across the landscape, connecting a bog here, a pond there, and a gracious old farmhouse around the bend.

The ride starts from Mattapoisett, an elegant, well-preserved harbor-front town on Buzzards Bay. At one time a shipbuilding center, the waterfront is now lined with attractive wooden homes, a few tastefully designed shops, and a fine park complete with a bandstand overlooking the harbor. As you leave town you'll head into a peaceful landscape of woods and prosperous farms to Rochester, an unspoiled rural village. The center consists of a good country store and a large green framed by a stately Gothic-style church and the old wooden town hall. Beyond Rochester you enter the cranberry bog country, with runs along Blackmore Pond and Mary's Pond for variety. The return trip to Mattapoisett is a smooth run passing small farms and fine old wooden homes.

Directions for the ride: 30 miles

1. Turn right (south) out of parking lot and go ⁶⁄₁₀ mile to traffic light (Route 6). There's a tall sculpture of a seahorse on the left corner imme-

diately before the light.

2. Turn left on Route 6 and go $^6/_{10}$ mile to an unmarked road that bears right.

3. Bear right on this road and go $^2/_{10}$ mile to crossroads and stop sign.

4. Turn right at crossroads. After $^1/_4$ mile the main road turns almost 90 degrees right at another crossroads onto Beacon Street. Stay on main road for 1 mile to Route 6, at traffic light. You'll follow Mattapoisett Harbor on your left. When you come to Route 6, notice the graceful white grange hall on the far left corner.

5. Cross Route 6. Just ahead the main road turns 90 degrees left at a crossroads onto Acushnet Road. Stay on main road for $^4/_{10}$ mile to end.

6. Turn left at end (still Acushnet Road). Just ahead, the main road curves sharply right and then sharply left in quick succession. Continue $^1/_2$ mile to where Acushnet Road turns left, just after the Interstate 195 overpass.

7. Turn left on Acushnet Road and go $1^1/_2$ miles to Long Plain Road on right, just after the main road turns 90 degrees left. This is a beautiful run–and the rest of the ride is just like it! You'll pass a cranberry bog on your left.

8. Turn right on Long Plain Road and go $2^2/_{10}$ miles to end (merge right; there is no stop sign here). You'll pass through a wooded area where the trees arch across the road in a vaulted green canopy.

9. Bear right at end, and go $3^3/_{10}$ miles to stop sign (merge right on Route 105). After $2^4/_{10}$ miles, look for a sculpture of a family of horses on the left, set back from the road. When you come back to Route 105, you're in the center of Rochester. Here the short ride turns sharply left and the long ride bears right.

10. Bear right on Route 105. The country store is just ahead on your right. If you don't want to stop there now, you'll go by it again toward the end of the ride. Continue on Route 105 for $2^2/_{10}$ miles to crossroads just before the Interstate 195 overpass (Pumping Station Road on right, County Road on left).

11. Turn left on County Road. After $^3/_{10}$ mile, Point Road bears right, but curve left on the main road. Go $^1/_2$ mile to Blackmore Pond Road on right.

12. Turn right on Blackmore Pond Road and go $2^6/_{10}$ miles to end. You'll pass Blackmore Pond on your right. **CAUTION:** Watch for bumps and potholes for the first mile.

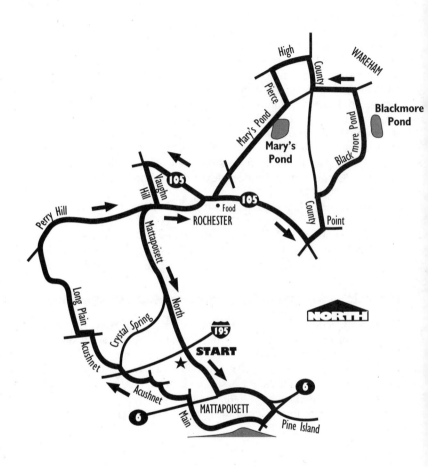

13. Turn left at end and go $^8/_{10}$ mile to crossroads and stop sign (County Road, unmarked).

14. Turn right on County Road and go 1 mile to High Street on left (sign may say TO OUTDOOR WORLD).

15. Turn left on High Street and go $^9/_{10}$ mile to Pierce Street on left.

16. Turn left on Pierce Street and go 1 mile to end (Mary's Pond Road).

17. Turn right at end and go $2^7/_{10}$ miles to end, at stop sign (merge right on Route 105). You'll pass Mary's Pond on your left; then you'll go by a picturesque old wooden mill on the left, opposite a smaller pond. When you come to Route 105, you're back in Rochester, and the country store is 100 yards to your left.

18. Bear right on Route 105. Just ahead is a fork. Bear right, staying on Route 105, and go $1^1/_2$ miles to crossroads (Vaughn Hill Road). Just after the fork is the distinctive Gothic-style church overlooking the Rochester town green.

19. Turn left on Vaughn Hill Road and go $1^1/_{10}$ miles to end (New Bedford Road).

20. Turn right at end and go $^1/_{10}$ mile to Mattapoisett Road on left.

21. Turn left on Mattapoisett Road. After 3 miles Crystal Spring Road bears right, but continue straight for 1 mile to parking lot on right.

Directions for the ride: 18 miles

1. Follow directions for the long ride through number 9. Here the short ride turns sharply left on Route 105, but if you bear right, a great country store is just ahead on your right.

2. Make a sharp left on Route 105. You'll immediately see the distinctive Gothic-style church and the Rochester town green on your left. Go $1^1/_2$ miles to crossroads (Vaughn Hill Road, unmarked).

3. Follow directions for the long ride from number 19 to the end.

Marion Ride

Number of miles: 17
Terrain: Flat.
Food: Grocery and restaurant at the center of town.
Start: Corner of Spring and Main streets in the center of Marion, about a mile south of Route 6. Park where legal on Spring Street, facing north, across from either the town hall or the elementary school.
How to get there: From Interstate 195, take exit 20 (Route 105, Marion). Turn right (south) at end of ramp and go about ½ mile to fork where Front Street bears left and Spring Street bears right. Bear right for ²/10 mile to Route 6. Go straight for ⁹/10 mile to end (Main Street).

This is a one-town ride on which you explore Marion, one of the series of waterfront communities along Buzzards Bay between the Rhode Island border and the Cape Cod Canal. Midway between New Bedford and the Canal along both sides of Sippican Harbor, Marion is a yachting center and the site of Tabor Academy, a prestigious private school. The expansive harbor divides the town into two portions, with the center of town on the western shore. Just south of town is Converse Point, a long, slender peninsula with mansions and estates along the tip. On the eastern shore of the harbor is Sippican Neck, a much larger peninsula rimmed with estates and large, gracious homes. One of the estates, Great Hill, matches anything to be found along the Massachusetts coast. It makes up its own 300-acre subpeninsula, with a majestic mansion overlooking the bay, narrow lanes hugging the shore, and a hill 125 feet high with spectacular views. Unfortunately the estate is open only on weekdays from 9:00 A.M. to 3:00 P.M. It's worth doing this ride during the week just to see the estate.

The ride starts off by going through the unspoiled, untouristed center of town, with a white Victorian town hall, several churches, and cedar-shingled homes and shops. You'll bike along the shoreline, passing Tabor Academy with its Tudor-style main building directly on the water. From here you'll swing over to Sippican Neck, bike to its tip along traffic-free roads, and return along its opposite shore, passing the Great Hill estate.

Directions for the ride 🌊🌊🌊🌊🌊🌊🌊🌊

1. From the end of Spring Street, turn left on Main Street and go $^2/_{10}$ mile to crossroads and stop sign (Front Street).

2. Cross Front Street and go $^8/_{10}$ mile to another crossroads and stop sign (Front Street again, unmarked). The road turns 90 degrees right twice on this stretch, bringing you back to Front Street. Here the ride turns right, but if you turn left and go $^2/_{10}$ mile you'll come to the town beach.

3. Turn right on Front Street and go $1^4/_{10}$ miles to traffic light (Route 6).

4. Turn right on Route 6 and go $^7/_{10}$ mile to Creek Road, which bears right.

5. Bear right on Creek Road and go $^4/_{10}$ mile to end (Point Road).

6. Turn right on Point Road. After $2^6/_{10}$ miles a private road turns left through two pillars and the main road curves sharply right. Continue on main road for $^3/_{10}$ mile to Planting Isle Road, a narrow lane on the right.

7. Turn right on Planting Isle Road, which leads to an island connected to the mainland by a causeway. Go $^4/_{10}$ mile to the far end of the causeway, where the road becomes private, and backtrack to the main road. **CAUTION:** Watch bumps and potholes at the beginning.

8. Turn right on the main road and go 1 mile to end, at the tip of Sippican Neck. At the very end is a country club where the road becomes private; turn around at this point.

9. Backtrack $2^6/_{10}$ miles to Delano Road on right.

10. Turn right on Delano Road and go $3^1/_{10}$ miles to end (Point Road). After 1 mile the road curves sharply left along the ocean. (At this point the entrance to the Great Hill estate is on your right; explore it if it's open.)

11. Turn right on Point Road and immediately cross Route 6 at traffic light. Go 1 mile to end (County Road). You'll pass a cranberry bog on the left.

12. Turn left at end onto Country Road and go $^3/_{10}$ mile to crossroads and stop sign (Route 105, Front Street).

13. Turn left on Route 105. Go $^7/_{10}$ mile to fork where Route 105 bears left and Spring Street bears right.

14. Bear right on Spring Street. Just ahead Mill Street bears right, but continue straight for $^1/_{10}$ mile to Route 6, at stop sign.

15. Cross Route 6 (**CAUTION** here) and go $^9/_{10}$ mile to end (Main Street). At the end notice the town hall with a bell tower on the right.

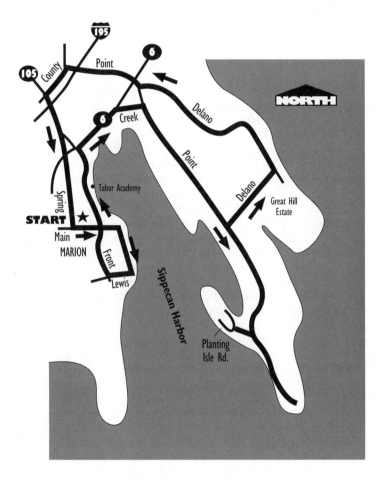

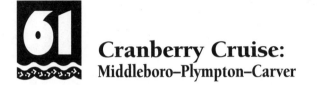

Cranberry Cruise:
Middleboro–Plympton–Carver

Number of miles: 28 (18 without Carver extension)
Terrain: Flat, with a couple of short hills.
Food: Grocery store and snack bar in Plympton. Grocery store in Carver. McDonald's across from starting point.
Start: Osco Drug, junction of Routes 105 and 28 in Middleboro, just north of Interstate 495.

This is a tour of the heart of the cranberry-growing country, midway between Taunton and Plymouth. Biking through the bogs, which are crosshatched by narrow, straight channels and have rustic little wooden sheds next to them, is a true pleasure. Narrow, untraveled lanes wind past peaked-roof, cedar-shingled homes and scrub pine from one bog to another across one of the most appealing rural landscapes in Massachusetts. The nicest time to do this ride is during the harvest season in October, when the berries form a deep red carpet across the land, or during the spring, when the bogs are flooded ponds.

The ride starts from Middleboro, a handsome town with large old wooden homes along the main street leading into the center, a dignified white town hall with a graceful dome, and a stately white church across from it. A fascinating place to visit is the Middleboro Historical Museum, with a display relating to the lives of Tom and Lavinia Thumb, the most famous midgets in history. Lavinia was born in Middleboro. Two miles out of town you'll pass a large green with a magnificent white church standing over it, unusual because it stands in splendid isolation. A little farther on is the Eddy Homestead, a Federal-style mansion built by Zachariah Eddy, a prominent local lawyer. From here you'll head along inviting narrow lanes to Plympton, an unspoiled gem of a town. The long green, with a monument in the middle, is framed by a fine old church and country store. The rest of the ride brings you past dozens of bogs on country lanes, passing through Carver, the number-one cranberry town in the state. The tiny center of town has a little park with a handsome Civil War monument.

Directions for the ride: 28 miles 🌸🌸🌸🌸🌸🌸🌸

1. Turn left (north) out of parking lot onto Route 105 and immediately cross Route 28 at traffic light. Go ⁶/₁₀ mile to another light (Wareham Street on right) in the center of town. The handsome, pillared town hall is on your left shortly before the intersection.

2. Go straight at light for ⁴/₁₀ mile to crossroads where Route 105 turns right. If you want to visit the museum, turn right 1 block past the light on Jackson Street. The museum is just ahead on your left.

3. Turn right and stay on Route 105 for 1⁶/₁₀ miles to traffic light (Route 44). You'll pass a magnificent church and green on your left just before the light.

4. Cross Route 44. After ⁷/₁₀ mile, Route 105 turns left, but continue straight for 1⁴/₁₀ miles to fork.

5. Bear left at fork onto Plympton Street (unmarked). Go 2²/₁₀ miles to blinking light where the main road curves sharply right and a smaller road turns left.The Eddy Homestead is just beyond the fork, on the far left corner of a crossroads.

6. Turn left at blinking light and go 1²/₁₀ miles to end (Route 58), in the center of Plympton. **CAUTION:** Watch for bumps and potholes at the beginning. When you come to the end, the short ride turns right and the long ride turns left.

7. Turn left on Route 58 (there's a pizza shop if you turn right and proceed ¹/₁₀ mile). Go ¼ mile to Main Street (unmarked) on right, immediately after cemetery.

8. Turn right on Main Street and go ⁷/₁₀ mile to Crescent Street, which bears right up a short hill.

9. Bear right on Crescent Street and go ³/₁₀ mile to Upland Road, which bears right up another short hill.

10. Bear right on Upland Road and go 1²/₁₀ miles to end.

11. Turn right at end and go ¹/₁₀ mile to Brook Street on left, at traffic island.

12. Turn left on Brook Street. After ²/₁₀ mile Mayflower Road bears right, but curve left on the main road. Go ⁴/₁₀ mile to fork where Spring Street bears left.

13. Bear slightly right at fork up a little hill. Go $^8/_{10}$ mile to end, at yield sign (merge right on High Street).

14. Bear right on High Street and go $^7/_{10}$ mile to your second paved left (Gate Street), at traffic island.

15. Turn left on Gate Street and go $^1/_2$ mile to end, at stop sign.

16. Go straight at stop sign and immediately bear left on Route 44. (Don't turn 90 degrees left directly at the stop sign onto Plymouth Street.) Go $1^3/_{10}$ miles to fork where Route 44 bears left and Center Street bears right. Notice the unusual wooden church on your right as soon as you get on Route 44.

17. Bear right at fork and go $^1/_2$ mile to Pond Street on left.

18. Turn left on Pond Street and go $1^1/_{10}$ miles to end (South Meadow Road).

19. Turn right at end and go 1 mile to end (Route 58).

20. Turn right on Route 58 and go $^1/_2$ mile to West Street on left, immediately before traffic light. This is the center of Carver. A convenience store is on the far side of the intersection, and a park with a Civil War monument is on the near side.

21. Turn left on West Street and go $1^1/_{10}$ miles to end (Holmes Street on left).

22. Turn left on Holmes Street and go $^3/_{10}$ mile to fork (Cross Street bears right).

23. Bear right on Cross Street and go $^8/_{10}$ mile to end.

24. Turn right at end and go $^3/_{10}$ mile to fork where Carver Street (unmarked) bears left.

25. Bear left on Carver Street and go $^9/_{10}$ mile to end (Purchase Street).

26. Turn left at end and go $1^7/_{10}$ miles to end (Chestnut Street).

27. Turn right on Chestnut Street and go $^3/_{10}$ mile to where the main road curves left and a narrow lane goes straight.

28. Go straight onto the lane (still Chestnut Street) for $2^2/_{10}$ miles to end (Wood Street). You'll pass Woods Pond on the right after $^7/_{10}$ mile.

29. Turn left on Wood Street and go $1^2/_{10}$ miles to diagonal crossroads and stop sign (Wareham Street).

30. Turn right on Wareham Street and go $1^2/_{10}$ miles to traffic light (Route 105), back in the center of Middleboro.

31. Turn left on Route 105 and go $^6/_{10}$ mile to Route 28, at traffic light. Osco Drug is on far side of intersection on right.

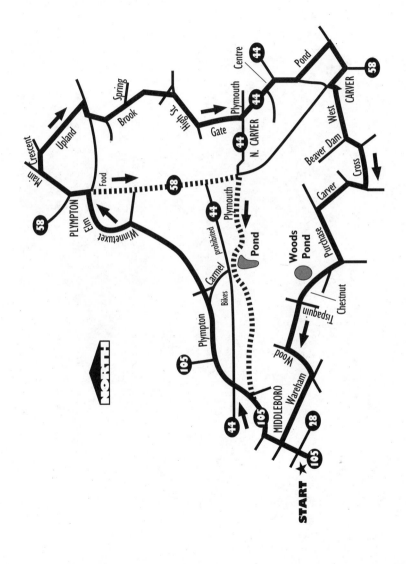

Harvesting cranberries in Carver

Directions for the ride: 18 miles

1. Follow directions for the long ride through number 6. Here the ride turns right, but it's worth turning left to see Plympton.

2. Turn right on Route 58 and go $2^3/_{10}$ miles to traffic light where Route 44 East turns left. Here the ride turns right, but if you turn left on Route 44 and go $^1/_4$ mile you'll pass through North Carver, another delightful village with a handsome white church.

3. Turn right at traffic light on Plymouth Road. Stay on the main road for $2^2/_{10}$ miles to fork where Carmel Street turns right underneath Route 44 and the main road bears slightly left.

4. Stay on the main road for $2^6/_{10}$ miles to stop sign (Route 105), at a five-way intersection. Notice the one-room schoolhouse on the left at the intersection.

5. Bear slightly left on Route 105. After $1^4/_{10}$ miles, Route 105 turns left at crossroads. Stay on Route 105 for 1 mile to Route 28, at second traffic light. Osco Drug is on the far side of the intersection on the right.

Pilgrim's Progress:
Plymouth–Carver

Number of miles: 28 (9 without extension to Myles Standish State Forest and Edaville Railroad)
Terrain: Gently rolling, with a few short hills.
Food: Country store in South Carver. Snack bar at Edaville Railroad.
Start: Shaw's Supermarket, on the south side of Route 44, in Plymouth. It's $^4/_{10}$ mile west of Route 3 (take exit 6B).

This is a tour of Plymouth and the scrub-pine and cranberry-bog country surrounding it. You'll go past or near many of the town's historic landmarks. Outside of town you'll go through the Myles Standish State Forest, a large, unspoiled area of pines and ponds, and then go past the Edaville Railroad, a narrow-gauge railway looping through a large expanse of cranberry bogs.

The cranberry-growing area is a uniquely beautiful part of the state to explore by bicycle, especially during the harvest season in October when the berries turn the bogs into a crimson carpet. Surrounded by pines and sandy banks, with little wooden sheds next to them, the bogs have a trim, rustic appeal. Narrow roads guide the bicyclist from bog to bog past cedar-shingled, cozy-looking homes.

You'll start the ride by visiting the Pilgrim Monument, a soaring, Victorian granite statue built in 1889. From here it's just a couple of blocks to the waterfront, where you'll go by Cranberry World, a museum of the cranberry and the cranberry industry. It's free and worth seeing. Just ahead is Plymouth Bay Winery, which manufactures and sells wine from locally grown grapes and cranberries. Stop in for a taste of cranberry wine. A little farther along the waterfront are the *Mayflower II* and Plymouth Rock. When you see the *Mayflower II* you'll be surprised at how small it is. Plymouth Rock is just a plain old rock covered by an ornate pillared portico. Within a couple of blocks are numerous other attractions and historic buildings, including a wax museum depicting Pilgrim life; the Federal-era Antiquarian House; and the outstanding Pilgrim Hall

Museum, one of the oldest in the country, founded in 1824. It contains extensive displays of Pilgrim possessions and artifacts.

Leaving Plymouth you'll head to the Myles Standish State Forest, an extensive wilderness area of scrub pine spreading up and over an endless succession of bubblelike little hills and hollows. Biking through this terrain is a lot of fun if you use your gears properly, roller-coastering down one little hill and over the next one. Several small ponds lie nestled in the pines. Beyond the forest you abruptly enter cranberry-bog country. After a few miles you'll come to the Edaville Railroad, which is touristy but fun. On the grounds is a museum with a fine collection of railroad memorabilia, antique toy trains, fire engines, and antique cars. Beyond Edaville you'll go through a long string of bogs and pass near Savery Avenue, the first divided highway in America, built in 1861. The road consists of two narrow lanes with pine trees between them and on each side, extending ½ mile alongside Route 58.

Directions for the ride: 28 miles

1. Turn left from the west end of the parking lot onto side road (don't get on Route 44). Go ²⁄₁₀ mile to end, at traffic light (Summer Street, unmarked).

2. Turn left on Summer Street and go ⁷⁄₁₀ mile to Oak Street on left, just after cemetery on left.

3. Turn left on Oak Street and go ⁴⁄₁₀ mile to end (Samoset Street, Route 44). You'll pass an old wooden school on left after ¹⁄₁₀ mile.

4. Turn right on Route 44 and go ¹⁄₁₀ mile to crossroads (Allerton Street). Shift into low gear as you approach it.

5. Turn left on Allerton Street up a short, steep hill. **CAUTION** turning left. Just ahead, the Pilgrim Monument is on your left. From the monument continue ²⁄₁₀ mile to end (Route 3A).

6. At end jog right and immediately left on Lothrop Street. Go ²⁄₁₀ mile to end (Water Street, unmarked). When you come to Water Street, the ride turns right, but if you turn left and go 100 yards you'll come to Cranberry World, which is free and fascinating.

7. Turn right on Water Street and go ¼ mile to rotary. You'll pass the Plymouth Bay Winery on your right.

8. Go straight at rotary, paralleling Plymouth Harbor. After ¼ mile you'll pass the *Mayflower II* and then Plymouth Rock on your left. Pilgrim Hall

Museum is opposite Plymouth Rock. Continue past the rock ¹/₁₀ mile to Leyden Street (unmarked), which bears right uphill.

9. Bear right on Leyden Street and go ¹/₁₀ mile to traffic light (Route 3A, Main Street). Notice the fine old homes along this street.

10. Cross Route 3A and turn immediately left. If you go straight instead of left, you'll go up Old Burial Hill, a well-landscaped cemetery with most of its gravestones dating back to the 1700s. The view from the top of the hill is impressive.

11. After turning left, go 1 block to Summer Street on right. **CAUTION:** There's a sewer grate with dangerous slots at the intersection.

12. Turn right on Summer Street, passing the Governor Carver Inn on your right, and go ⁴/₁₀ mile to Billington Street, which bears left downhill. Immediately after the Inn, on the left, is a beautifully landscaped park with the restored Jenney Gristmill; the original was built in 1636.

13. Bear left on Billington Street and go ¹/₂ mile to fork.

14. Bear left at fork, going underneath Route 3, and go 1⁴/₁₀ miles to Black Cat Road (unmarked) on right, opposite cranberry bog. You'll pass Lout Pond on the right. The short ride turns right on Black Cat Road and the long ride goes straight.

15. Continue straight for 6 miles to fork where the main road goes straight and another road bears left, at the top of a tiny hill. **CAUTION:** Watch out for sandy spots on the second mile of this long stretch.

16. Continue straight on the main road for 1 mile to a traffic island on right, opposite the headquarters of the Myles Standish State Forest on your left.

17. Turn sharply right opposite the State Forest headquarters and go 1½ miles to fork where Federal Road (unmarked) bears left and the main road curves right.

18. Curve right on main road and go 1²/₁₀ miles to end (Federal Furnace Road, unmarked). Here the ride turns left, but you can shorten the distance to 23 miles by turning right and going 7⁹/₁₀ miles to traffic light where the access road to Shaw's Plaza (unmarked) turns left, at top of hill. Turn left and go ²/₁₀ mile to supermarket on right.

19. Turn left at end and go ⁴/₁₀ mile to fork where Tremont Street bears left and Lakeview Street bears right. This is South Carver. A small grocery store is at the intersection.

20. Bear right at fork and go ⁶/₁₀ mile to end (Route 58, South Main Street), passing Sampson Pond on your right.

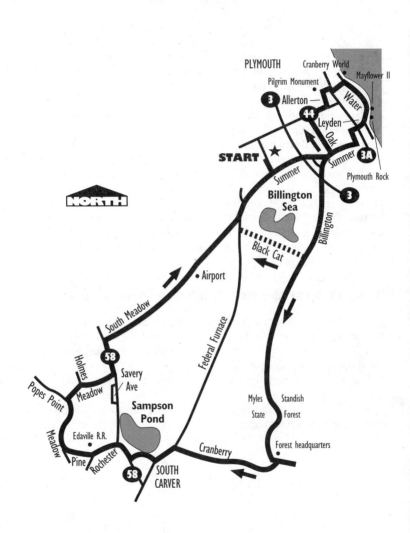

21. Turn right at end and go ¼ mile to Rochester Road on left (sign may say EDAVILLE RAILROAD).

22. Turn left on Rochester Road and go ⁶⁄10 mile to Pine Street, which bears right (sign says TO EDAVILLE RAILROAD). It's the second right.

23. Bear right on Pine Street. The Edaville Railroad is just ahead on the right. Continue ⁷⁄10 mile to end (merge right on Meadow Street).

24. Bear right on Meadow Street and go 1³⁄10 miles to large traffic island where Meadow Street turns right.

25. Turn right (still Meadow Street) and go 1⁸⁄10 miles to end (Route 58). Here the ride goes left, but if you turn right and proceed ²⁄10 mile you'll come to Savery Avenue on the right.

26. Turn left on Route 58 and go ⁷⁄10 mile to South Meadow Road on right. There may be signs pointing to the airport and Carver High School.

27. Turn right on South Meadow Road and go 5²⁄10 miles to end (Federal Furnace Road). You'll pass the Plymouth Airport on your right.

28. Turn left at end and go 1⁴⁄10 to traffic light at top of hill.

29. Turn left on the access road to Shaw's Plaza (unmarked) and go ²⁄10 mile to supermarket on right.

Directions for the ride: 9 miles

1. Follow directions for the long ride through number 14.

2. Turn right on Black Cat Road and go 1⁷⁄10 miles to end (Federal Furnace Road). You'll go past Billington Sea, a freshwater lake, and up and down several short, sharp hills.

3. Turn right on Federal Furnace Road and go 1⁶⁄10 miles to traffic light at top of hill.

4. Turn left on the access road to Shaw's Plaza (unmarked) and go ²⁄10 mile to supermarket on right.

63 Southeastern Shore:
Manomet–Cedarville–Cape Cod Canal

Number of miles: 34 (16 without Cedarville–Cape Cod Canal extension)
Terrain: Gently rolling, with several short, sharp hills and lots of little ups and downs.
Road surface: 8/10 mile of dirt road, which can be avoided.
Food: Grocery and snack bar in Manomet. Grocery and restaurant in Cedarville. Friendly's and McDonald's near the Canal. Cafeteria at Plimoth Plantation.
Start: Plimoth Plantation, Route 3A in Plymouth, 3 miles south of Route 44. From Route 3, take the Plimoth Plantation Highway exit (exit 4) and follow the signs. Park here only if you'll definitely be back before the plantation closes (currently at 5:00 P.M.). Allow five hours for the long ride and two and a half hours for the short one. I recommend getting an early start and visiting the Plantation after the ride.

Another good starting point is the Friendly's at the rotary immediately before the Sagamore Bridge, at the end of Route 3. If you start here, turn left out of parking lot to rotary, and begin with direction 17.

The southeastern shoulder of Massachusetts between Plymouth and the Cape Cod Canal provides ideal bicycling through a rural, unspoiled area of scrub pine, lots of lakes, cranberry bogs, a few farms, and refreshingly undeveloped coastline, with the exception of White Horse Beach. The long ride goes along a section of the bicycle path hugging the Cape Cod Canal, which is one of the nicest places in the state to bike. The ride has both a cultural highlight and a cultural low point—Plimoth Plantation, a superb reconstruction of the original Pilgrim colony, and Pilgrim I, a nuclear power plant.

You'll start from Plimoth Plantation, a successful attempt to portray as accurately as possible the village and the style in which the Pilgrims lived in 1627. Employees dress in period costume, imitate the Pilgrims' speech as well as it has been determined, raise farm animals, and reenact episodes from the daily life of the colony such as court sessions, trade with the Indians, and military drills.

Leaving the Plantation you immediately enter the delightful landscape of scrub pine and cozy, cedar-shingled homes characteristic of southeastern Massachusetts. The terrain is rolling but in miniature, with little ups and downs that are fun to bike through if you time your gear-shifting properly. You'll pass Little Long Pond and then enjoy a smooth, straight run past cranberry bogs to Manomet, the community where the shoulder of land protrudes farthest out to sea. You'll follow the shore along a steep bluff nearly 100 feet high, and then descend past the access road to the public shorefront behind the Pilgrim I nuclear power plant. It's worth visiting this spot to see what a nuke looks like—a monolithic concrete slab jutting up starkly from the otherwise unspoiled coastline, with the effluent gushing from beneath the building to the ocean along a concrete channel lined with people fishing. An information booth displays booklets extolling the benefits and safety of nuclear energy, and you can decorate your bike with free bumper stickers saying "Know Nukes" and "Build Pilgrim II." From here it's not far along the bay back to the starting point.

The longer ride heads south all the way to the canal through more of this beautiful woods-and-lakes landscape, passing weathered, cedar-shingled homes nestled in pine groves, a country church, and two old cemeteries. Then you'll enjoy biking along Little Herring Pond and 2-mile-long Great Herring Pond. Just beyond the canal you go through the tiny village of Bournedale, with a small, cupola-topped village hall and a charming country store.

The canal is a visual delight, curving gently between low hills with the graceful span of the Sagamore Bridge in the background. From the canal you'll head back to Plymouth, following the coast. Several small roads diverge from the main road to dip along the water's edge. In Manomet you'll go out to Manomet Point, which provides panoramic views of Cape Cod Bay. You'll go along White Horse Beach, a popular summer resort, and then rejoin the short ride just in time to pedal along the Manomet Bluffs.

Directions for the ride: 34 miles

1. Follow the entrance road at the back of the parking lot, climbing a short, steep hill. Go ³⁄₁₀ mile to end (Route 3A).

2. Turn right (south) on Route 3A and go $\frac{1}{2}$ mile to Clifford Road, which bears right midway up the hill.

3. Bear right on Clifford Road and go $\frac{8}{10}$ mile to fork (Doten Road bears left).

4. Bear right at fork (still Clifford Road) and go $\frac{4}{10}$ mile to crossroads and stop sign (Old Sandwich Road).

5. Cross Old Sandwich Road. After $\frac{7}{10}$ mile Russell Mills Road is on your right, but curve left, staying on the main road. Continue $1\frac{2}{10}$ miles to end.

6. Turn left at end. After 1 mile there'll be a road on your right (sign may say TO MYLES STANDISH STATE FOREST), but again curve left, staying on the main road. Go $1\frac{6}{10}$ miles to Oar and Line Road, which bears right.

7. Bear right on Oar and Line Road and go $\frac{4}{10}$ mile to fork, passing Little Long Pond on right. At the fork the ride bears left, but if you bear right for 50 yards you'll come to a captivating little beach on Long Pond.

8. Bear left at fork and go $\frac{4}{10}$ mile to crossroads (Long Pond Road, unmarked). Here the short ride goes straight on Clark Road, and the long ride turns right.

9. Turn right on Long Pond Road. Go $3\frac{1}{10}$ miles to unmarked fork where the main road curves left (becoming Hedges Pond Road) and Long Pond Road bears right onto a smaller road.

Here the ride bears right and soon reaches an $\frac{8}{10}$-mile stretch of dirt. If you wish to avoid this section, curve left on main road and go $1\frac{8}{10}$ miles to end (Route 3A, in Cedarville), then turn right and go $\frac{1}{10}$ mile to fork (sign may point right to Route 3). Bear right and continue $3\frac{1}{10}$ miles to the Bournedale Village Hall, a picturesque red building with a cupola, on your right. Just past the village hall, a road turns right opposite the country store. Resume with direction number 13.

10. Bear right on Long Pond Road and go $1\frac{6}{10}$ miles to end (merge left at stop sign; Carter's Bridge Road is on right). The road becomes dirt after $\frac{1}{4}$ mile. You'll see Little Herring Pond below on your right.

11. Bear left at stop sign (still Long Pond Road) and go $\frac{4}{10}$ mile to crossroads and stop sign (Herring Pond Road, unmarked). There's an old schoolhouse with a bell tower on your left at the intersection.

12. Turn right at crossroads and go $2\frac{6}{10}$ miles to Bournedale Village Hall, a picturesque red building with a cupola, on your right. It's $\frac{8}{10}$ mile after the end of Great Herring Pond. Just past the village hall, a road turns right opposite the country store.

13. Turn right on this road and go 100 yards to Route 6, at traffic light.

14. Cross Route 6. **CAUTION:** It is very busy. The Cape Cod Canal is in front of you. Carry your bike down the stairs to the bicycle path running along the bank of the canal.

15. Turn left on the bicycle path, following the canal on your right. Ahead of you is the Sagamore Bridge. Go $9/10$ mile to fork just before the bridge where the left-hand road bears up a steep hill. **CAUTION:** The bikeway is heavily used by both cyclists and noncyclists, including people fishing.

16. Bear left uphill at fork. Go underneath the bridge and into the parking lot of the Sagamore Recreation Area. Turn sharply left out of the lot and go up a moderate hill, paralleling the bridge on your left. Just ahead is a Friendly's on your left and a rotary.

17. Turn right at rotary, passing McDonald's on left. Immediately after McDonald's, turn left (sign may say TO ROUTES 3 AND 3A). After $2^6/10$ miles you'll come into Cedarville, where the road becomes Route 3A. Continue $1/2$ mile to Ellisville Road, a smaller road that bears right.

18. Bear right on Ellisville Road and go $1^1/2$ miles to Route 3A again, at stop sign.

19. Turn right on Route 3A and go $1/4$ mile to Center Hill Road, a smaller road that bears right. At the beginning you'll pass Ellisville Harbor State Park on the right. From here a footpath leads about $3/10$ mile to a bluff overlooking a tidal inlet and salt marsh.

20. Bear right on Center Hill Road and go $1^8/10$ miles to end, at stop sign (merge to your right back on Route 3A).

21. Bear right on Route 3A and go $2^1/2$ miles to Old Beach Road on right. It's a small road immediately before a snack bar on right. If you come to a large pond on your left, you've gone $2/10$ mile too far.

22. Turn right on Old Beach Road and go $1^2/10$ miles to Simes Road on left. The main road bears right at the intersection. You'll bob up and down several short, sharp hills.

23. Turn left on Simes Road and go $2/10$ mile to end. You'll turn 90 degrees left on this stretch.

24. Turn right at end and go $1/4$ mile to end (Manomet Point Road).

25. Turn 90 degrees right at end (sign may say TO WHITE HORSE BEACH, PRISCILLA BEACH). After $9/10$ mile you'll come to a little traffic island on left. Curve slightly right and go $3/10$ mile to the tip of Manomet Point.

26. Turn around and backtrack $3/10$ mile to the traffic island.

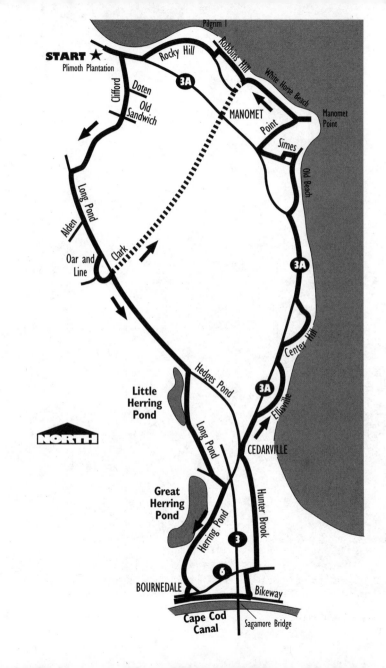

Cape Cod Canal

27. Turn right at traffic island, following the ocean on your right along White Horse Beach, and go 1$^1/_{10}$ miles to Robbins Hill Road on right. It's your first right after the road curves sharply inland.

28. Turn right on Robbins Hill Road and go $^6/_{10}$ mile to a large rock in the middle of the road.

29. Turn left immediately after the rock and go 100 yards to end, down a steep hill. **CAUTION** at bottom.

30. Turn right at end and go 2$^4/_{10}$ miles to end, at yield sign (merge right on Route 3A). After $^8/_{10}$ mile you'll pass the access road to the public shorefront behind the nuclear power plant. It's the third driveway on the right (a sign may point to shorefront and nature trail). All three access roads bristle with forbidding signs that say "exclusion area" and other dire warnings, but the third road is public and you won't be shot on sight if you venture down it. The shorefront is $^1/_4$ mile from the main road.

31. Bear right on Route 3A and go 1 mile to Plimoth Plantation entrance road on left.

32. Turn left on entrance road and go $^3/_{10}$ mile to parking lot.

Directions for the ride: 16 miles

1. Follow the directions for the long ride through number 8.

2. Continue straight at crossroads onto Clark Road (unmarked). **CAUTION:** There is no stop sign here. Go 4$^4/_{10}$ miles to traffic light (Route 3A). Notice the fine white church at the intersection.

3. Cross Route 3A and go $^7/_{10}$ mile to the second left, Robbins Hill Road. It's shortly after the first left, Rocky Hill Road. If you come to the ocean, you've gone $^1/_{10}$ mile too far.

4. Turn left on Robbins Hill Road and go $^6/_{10}$ mile to a large rock in the middle of the road.

5. Follow directions for the long ride from number 29 to the end.

64 The Cape Cod Canal Ride:
Bournedale–Buzzards Bay–Onset

Number of miles: 14
Terrain: Flat, with one moderate hill at the beginning.
Food: Grocery stores and snack bars in Onset and Buzzards Bay.
Start: Herring Run Recreation Area, Route 6 in Bourne, on the north side of the canal, across from the Bournedale Lodge Motel. It's 1 mile west of the rotary immediately before the Sagamore Bridge and 2½ miles east of the rotary before the Bourne Bridge, in a valley between two hills. If you're heading south on Interstate 495 or east on Interstate 195, take exit 2 (Route 6), which deposits you at the Bourne Bridge rotary.

CAUTION:

1. This ride has two brief sections on Routes 6 and 28, a busy four-lane highway. If traffic is heavy, it's safest to walk or ride through the parking lots of the businesses alongside the road, dismounting when necessary.
2. The bicycle path along the Cape Cod Canal is very heavily used on weekends in good weather by both cyclists and noncyclists. Keep alert for walkers, joggers, rollerskaters, children, dogs, and people fishing. When passing, call out "Passing on your left" or "Coming through" in a clear voice. Keep your pace moderate. I suggest getting an early start, so that you can enjoy the bikeway before it becomes busy.

This is a relaxing tour along the scenic Cape Cod Canal, the unspoiled woods and inlets just north of it, and the old beach resort of Onset. You'll start from the banks of the canal at the visitor's center, where there's an exhibit on the canal's construction and history. Just inland from the canal is the tiny village of Bournedale, with a charming country store and the little Village Hall, an ornate old building with a cupola. From here you'll head a couple of miles inland along winding, nearly untraveled roads through woods and then along the shore of Buttermilk

Bay, one of the many inlets along the edge of Buzzards Bay. You'll then head south to Onset, an old beach resort with some fine Victorian buildings set on a peninsula surrounded by little coves and inlets. Onset is not Hyannisport—it's middle-class rather than elegant and fairly congested. The views of neighboring peninsulas across the gracefully curving shoreline of Onset Bay, instead of just open ocean, give Onset a unique appeal.

From Onset it's a short ride to Buzzards Bay, which is a part of Bourne and the main commercial center for the southeastern corner of the state south of Plymouth. Here you'll get onto the bicycle path beside the Cape Cod Canal, one of the most enjoyable places to ride in Massachusetts. The bikeway is completely flat, and hugs the bank of the canal for its entire length. As a waterway the canal is beautiful, curving gently between low, wooded hills. The waterway is of uniform width (about 200 yards) and is crossed by the spidery steel spans of the Bourne and Sagamore highway bridges, as well as the striking vertical-lift railroad bridge that you'll see when you get onto the bike path. In good weather the canal is alive with pleasure boats and some sleek yachts, and if you're lucky you may see an enormous barge or cargo ship chugging along.

Directions for the ride

1. Go to the west end of the parking lot and cross Route 6 at the traffic light (**CAUTION** here). Go 100 yards to end, where there's a country store. This is the village of Bournedale.

2. Turn left at end and go $\frac{1}{10}$ mile to fork where Herring Pond Road curves right and Bournedale Road bears left. Immediately before the fork, the Bournedale Village Hall is on your left.

3. Bear left downhill at fork and go $2\frac{2}{10}$ miles to end (Head of the Bay Road), at a large, triangular traffic island. Shortly before the end you'll pass a farm on the left with an unusual stone tower.

4. Bear right at end and go $2\frac{6}{10}$ miles to end (merge right on Routes 6 and 28). You'll go along Buttermilk Bay on your left.

5. Bear right on Route 6 and go $\frac{3}{10}$ mile to traffic light (sign may say TO ONSET BEACH, POINT INDEPENDENCE). Here you will turn left by making a jug-handle turn—you bear right just before the light, curve left, and cross the highway at right angles. Use extreme **CAUTION** riding on Route 6.

6. Make jug-handle left turn at light onto Main Avenue. **CAUTION:** Bad railroad tracks as soon as you cross Route 6. Go $^7/_{10}$ mile to fork immediately after metal-grate drawbridge. **CAUTION:** Walk across if the road is wet.

7. Bear right at fork and go 100 yards to crossroads (Whittemore Avenue on left, North Boulevard on right).

8. Turn right on North Boulevard. On your right is Muddy Cove, an offshoot of Onset Bay, which is in turn an offshoot of Buzzards Bay. After $^1/_4$ mile the main road turns 90 degrees left. Continue less than $^2/_{10}$ mile to end (merge left).

9. Bear left at end and go $^1/_{10}$ mile to West Boulevard on right, just after playground on right.

10. Turn right on West Boulevard. Stay on the main road for $^9/_{10}$ mile to crossroads and stop sign, following the shore of Onset Bay. This is a pleasant run around the Onset peninsula and along Onset Beach.

11. Turn right at crossroads. This is the center of Onset. Go $1^9/_{10}$ miles to Routes 6 and 28, at traffic light. You'll pass an attractive stucco church on the right.

12. Turn right on Route 6 and go $^1/_2$ mile to rotary just after bridge over inlet, at yield sign. **CAUTION:** If traffic is heavy when you cross the bridge, wait for a break in the traffic and then ride across quickly in the middle of the right lane. This forces traffic behind you to pass you in the next lane, rather than to squeeze past you by inches in the right lane.

13. Go straight at rotary (don't bear left). Just ahead is a traffic light where Academy Drive turns right. Continue 100 feet to parking lot on right.

14. Turn right into parking lot, passing the old Buzzards Bay train station on your right. In front of you is the magnificent vertical-lift railroad bridge across the canal, built in 1935, one of the highest bridges of this type in the country. Just past the train station the parking lot turns to dirt. Continue 100 yards to the canal, where you'll pick up the beginning of the bicycle path. You'll have to walk your bike around a barricade meant to keep out cars.

15. Curve left onto the bicycle path, following the canal on your right. Use **CAUTION** on the bikeway. See **CAUTION** notice number 2 after the Start section of the ride description. Go $3^7/_{10}$ miles until you come to several flights of stairs going up the embankment on your left. The stairs lead to the parking lot that you started from. (The bicycle path continues another 3 miles to Scusset Beach.)

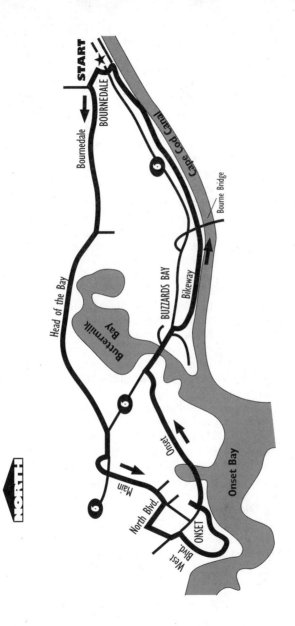

Appendix

Bicycle Clubs

If you would like to bike with a group and meet other people who enjoy cycling, join a bicycle club. Most clubs have weekend rides of comfortable length, with a shortcut if you don't want to go too far. Usually a club will provide maps and mark the route by painting arrows in the road so that nobody gets lost. Joining a club is especially valuable if you don't have a car because you'll meet people who do and who'll be able to give you a lift to areas beyond biking distance from home. To find out about clubs in your area, ask at any good bike shop. Addresses of clubs riding in eastern Massachusetts (subject to annual change) are as follows:

Bicycle Coalition of Massachusetts (formerly the *Boston Area Bicycle Coalition*), 214A Broadway, Cambridge, MA 02139 (phone 617–491–RIDE). A political action group devoted to improving conditions for bicyclists. Recently the BCoM lobbied successfully to allow bicycles on many of the Massachusetts Bay Transit Authority lines on weekends and off-peak hours (see Introduction for details).

Charles River Wheelmen, 19 Chase Avenue, West Newton, MA 02165. The main club for the Boston area.

Hostelling International-American Youth Hostels, 1020 Commonwealth Avenue, Boston, MA 02215. Biking in the Boston area; also hiking, canoeing, cross-country skiing.

Appalachian Mountain Club, 5 Joy Street, Boston, MA 02108. Mostly hiking, but some bicycle rides in the Boston area.

North Shore Cyclists, 18 Wheatland Street, Burlington, MA 01803.

Nashoba Valley Pedalers, Box 2398, Acton, MA 01720. Northwestern suburbs between Concord and Fitchburg.

Mass Bay Road Club, Box 791, Plymouth, MA 02362.

Granite State Wheelmen, 2 Townsend Avenue, Salem, NH 03079. Southern New Hampshire and nearby Massachusetts.

Narragansett Bay Wheelmen, Box 41177, Providence, RI 02940. Rhode Island and nearby Massachusetts.

Seven Hills Wheelmen, Box 24, Worcester, MA 01606.

Fitchburg Cycling Club, Box 411, Lunenburg, MA 01462.